THEY'RE YOUR PARENTS, TOO!

THEY'RE YOUR PARENTS, TOO!

How Siblings Can Survive Their Parents'
Aging Without Driving Each Other Crazy

Francine Russo

BANTAM BOOKS

NEW YORK

Copyright © 2010 by Francine Russo

Published in the United States by Bantam Books, an imprint of
The Random House Publishing Group, a division of
Random House, Inc., New York.

BANTAM BOOKS and the rooster colophon are registered
trademarks of Random House, Inc.

LIBRARY OF CONGRESS CATALOGING-IN-PUBLICATION DATA
Russo, Francine.
They're your parents, too!: how siblings can survive their parents'
aging without driving each other crazy / by Francine Russo.
p.   cm.
Includes bibliographical references and index.
ISBN 978–0-553–80699–1
eBook ISBN: 978-0-553-90718-6
1. Aging parents—Care. I. Title.
HQ1063.6.R88 2010
646.7'80846—dc22   2009036609

Printed in the United States of America on acid-free paper

www.bantamdell.com

2   4   6   8   9   7   5   3   1

First Edition

Book design by Christopher M. Zucker

To the memory of my beloved husband,
    Christian Scott Ward,
whose love, encouragement, and writer's eye
sustained me through some of the harder
moments of creating this book

CONTENTS

INTRODUCTION

My Uneasy Journey into the Twilight

BY THE TIME MY PARENTS were in their late seventies, I had lived two hours away for more than thirty years. I called most Sundays. I brought my daughters down for an afternoon every few months and on holidays. That was about as much closeness as I could tolerate, given some pretty uncomfortable family dynamics. I told myself that I was much more independent and grown-up than my younger sister, who bought a house a few blocks from my parents and lived near them all those years. Not exactly.

When my mother started having serious health problems, my sister, my only sibling, was the one who helped out. I was relieved that she was there. I felt, a little guiltily, that I was off the hook. In fact, like so many people I've met since, I was clueless. I thought I'd left my first family, for good. No one told me that whether I wanted it or not, whether I embraced it or fled from it, my family would, in some form, come back to me. I had no idea that I was entering a new developmental crisis in the life of my original family, or that there even was such a crisis lying in wait.

I didn't realize that something new was expected of me when my parents got old, that I would need to make a developmental leap, emotionally. They were still my parents, and I was still their child—with many of our old reactions to one another intact—but now I needed to understand that they were also simply two elderly people, who perhaps needed something from *me*.

It also never occurred to me to suddenly step up and give my sister support. We weren't close; we talked only a couple of times a year and saw each other on holidays. Getting together with my family provided some deep satisfactions, but being with them was also profoundly uncomfortable. Our family dynamics were riddled with anger, criticism, guilt, neediness, and indirection, but also love. And the love would prove significant. In my own defense (and this is true in so many families I've met since then), understanding the new psychological demands of this time are far from easy. Even in the healthiest families, our parents' aging and mortality evoke outsized, often distorted feelings in all of us. And even at the best of times, family dynamics are hard to change.

I didn't manage all this very well. After my mother died, my father's hurt at my lack of involvement, my sister's anger—and an avalanche of my own feelings of guilt, regret, and sorrow—descended on me. Bit by bit, I struggled to mend my relationship with my father before he died and, in general, to respond better to the new demands of this time of life. It felt good to be there for my father in this new way. After he died I was surprised to discover how much my relationship with my sister mattered to me, given how little contact we'd had. I am still in the process of repairing that relationship.

Up until this point I'd considered myself psychologically astute and self-aware. In my work as a journalist, I regularly covered subjects rooted in human relations: family, marriage, and individual development. In my years of reporting for major magazines, I'd interviewed many psychologists, therapists, and researchers. I knew a lot, but not about this.

WHY I WROTE THIS BOOK

In the years after my mother died, I did a lot of soul-searching. I struggled to understand what had gone wrong, what I could have done differently. As I tried to figure this out, I noticed in my work that many other people were wrestling with the same issues. They wrote to me at my "Ask Francine" column in *Time* magazine about conflicts they were having with their sisters and brothers as their parents needed care or when they died. My readers were confused, conflicted, yearning, angry.

I thought it would help me, and others as well, if I could understand these sibling struggles. I began researching a story for *Time* about how siblings related to one another over caring for their parents. Even before its publication, the story was huge. As I reached out to potential interview subjects, I was flooded with messages and mail from people who wanted to talk, to vent, to ask for help. Clearly I'd tapped into a huge reservoir of untold stories and difficult emotions. Some of these adult children were intensely protective of their aging parents; others were angry. Many were fuming at their siblings for not helping; others were desperately competing to be their mother's caregiver. Some had been surprised and thrilled to rediscover a sister or brother as a new best friend. Still others were lonely and seeking closeness with a sibling even though they'd never been close before.

I learned, among other things, that what had happened in my family was far more complicated than my own mistakes and more common than I had known. Over time I realized that there were things I could have done differently for a more positive result. I also learned there were dynamics in my family—our roles, our complex feelings about one another, our ways of operating—that we'd been acting out our entire lives without being conscious of them. Most of these I could never have changed, no matter what I did. Yet understanding them better could have helped me do more of what was possible and reduce my distress over what was not.

Besides talking to siblings, I talked to many experts. They were seeing different versions of my family's story all around them. Some were struggling with similar issues in their own families. A few confessed to having the same problems, the same blind spots, the same reactions to their aging parents and clashes with their siblings. "This is so difficult," one mediator told me, "that even those of us who do it for a living have trouble with it."

What is the "this"? It's the new life crisis of our original family that I think of as the twilight transition. These years of our parents' decline are the final phase of the family in which we grew up. They are the transition to a new day, a new epoch in which we and our siblings will be the oldest generation of our family. In this transition, one, if not both, of our parents are here, yet not here, at least not the way they were. Our roles and those of our sisters and brothers need to change, but change comes hard. It's all too easy for our emotions to be blown out of proportion. At moments, past and present can blend in disorienting ways. It's scary. The end of our old family as we knew it is near; what the next generation will bring is unknown.

THE TWILIGHT TRANSITION IS NOW A NORMAL PASSAGE FOR FAMILIES

I researched the twilight transition intensely for years. I read about family psychology and adult development. I spoke to psychoanalysts, family therapists, health-care workers, and other professionals in the field of aging, from assisted living experts to family law attorneys. They confirmed that the family dynamics I was finding everywhere were real, and they helped me better understand specific pieces of the puzzle. But no matter who I asked, they told me they knew of no one who was looking at the full picture. That's what I wanted to explore: the emotional dynamics of the last developmental transition of our *first* family, when we reengage so intensely again with our parents, our sisters, and brothers.

The experts who work face-to-face with the elderly and their families were my astute guides. Family therapists, social workers, geriatric care managers, home aides, senior-living employees, hospice counselors: These professionals gave me tremendous insight and a sense of context. But the people struggling through the twilight, or recently emerged from it, taught me the most. I interviewed scores of adult siblings in person, by telephone, sometimes by email correspondence, talking to as many as possible within each family. It was startling at times to hear sisters and brothers give such different accounts of the people in their families and the meaning of events, past and present. It was rare that I thought one was "right" and one was "wrong." Each had grasped part of a complex picture. No one was in possession of the whole truth. What they taught me most of all was compassion—for all of them, even those who were not behaving well by most people's standards. Who was I to judge?

GETTING TO KNOW THE FAMILIES IN THIS BOOK

I'm enormously grateful to the families you're about to meet in these pages. Many I spoke with over several years. They were generous with their time and their emotions. They were willing to open their deepest feelings to view. Many were open to questioning themselves, reexamining their family histories and their long-held assumptions in a new light.

I have worked hard to disguise their identities and have changed names and details in order to preserve their privacy. In telling their stories, it is impossible to do justice to the full complexity and richness of even one family. With each story, I have chosen to emphasize a particular dynamic out of a multilayered family interaction. Generally, I spotlight the sibling relationship although the relationships with parents are always implicit, sometimes explicit. At any one moment, a thorny tangle of issues and emotions are operating all at once. These dynamics are so complicated that I could have devoted an entire book to a single family. Instead I have chosen to show many different kinds of families, from close to conflicted, from deeply troubled to fairly healthy. I have included families large and small from different ethnic and economic groups.

Obviously I describe scenes at which I could not have been present. In doing this, I try to capture the drama of what was told to me, usually with details supplied by several of the participants. In one instance, I recount a story as related to me by an involved social worker. The great majority of the quotations are verbatim.

I do not explicitly identify people's ethnic identities, but I often imply their backgrounds by their names and in their narratives. Certain things I talk about—assumptions about caregiving, gender roles, religious beliefs—do differ by culture. In researching these cultural differences, I learned that, despite variations in customs and beliefs, the family dynamics I am probing in the twilight—facing our parents' mortality and loss, reawakened sibling rivalry, conflict about fairness—these are universal.

WHEN OUR PARENTS ARE GONE, OUR SISTERS AND BROTHERS REMAIN

As we struggle through the twilight, stirred by the tumultuous feelings evoked as our parents fail and eventually die, how we behave toward our siblings now is likely to determine who we will be to one another in the next generation.

It's very hard for any one person to grasp the "big picture" of their family. Rarely does one sibling fully understand a sister's or brother's relationship to their parents or the complex dynamics that bind them to each other. As you will see in the following accounts, and as family relationship experts will attest, very few people comprehend the complexity of their own motivations and behavior toward their parents and siblings. How could they? This picture is so vast and thickly layered with everything from our parents' value systems, the quality of their marriage, and their treatment of each child, to our individual relationships with each parent and sibling, and our multiple roles within our family.

Whether or not we're the primary caregivers for our parents, whether we have close ties to siblings or we remain distant, both figuratively and literally, we can make this passage smoother by simply making an effort to understand what motivates us and them. Are we overburdening ourselves with caregiving because we feel guilty or needy? Are we avoiding involvement with an aging parent because it's too hard to face their mortality, and therefore our own? Are we watching a sibling struggle with the lion's share of responsibility because we're angry at our parent? Or because this sibling won't let anyone else help?

HOW THIS BOOK IS ORGANIZED

The four parts of this book reflect the phases of the twilight transition, as most families encounter them. At the end of each chapter you'll find strategies for improving sibling interactions over specific issues. Throughout the book, you will find boxes that offer research sidelights and statistics, and practical suggestions, as well as the occasional note on usage.

In Part One, I'll take you through our initial confrontation with our parents' aging and explore why it can be so difficult to get an accurate take on how our parents are doing, and why siblings may view their parents' changing needs so differently.

Part Two deals with how we react when certain siblings assume and others avoid various aspects of caring for their increasingly needy parents, from simple needs to more complicated medical or legal requirements. Day-to-day decisions about caregiving, huge issues about life, death, and money can touch on deeply felt emotions about duty, fairness, love, and power; they can bring siblings together or inflame long-buried resentments. But as you'll see, learning to understand these dynamics better and to communicate more effectively can help us through these emotional minefields.

Part Three moves further into the darkest part of the twilight, as we watch our parents decline and die. For many people, this is the roughest and most emotional passage, often made more painful by dementia. How we behave toward one another as we prepare to gather at the deathbed can affect our relationships for years to come.

Part Four sifts through the emotional challenges of grief, recovery, and the reinvention of our original family. Given the unique relationship between any child and parent, each sibling will experience the loss of a parent differently. If we respect these differences, we have a better chance of maintaining strong and healthy ties to one another after our parents die. The often loaded issue of inheritance also figures into this final phase, as does the emotional legacy of our parents.

By the end of this life passage, many of us will have learned to value one another more now than before the twilight years. If we have a connection with a sibling—a cherished bond worth preserving, or perhaps a fractured one in need of repair—now is our opportunity. Our siblings, no matter how we view them and how they view us, are our last link to our first family, and our best hope for its survival.

PART 1

CONFRONTING A NEW

FAMILY PASSAGE

CHAPTER ONE

THE LAST TRANSITION
OF OUR FIRST FAMILY

DOTTIE, FIFTY-SEVEN, A LIBRARIAN and local historian, and Arlene, fifty-five, a financial planner, brought their cars around to the rutted front drive of the old Kansas farmhouse to move their mother to the assisted living home. Mrs. Keller, an impressively tall ninety-one-year-old woman, hobbled out on her cane, her face stony. Her daughters each took a deep breath. This moment was the climax of a year of contentious family meetings and a decade of seismic shifts in their family since their father's death.

Once their mother was widowed, their brother Donny, fifty-two, had taken the lead because he was there; he'd continued their dad's pet-supply business and helped out their mom with chores. The four sisters, at various distances and busy with families and careers, saw their mother more regularly than before. At first these were the only differences, but then the pace of change accelerated: Mom's fender bender in the grocery parking lot, several falls she took in the decrepit house, an oven mitt on fire in the oven. The five siblings gathered for a series of family meetings in Donny's living room to figure out what to do. Usually having all five together was a cause for joy, but not this time. Several thought Mom should move out for her own safety. Opinions differed. Tears were shed. Yet through it all they worked hard to reach a consensus. Dottie was the last to agree to the move, three months after her siblings. "I got sucked into it," she admitted, "taking Mom's side, that she should die in that house. I couldn't see how she'd changed. She was the mother of my past, my comfort. I couldn't let that go."

Once the decision was made, the siblings worked together: finding the right place and then persuading Mom, applying firmness and the gentle persuasion of a family prayer meeting. On their own schedules, each spent hours packing up. During that time the siblings felt close, as they would again in the future. But when the critical moment arrived, each was swept up in tumultuous feelings.

Dottie, a sweet-tempered woman with unruly curls, was chafing because her *younger* sister, was taking charge. She was floored when Arlene, crisp and efficient, declared, "Mom will go in the car with me. You follow."

"I just shut down," Dottie said, "and my sister rolled over me and my feelings by sheer force of personality."

For Dottie, it was hard not being with her mother for this momentous ride. For Arlene, sitting at the wheel and seeing her mother's stricken expression was awful. "Mom," she asked before she pulled out, "would you like to say a prayer?" Her mother nodded.

"Lord," the older woman prayed, "please give me the courage to accept where I am going to live." Arlene started the car and drove silently, swept with admiration for her mother and grief for what they were losing. As soon as they got there, she channeled her emotions into a whirl of activity, setting up her mother's new home in the assisted living center.

When Dottie arrived, Arlene was in a frenzy of hanging pictures. Dottie stood there gaping. She'd taken photos of the farmhouse walls to help place the pictures in a familiar way. Now she froze, unable to help. Then, one after the other, their sisters showed up and shouted that Mom said she wanted a different picture up.

"But Mom just told me she didn't *want* that one now," Arlene repeated with increasing desperation.

Finally Arlene just walked out. "I couldn't take it anymore," she said. "I was working so hard to make it good for my mother, and they criticized everything I did. The feelings just got to me. This was the end of a huge part of my life, my mom moving out of the place where I grew up, that was in our family for sixty years. It was huge."

Dottie felt even worse, especially after Donny took Arlene outside alone to talk business, seeming to exclude the rest of the family. The next day, Dottie took off to camp in the woods alone. "It was so hard to come out of that terrible deep hole," she said. "It took me weeks to recover."

A FAMILY REUNION UNLIKE ANY OTHER

Like so many of us, these siblings were struggling through one day in the long developmental transition of their original family. As we come together to deal with the needs of our aging parents, sweeping emotions like theirs—anger and helplessness, childlike needs and rivalries in tandem with mature behavior and life-changing decisions—often go with the territory. As we are thrust into prolonged and intimate contact with our sisters and brothers after decades in separate homes and lives, all our family history crashes down on us as we each look mortality in the face, up close—our parents' and our own.

"It's like being put down with your siblings in the center of a nuclear reactor and being told, 'Figure it out,'" Sara Honn Qualls told me. The University of Colorado geropsychologist, a practitioner in the emerging field of the psychology of aging, is one of a host of experts who have embarked on trying to understand this late-life convergence of the family.

This transition unfolds over several years, even decades, as we and our siblings reunite around our aging parents and their new needs. Over time we share or resist responsibilities for their health, well-being, and property, making decisions from the mundane to the literally life-and-death. But the twilight is not only a matter of solving practical problems and meeting practical needs. It is an existential crisis through which we will be transformed from the children of our parents to the elders of our family. It requires a critical recalibration of our sense of who we are and what our family is. It demands that we accept change and grow as people. How we navigate this passage with our siblings determines, in large part, whether we remain a *connected* family after our parents die, and what our connection will be like.

Just think about the enormity of this. Decades of life and change, the addition of partners and children, have made us different people from the sons and daughters, sisters and brothers we were. One of our parents is probably gone; both may be frail. Making our original family work together at this point can be like trying to crunch together a machine from a group of scattered and reshaped parts. It just doesn't function the way it used to; we have to adapt what we've got to make it run. Even harder, our parents' decline and dependency evokes powerful emotions from our earliest days, feelings that pull us backward when we need most desperately to push forward and be more adult than we've ever been.

The Kellers' reactions are typical. Before they reassembled to deal with their increasingly frail mother, they had all gone different ways. There were marriages, divorces, remarriages, kids, and grandkids. By the time Dottie moved back to their hometown, twice-divorced and still a dreamy romantic, her younger sister, Arlene, had become a player in their town, a trusted financial adviser and confident leader. As Dottie found out, being older didn't count for much anymore. Many things about these people and their relationships were different. As they confronted their mother's new dependency, and glimpsed her mortality, they found themselves acting out of old needs, reenacting old rivalries. They felt sad, angry, hurt, and confused. Yet, as I can attest after interviewing scores of siblings from twilight families, the Kellers did reasonably well overall.

These Kansas siblings are pioneers: We *all* are. "There are no role models for this," social worker Lynn Cibuzar told me. She and I were sitting at the conference room table of DARTS, a Minneapolis-area nonprofit serving seniors and their families. Cibuzar had led countless family meetings around that table to help beleaguered and conflicted sibling groups, with or without their parents, to hammer out how to work together, both for their parents' sake and for one another's, as they coped with everything from elder care and housing to powers of attorney, from medical decisions to inheritance. "As families," Cibuzar lamented, "we have no models for this. We're all struggling through something new. I tell people, 'This is not just your sister's fault. We have to see the bigger picture, all the forces that have brought us here.'"

NEW TIMES, NEW KINDS OF FAMILIES

One or two generations ago, the Keller family would probably not have gone through this long renegotiation of their family relationships over their parents' old age. The odds are overwhelming that their mother would not have lived to be so old. But if she had been one of the rare old people, she would probably have been healthy, then died after a brief illness. If she needed assistance longer, an unusual occurrence, one of her homemaker daughters would have cared for her. There were no senior housing, assisted living, or continuous care centers. There was a mere handful of "old age homes."

"It was a barren landscape," Elaine Brody told me. In 1957, this pioneering gerontologist was doing intake interviews at one of these few old age homes. The word *caregiving* did not exist then, she told me. Most old people were poor; the Social Security Act of 1935 came too late to help them when they could no longer work. In fact, many states had (and still have on the books) laws requiring their "legally responsible relatives"—their children—to support them. Over the following decades, the Philadelphia Geriatric Center, as this old age home came to be called (it has since been reconstituted as the Abramson Center for Jewish Life and the Polisher Research Institute), established a number of firsts: an apartment building for old people, geriatric hospital, assisted living center, and, in 1974, a model Alzheimer's facility.

In the 1970s, Penn State gerontologist Steven Zarit, then a young professor at the University of Southern California, witnessed the first swell in the elderly population while operating a community counseling program for the Andrus Gerontology Center in Los Angeles. The children of people with dementia begged Zarit to help because they had nowhere else to turn.

Many old people themselves were surprised to be alive. "I never thought I'd live this long," bemused old folks told social workers. In fact, as Purdue University family studies expert Karen Fingerman noted, the parents of baby boomers, our parents, were the first generation in history to experience old age as a normal stage of life. They were the first to enjoy the benefits of social security and to look forward to retirement; the first to move far from home to enjoy it.

The New Old People

During the twentieth century, the average person's life expectancy shot up by three decades. Thirty more years of life! Between 1950 and 2000, the percentage of people seventy-five and older doubled from 3 to 6 percent of the U.S. population, and people over eighty-five are now the fastest-growing demographic group.

When our grandparents or great-grandparents got sick, they usually died quickly from infectious diseases, such as influenza or diphtheria. Or they died from mostly untreatable conditions, such as heart disease, ulcers, or cancer. It was our parents who saw the invention of antibiotics to treat the diseases that used to kill people. They were among the first to receive new vaccines to ward off killer epidemics, such as cholera and smallpox. Better nutrition, health information, water, and sanitation also helped keep them alive. Then the introduction of Medicare in 1965 gave them unprecedented access to medical care.

Because of medical advances in the treatment of chronic health conditions, more and more of our parents have been able to survive into old age. But there's a dark side to this progress. Those who get to be very old, whose numbers are increasing rapidly, have a much greater probability of developing Alzheimer's or another dementia. More than 40 percent of people over eighty-five are now afflicted, according to the Alzheimer's Association. These revolutionary changes mean that most of our parents need or will need some kind of care, probably for years. We are the ones who will care for them— 34 million of us currently, according to the National Alliance for Caregiving, AARP, and MetLife.

The New Adult Children

On the other side of this social revolution, today's midlife adults, beginning with those of us born between 1946 and 1964 and defined as baby boomers, are dramatically different as adult children from those in previous generations. We grew up in tremendous prosperity in what scholars tell us were the most child-centered homes in history until that time. We became the best-educated generation. Better education in turn prompted many of us to move far from home, first for college, then for career, and newly accessible air travel facilitated these moves. At least half of us live fifty miles or more from our parents. This makes us the first native-born generation, Fingerman observed, whose relationships with our parents have been so affected by geographic distance.

Sweeping social changes have also shaped our generation. The women's movement, which made it normal for women to work, collided with the traditional assumption that women would be responsible for caring for their parents. Certainly, today's daughters are less available for caregiving. Male or female, we are also less on hand because of new kinds of family lives and career trajectories. Many of us have had our children later and are still raising kids when our parents get old, hence the "sandwich" generation. With more divorce and remarriage, more single-parent families and untraditional kinds of households, increasing numbers of boomers are juggling more competing responsibilities with supercharged demands.

All these historical developments complicate our relationships with our aging parents. Although studies show that we remain emotionally close even when we live far away, physical distance can add tensions to our relationships because we cannot always give our parents the time and attention they would like or we might like to give them. Moreover, many of us became better educated than our parents, and this difference is yet one more factor with the potential to create emotional distance between us as well as physical. Ambivalence in our relationships is common.

The culture in which we were brought up has also given us a sense that we have control over the important things in our lives. We are problem solvers. If something is broken, we are convinced we can fix it. Are we, therefore, psychologically prepared for the aging of our parents? Those who have studied us, such as Brandeis University researcher Margie Lachman, say that we enter midlife with a sense of mastery of our world. But most of us also enter midlife with at least one living parent. What happens between this point and our last parent's death profoundly challenges our sense of mastery.

THE FAMILY WE LEFT: THE HOUSE OF CHILDHOOD

When we reassemble with our siblings around our parents' new needs, we understand at one level that neither we nor our family is the same, but we often relate to one another as if we were. The old ways of relating are what we know, so slipping into them is automatic. We come back together, whether sitting in a parent's or sibling's living room or by phone or email, in what I call the house of childhood. This metaphorical structure contains the roles and rules and beliefs we learned as children, the way we learned to communicate and interact with one another.

A family is a living organism, a system, composed of complex networks of interactions. This way of understanding families was developed by the first family therapists in the 1950s. By now we've all imbibed a little of this point of view. Most of us are familiar with the idea that each of us has a different role in our family. I'm the achiever, you're the rebel, our younger sister is the peacemaker, and our little brother makes everyone laugh when things get tense. But it's far more complicated than that. In every family there is a kind of emotional division of labor. Each person has a specialized part in keeping the family going. If we each do what we've learned to do, our family remains stable.

Every family is a separate country with its own laws, governing powers, and assumptions. In its emotional life, one family can be as different from another down the block as a middle-class, secular family in New York is from an impoverished Muslim family in Afghanistan. Our parents pass down the rules, although they may not themselves be able to articulate them. The rules are rarely spelled out. Yet they implicitly dictate how we should feel about people, what we are allowed to talk about and how, and what we are permitted to do. If we break the rules, we risk punishment: anger, coldness, even banishment.

Parents lay down the belief system—that we're all here to help one another, for example, or that asking for help is weakness. They also define our values: what's important—education, for example, or money, public opinion, or kindness. Parents also spell out how different people in the family are to be regarded. If one of us is uncharacteristically successful or uncharacteristically badly behaved, our family generally finds a way to dismiss this departure from our worldview. If the child considered not so smart scores well in a test, for example, well, that test must have been really easy. As children, each of us has to find a way to fit in, play a part that is needed or, at least, not already taken.

Family systems take in events and forces from generations before us and the new families we create after we leave home. They include our parents' habits, values, attitudes, and much more, things both conscious and unconscious. It would be impossible to detail here all the elements in even one family. We can, however, consider some very simplified examples of how families work.

In one stable, loving family, the immigrant father, a highly successful business owner, affectionately cares for his wife, son, and daughter. He takes pride in his role as provider and is also proud of his wife, who is better educated than he is. The wife, who feels weak, looks to her capable husband to protect and care for her but feels, not so secretly, that she's the smarter one. Knowing he's somewhat insecure, she caters to his need to be in charge, although, at some level, she resents it. She rarely challenges him, and he gets angry when she does. All the relationships in the family reflect aspects of this primary relationship. The son, like his father, works hard to be successful and take care of other family members. He is obedient and strives hard to get his father's approval, but he never feels fully approved because his father, though proud of him, also feels ambivalent about his son surpassing him. When the father is brusque or harsh, the mother does not stand up for her son but comforts him when they are alone. The son and mother feel allied in being the smarter ones, an unspoken assumption that everyone understands. To the daughter, the mother communicates that achievement is not important for women, who are weaker than men. The daughter blames her mother for keeping her down and gets lots of attention by complaining. She looks to her father and brother to give her affection and take care of her. Both do. The father feels freer to be affectionate to his daughter, and she can let him be strong without resenting him. Her brother enjoys the role of being the benevolent older male, a junior version of his father. In this complex network of relationships, they all get some of their needs met. When the parents get old and the father dies suddenly, the son will embrace the idea that it is his place to care for his mother, and his sister, who does not see her job as caring for others, will automatically cede this role to her brother.

In another family, the parents' marriage is more troubled. The father, a brilliant doctor, enjoys feeling adored and marries a beautiful, emotionally fragile woman who worships him. Yet he really doesn't like catering to other people's needs and comes to resent his wife. He is impatient with his less brilliant son, who flounders in and out of school. The son, who feels he can never compete with his father, feels relieved of trying. He acts out and gets negative attention from his father and love and solicitude from his mother, who looks to him for the sense of importance and affection she misses from her husband. Mother and son form a tight alliance of the undervalued. The father dotes on his smart, pretty daughter, his second-born, and makes her his confidante, looking to her for the easy companionship he can't get from his wife. He praises how well she deals with her mother and brother, and implicitly relies on her to take care of them. She has learned that she will get love from everyone as long as she is well behaved and has no needs of her own. She also acts as a buffer between her parents, who don't fight so much when she is there. So around and around they go, getting their needs met as best they can and keeping the family stable. But shortly after the children leave home, the marriage collapses.

There are endless permutations of these self-perpetuating family interactions. If one person, or an alliance of two or more, always takes on more work or responsibility, the others in the family will always do less, however much the workers complain. Their doing less will result in the others doing more. If some people in the family are seen as angry or needy, the others will mollify them or take care of them, not allowing themselves to get angry or get their own needs met, and the cycle will continue.

The Crunch of Change

Families, by their nature, resist change. Because of established dynamics, which provide the family's foundation, the family and its members cling to the status quo, even when that "status" is anything but stable. Yet adapting to change is critical to family health and growth. Nothing ever really stays the same. Little kids turn into adolescents. New people—brides and babies and in-laws—enter the family, and other people leave it, through death or divorce. What happens in each part affects all the other parts. Healthy families do change when they need to, although the earth rumbles a little under them before it feels firm again. Some family shifts are brought on by unhappy events. But even the happy ones, such as a birth or a marriage, can precipitate an anxious transition.

It was psychoanalyst Erik Erikson who first suggested that in order to grow as people and reach the next level of maturity, we may have to go through a developmental and emotional "crisis," a period of confusion or anxiety before we make the leap to solid ground. Think about it. Every major step forward involves not just gain but loss. When I get married, for example, I lose the freedom to be with other partners, and I also lose my sense of myself as a single person who has to be responsible only for myself. I have to transform my *identity* to include being part of a couple and someone whose first allegiance is to my husband or wife rather than to my father and mother. These are my psychic challenges as a person.

As newlyweds, we two also have to adjust to each other to become a new family. We assimilate, blend, or change the dynamics we bring with us from our original families. These are our psychic challenges as a *family*. As we move forward, every major transition subjects our little world to unsettling tremors before settling down again; the parts and the whole change and adjust in response to one another. Families, in other words, like individuals, experience "crises" of development, transitions that can lead to growth.

THE TWILIGHT:
A DIFFERENT KIND OF FAMILY TRANSITION

When family therapists talk about these crises, they invariably focus on the nuclear family—you and me and our spouses and kids—and how each of us is stressed by the changes at our time of life: our kids leaving home, for example, or our parents getting old and needing care.

A great deal has been written about these important family transitions, from the birth of our first child to the "empty nest" and the death of a spouse. These major life shifts demand psychological adjustments and emotional growth. But until now, we have heard almost nothing about this stressful passage of our *original* family. Yet for adult children, this reengagement as our parents are fading reawakens visceral emotional needs rooted in our childhood.

Until quite recently, there has been little or no reason to discuss this phenomenon. It did not exist in its present form for most families. Now, however, because of the convergence of historical and social forces I described, as record numbers of boomers come together to address the decline and death of their parents, there is a pressing need to understand this transition.

This new phase of family life is unlike any we've experienced before. Other family transitions, however difficult they are, usually start with a relatively continuous core. Two people in a relationship get married and have children, who eventually grow up and leave home. At every point, as the family expands or contracts, its core members, usually the parents at the center, remain more or less constant and changes are gradual, unless they divorce or one of them unexpectedly becomes seriously ill or dies. But the very nature of this twilight passage is its discontinuity. When we come together, sisters and brothers around our aging parents, it is this core of our original family that is crumbling: One of our parents has died or both are frail and unable to play the roles they once did. The family we grew up in, that network of continuous, intimate relationships, has not been operating as it used to for decades.

What this means is that we may now face many obstacles to working together as a family. Some of these are external: for example, living far apart. Some obstacles are internal, such as unresolved anger or guilt toward a parent or sibling. What's required of us in this new transition? A lot, if we are to come through it successfully. As we seek some shared sense of duty and fairness in the division of responsibilities, power, and property, we need to come to terms with our relationships with our parents. We also need to rework our relationships with one another.

How do we get through it? What are the challenges for each of us and for our family as a whole? Experts, as I have said, are only just beginning to address this. When I first looked for research about this family transition, I found very little: a few studies of caregiving and a few about adult siblings, but nothing that went to the heart of the matter I was investigating. In fact, in the 1990s, it seemed as if the research community was ignoring this important phase in life. Consider the MacArthur Foundation's MIDUS (Midlife in the United States) study, the scholarly community's most extensive look at boomers in midlife. In 1994, when this massive project was initiated by top experts in many fields, they asked participants hundreds of questions about their lives, including queries about their health, marriages, religious feelings, and sexual attitudes. But they did not ask a single direct question about caregiving, reactions to a parent's death, or relations with siblings. "As I get older, I wonder why we didn't ask this at MIDUS," said Elaine Wethington, fifty-five, a sociologist who participated in MIDUS. I was speaking to her, coincidentally, on the day on which she had flown home to pick up her eighty-six-year-old mother from the hospital following surgery.

I asked leading family therapists about this idea of a new family transition and I searched the literature in the field, but no one seemed to be looking at this period as a developmental crisis of the original family. Then, in 2004, University of Rochester geropsychologist Deborah King and psychiatrist Lyman Wynne, who both worked with elders in therapy, published a paper on what they called "family integrity." Wynne, an eminent pioneer in the field, was an old person and the head of a family, as he himself pointed out when I spoke to him shortly before his death in 2007. His and King's primary concern was with the emotional health of the elder of the family, the parent of middle-aged children who had left the nest decades before.

For any family to succeed in this phase of life, King and Wynne said, its family system, and every person in it, had to make three major leaps. First, they had to adapt their relationships to one another's current time of life. They also had to resolve their family conflicts or accept relationships as lost or damaged beyond repair. Finally, they had to create meaning and connection by sharing and passing down family stories and traditions. King and Wynne, as I said, were looking at this late-life family transition with a focus on the aging parent. I am looking at it from *our* point of view: We who are now middle-aged children. As people in midlife, our challenges are a little different; our parents' role will grow smaller, and ours will grow larger. We will not only care for them but also make decisions for them, bury them, and mourn them. We will inherit their property, their values, traditions, and history. To do all these well, we must meet these considerable challenges:

- adapt our roles and relationships as adults in a changing family

- confront our old conflicts with our siblings and parents, and resolve them, let them go, or work around them

- make peace with the loss of our parents and with their legacies, positive and negative

- redefine and pass on our family history and traditions

If our parents are able to take the lead as we begin, realistically dealing with their aging, for example, or making amends for past injustices, they will make it easier for us to do our part. If they have been emotionally healthy parents and generally good role models, we will be better prepared to meet these challenges, though confronting them may still be very hard. Not everyone will be able to make these leaps. But if we succeed, the payoff is profound. We emerge with a deeper, richer sense of self and of human life. We can accept the loss of our parents as part of the natural cycle of life and move forward with our own lives. And we are likelier to advance with an enduring and sustaining connection to our sisters and brothers in the next generation.

CHAPTER TWO

ACKNOWLEDGING OUR PARENTS' AGING

A SHORT, WIRY WOMAN with a feisty spirit, Tonya had moved back home to Louisiana to care for her ninety-year-old father. After the fifty-seven-year-old nutritionist moved in, she tried to talk to her brother, Ricky, about making some changes in the house.

He deflected her. Just turning sixty, Ricky, a high school football hero turned graying car dealer, joked self-consciously about needing reading glasses and his sciatic nerve acting up. But he reserved the big guns of his defensive comedy for his father. When the old man fell asleep in his chair with his mouth hanging open, Ricky mimicked him. When his father couldn't hear him, Ricky shouted histrionically and looked toward Tonya to share a laugh at his expense. Tonya was not amused.

"Dad is becoming increasingly frail," Tonya told me. "I've seen him stumble, wobble, refuse to use a cane at times, and fall twice. My brother does not realize that he needs adaptations in the household." She believed that her brother's anxiety about his own aging blocked his ability to deal with the reality of his father's decline. "It's a tough mirror for a son to look at," she said.

SISTERS AND BROTHERS, MOTHERS AND FATHERS

To avoid awkwardness or repetition, I may say "sister" or "brother" when I am speaking generally of a sibling. Frequently I also say "mother" or "father" to refer to either parent. I use "mother" more frequently because the demographic reality is that women outlive men by seven years on average. Also, when women are widowed or divorced, they remarry less frequently than men. So most boomers are likely to be relating to a widowed or single mother rather than a father. In addition, with a majority entering midlife having lost at least one parent and since a well parent usually cares for the less healthy one, most adult children will be involved with the care of one parent rather than both. For the most part, I use the singular and plural of parent interchangeably.

CHANGING ROLES, SHIFTING RESPONSIBILITIES

When does the twilight of the family begin? There is no clear border. Siblings may wake up to its arrival at different times, even years apart. In the absence of a crisis, no one wakes up one morning and says, "Today my mother is old. We'd better talk about what comes next."

Often no one in the family wants to see that a change has come. As adult children, we don't want to see our parents as people with failing bodies who are likely to need assistance and care. After all, *they* are the people who have always cared for *us*, raising us as children, being our parents throughout our lives, loving, approving, criticizing, demanding. But a revolution is at hand. They will always be our parents, but these times demand a rebalancing of the care equation and our respective roles. More and more, our parents will become dependent on us. Making this shift internally requires a major psychic leap—jumping over or storming through some major emotional barriers—including acknowledging the limits of life and giving up the myth of our powerful, protecting parents.

The death of our parents confronts us more viscerally than ever before with our own mortality. As middle-aged people, we resist this fact. As human beings, we naturally fear our own death. As people in this culture, we have lots of company in denying death as a natural part of life. We're unprepared to deal with it. So we have a major threshold to cross before we can realistically plan for our parents' aging.

Our parents' death also brings about our final separation from them. How emotionally prepared we are to let them go, to see their health and aging in a clear-eyed way, depends on how emotionally separate from them we have become. In any family, each sister or brother is likely to be at a different stage of readiness. To the extent that any of us still look to our parents to fulfill our emotional needs (for love, encouragement, vindication, a force to be resisted, a shoulder to cry on), we resist seeing that our time with them is running out. Anxiety colors our ability to accurately assess our parents' health or talk to one another about what, if anything, we should do to help them. Our parents may also set up hurdles, such as denying their frailty, hiding their symptoms, or refusing to adapt to their changed circumstances. Living far away from them can add another layer of complication to recognizing their aging and to reaching a consensus about it with our siblings.

If we manage this phase well, we will be able to be appropriately helpful to our parents, neither treating them as helpless children nor refusing to make any accommodation to their new time of life. As each of us makes this shift of perception and role, we become more fully adult. We enhance our ability to look forward, to plan, and to work cooperatively as a family that will soon enter a new era with a new generation in charge.

STRUGGLING AGAINST MORTALITY

We live in a generation and in a culture that does not accept aging and death as a natural part of life. Even a generation ago, this was less true. My father, who was born in 1918, lost a beloved older sister when she developed rheumatic fever at the age of sixteen. He also lost a baby brother who died within a few days of birth. His generation, who lived through World War II, knew death intimately.

Some in our generation have also seen death close up, having lost people we loved to illnesses such as AIDS or breast cancer, and we have seen the limits of what medicine can do. Yet there remains a widespread resistance in our culture to acknowledging these limits. We live in the age of prevention and cure. Whatever it is, we think we can be vaccinated against it or take something to make it go away. As for what can't be treated right now? By the time we need it, we're sure there will be a cure for cancer and for Alzheimer's. Scientists are working on it right now; every day brings a newspaper headline about an advance in medicine. Even though many of these "breakthroughs" prove illusory, some of us seem to believe we can eliminate old age itself.

As a culture, we shrink from death and sanitize it. "Even in a hospital," geriatric care manager Rona Bartelstone of Senior Bridge told me, "they cover up the body and take it right out. I have a friend who, until the age of fifty, never saw a dead body. She nearly had a panic attack when we went to a wake."

It's no secret that our culture worships youth and despises aging. Studies show that we think of ourselves as ten years younger than we are. We spend millions of dollars a year on wrinkle creams, Botox, and plastic surgery to erase the evidence of our years. We join gyms and exercise to keep our bodies healthy, limber, and, well, youthful. Scholars of midlife, such as Brandeis psychologist Margie Lachman, see such efforts as our attempt to be in charge of the aging process rather than let it be in charge of us.

Boomers especially are used to being in charge. We've come pretty far in the world, maybe as far as we will go. On the other hand, no matter how hard we work to stay young, inevitably our bodies tell us we're not as young as we used to be. We're a little slower, less flexible, less energetic. We see the first signs of chronic ailments: arthritis, diabetes, high blood pressure, or cholesterol. Knees give out; back problems are legion. Scholars who have studied people our age have found this to be a time of transition and contradiction. It is a time to be confident, but also a time to worry, because we are beginning to confront the limits of what we can control.

In midlife, studies show, we become especially anxious about both our physical decline and our mortality. This is a time, Purdue family studies researcher Karen Fingerman says, when we begin thinking of how many years we have left rather than how many years we've lived. In fact, *we* fixate more on death than old people, who, for the most part, have accepted its inevitability and live in the moment. When WellPoint, a health company, commissioned Roper to poll more than a thousand seniors and their adult children, they found that the younger generation believed their parents worried more about aging issues than they actually did by a margin of 53 to 33 percent. It seems we boomers confront our parents' approaching death just when we are most anxious about our own mortality.

So pervasive is the need to deny the reality of death that even those of us who have lost one parent often behave as if our other parent will live indefinitely. When University of Texas sociologist Debra Umberson interviewed adults who had lost a parent, she called it "striking" that many of them neither felt nor acted as if their surviving parent's death was inevitable. Having even one living parent, she observed in *Death of a Parent: Transition to a New Adult Identity,* serves psychologically as a buffer against death.

A certain degree of denial is useful. As Ernest Becker points out in his classic study, *The Denial of Death,* human beings cannot look at this terrifying prospect on a regular basis or we would not be able to live, work, raise our families, and accomplish so much. Avoiding the constant awareness of our parents' mortality can also be a healthy thing, family therapist Mario Tonti suggested in *Siblings in Therapy*. It lets people relate to their parents without being weighed down by fear of their death or worry about someday having to care for them. "Most children," he said, "are not prepared for their parents' becoming frail or disabled." Yet a complete disregard of the aging process makes it difficult to have any kind of reasonable planning or discussions with our parents while they can still make their voices heard. And it makes it hard for us to deal with our siblings about this very loaded subject.

READY OR NOT: CONFRONTING
THE FINAL SEPARATION FROM OUR PARENTS

As I mentioned earlier, our capacity to deal with our parents' aging realistically depends on how separate from them we have become emotionally. Do I, as an adult child, still rely on my mother to be there for me whenever I feel down or doubt myself? Do I still need to prove to my father that I've made the right choices in my life despite his predictions? Are we still declaring internally to them: "Look at what I've achieved"?

I have talked to people who resisted for a long time letting in the idea that their father might be getting old and others who overreacted in the opposite direction, leaping into protective mode at the slightest hint he was slowing down. Sometimes these were siblings reacting to the same father. The less each of us has separated from our parents emotionally, the harder it is to tolerate the idea of their death, which is the ultimate separation from them and the culmination of a lifelong process that began when we were born.

Peekaboo: From Helpless Infant to Adult
Picture a little girl of two running headlong down the street. She stops, looks back toward her parents, and smiles. She's as-

sured herself that she can be half a block from them and still be okay. But if she doesn't see them, she will be stricken with terror: If her parents lose her or abandon her, she will die. A two-year-old can't survive without adults to feed and protect and care for her. So of course she's scared.

Yet she has already come a long way toward separating from her mother. She is no longer a part of her mother's body. She has learned to tolerate her mother's absence for a second; that's partly what the infant game of peekaboo teaches. She has probably learned she will be okay if her mother is in the next room or even in another building, because she now knows her mother always comes back.

In childhood, adolescence, and young adulthood, this process of physical and emotional separation will progress in stages. If her family is relatively healthy emotionally, she will gradually learn that she can survive having some of her needs frustrated. This can happen at any time and certainly when she has to share her parents with a sibling. She will learn that she can have her own will, that she can want and feel things different from what her parents want and feel, maybe even in opposition to what they want and feel, and still be okay. Eventually, she will develop the ability to make her own judgments, take care of her own needs, and take responsibility for her own actions. In other words, she will have become *emotionally separate,* a person who can relate to others, adult to adult. Psychoanalysts refer to this process as "separation/individuation." Family therapists call it "differentiation." The concepts are not identical, but I am using *emotional separation* as an umbrella term to describe this process of emotional growth that continues throughout our lives.

As this little girl becomes an emotionally separate woman, she will not be an island to herself, unconnected intimately to others. Ideally she will be able to be herself and have maturely interdependent relationships with others, accepting that they have their own agendas and needs that have nothing to do with her. This is the ideal, anyway. No one achieves this fully. We're fallible people raised by equally fallible people.

Young Adult to Midlife: Milestones
Toward Seeing Our Parents as People

In the process of separating from our parents, it takes us a long time to recognize that they are people like us. As small children, we see them as giants, all-powerful and all-knowing, the source of everything we need. As we grow up and begin taking responsibility for our own needs, mistakes, and accomplishments, we start to see our parents more realistically. Somewhere along the way, in our thirties, forties, or even later, we begin to see our parents as people with needs and struggles of their own, people with roles apart from being our parents, who have both strengths and limitations. As middle-aged adults, suggested therapist Donald Williamson, author of *The Intimacy Paradox: Personal Authority in the Family System,* we develop the capacity to see their vulnerabilities, to stop judging them primarily as parents; we begin to feel compassion for them as fellow human beings.

These evolving perceptions of our parents mark major developmental steps, even crises for us. In order to see who our parents really are, we have to give up who we thought they were. Some of us experience crushing disillusionment; recovering can take years. But, in some way or form, all of us have to mourn these lost parents of our child's eye: the people who had the power to make us happy, protect us from hurt, and the people whose fault it was if we were unhappy. Until midlife, Williamson observed, "the kids just aren't ready to let the parent go as parent." Even then, it doesn't necessarily come easy.

Sam's story shows one of the many ways this recognition can come. Learning that his tough ex-marine father was not the commanding presence of his youth came as a jolt, but also a relief: His father was human after all.

SAM: COMING TO KNOW HIS FATHER, MAN TO MAN

Sam, a fifty-year-old film-score composer in Los Angeles, grew up in Texas in the sixties, the arty younger son of a former marine officer and corporate executive who just didn't "get" what his "crazy kid" was about. His parents, Romanian immigrants, had high expectations for Sam and his sister, who had both tested as "gifted" children. Praise was scarce because Dad did not want his kids to get a "swelled head." Sometimes attention seemed scarce, too. Sam, looking relaxed with his mop of black hair falling gently about a round, smiling face, grinned. "I once did poorly on a course in high school just to get my Dad's attention." Not too poorly—and only once.

His father had hoped Sam would get a corporate job after college, and he fretted and fumed about his son's starving-musician lifestyle. But Sam obviously felt secure in his parents' love. "Whatever our differences," he said, "I always felt my dad had my back." Clearly, he felt safe being separate, having different wishes and opinions from his father.

Although Sam felt closer to his mother, he thought of his father as a "good guy" who was uncomfortable as a parent and didn't know how to talk to his kids. "Dad was funny and quick-witted with his peers," he explained, "but he played 'father' to us as he saw it." Long into Sam's adulthood, his mother was a "buffer" between them. When his father answered the phone, Sam reports with a smile, "Dad would say, 'Hi. Got a job? Here's your mother.'"

Then Sam's mother died of cancer. Sam was only thirty-two years old, his father seventy. Struggling with grief for his mother, he reached out to his father, realizing they had to find a new way to relate. He proposed a father-son road trip to get to know each other. That weeklong jaunt across the Southwest marked the start of their first adult-to-adult conversations. His father told him of his anger and sadness that Sam hadn't gotten married before his mother died, that the medical establishment had failed her. "I saw his vulnerabilities,"

Sam said. "He was a tough guy. When my mom died, his whole life plan fell apart. He was alone and had no anchor. My dad always had the answers, and now he didn't."

With this realization, Sam let go of the powerful and demanding parent he'd imagined his dad was. "It leveled the playing field," he said. He realized maybe *he* could help his *father*. That didn't mean his father's approval no longer mattered. It did, but not having it didn't keep Sam at a distance. With greater equality between them, he found it easier to tell his father more about his booming career as a film and television composer. "My dad didn't think his kid was so 'crazy' after all," Sam said with a grin.

WHEN SEPARATING IS STILL A STRUGGLE

Even by the age of thirty, Sam had achieved a high degree of emotional separateness. This was because his parents, whatever their limitations, did not convey that their love, their well-being, or his own were at risk when he voiced opinions different from theirs or made choices of which they didn't approve. So as an adult Sam could see his father with some clarity, even if not completely objectively. Other people I met, even in their sixties, had not been able to give up their child's-eye view. They had grown up in families with much less emotional separation.

Safe to Be Separate? Our Parents' Lessons

Emotional separateness, the pioneering family systems thinker Murray Bowen said (although he called it "differentiation"), is not just a quality of individuals but of families—and families vary greatly in how much of this healthy quality they have and foster.

In a perfect family, the needs we all have to be close and to be separate would be in balance. The ideal parents (who would have to have had ideal parents themselves) would support their children while encouraging their individuality. They would make their children feel safe, protected, and loved, allowing them to have feelings and opinions different from their own. Children who grew up in this ideal family would learn to see clearly and think for themselves rather than to react emotionally *to* or *against* what their parents and siblings want or don't want, need or reject.

In families with little emotional separation, people bounce off their parents' and siblings' feelings constantly, anxious to be what other people in the family need them to be: ultra-responsible, frail, obedient, rebellious, or something else. To take just one example, let's say the parents share the belief that people can't take care of themselves. In this family, some of the people will be appointed caretakers, who will always be taking care of others, hoping that someone someday will take care of them; others will be labeled people who need help. In such a family, parents and children will be so tightly interdependent that they won't know where one ends and the other begins; they won't have good boundaries.

If we grew up in a family that lacked this kind of differentiation between people, the normal milestones toward seeing our parents as people come harder for us. Even when she was well past fifty, Hillary, for example, related to her mother as the towering figure of childhood and viewed her aging through a distorting lens.

HILLARY: EXAGGERATING HER MOTHER'S FRAGILITY

Hillary, a fifty-six-year-old tennis pro, described a family where it was very hard for her or her sisters to feel okay if they did not agree with Mother. "Mother and I were very good friends when I was in college," she told me. "But looking back, I realized most of my opinions were hers, not mine. If you saw things the same way, you had a wonderful relationship. Otherwise, it fell apart. I thought she was the most wonderful woman in the world. Yet I questioned whether she loved us."

Hillary's parents, both from prominent Dallas families, were a glamorous society couple, very involved with each other but not especially interested in parenting. Mother made it known that but for the burden of husband and three daughters, she could have been a great artist. When they were with their mother, the girls had to conform to all her beliefs and wishes. On the other hand, when they were out of her sight, she didn't seem to care what they were up to, even if they stayed out after dark or got into fistfights with one another. This lack of attention made them feel unsafe, and they clung more tightly to their parents, wanting never to displease them.

Hillary gave a vivid illustration of how hard it was to feel separate from this indomitable force even in her fifties, when her mother was seventy-five. She got a knot in her stomach just talking about their annual drive to her sister's house at Christmas. She would be at the wheel, her mother in the passenger seat, and her husband in the rear. "During those rides, I was torn in two," she said, "between being the adult person I was with my husband and being the person my mother wanted. I had to make sure everything was okay for Mother, that the radio was not too loud or too soft, that I did not drive too fast or too slow. I'd get tenser and tenser trying to please her. I felt somehow that if I did not please her, she would *die*."

Fused or Conflicted: Distorted Perspectives

When our parents are too little involved with us, family therapists say, we tend to cling to them, looking for security. Like Hillary, we think and live in accordance with our parents' beliefs and wishes. Therapists describe us as "fused" or "enmeshed." To the extent that we feel as adults that we are responsible for making our parents happy and satisfying their needs, we are not fully separate.

Was Hillary's mother really so fragile that a slightly uncomfortable car ride would do her in? Of course not. This daughter's terror of losing her mother made it hard for her to gauge her mother's actual condition as a reasonably healthy woman whose failing vision made driving long distances herself a bad idea. At any age, therapist Donald Williamson explained, when people do not feel emotionally separate from a parent, they react out of a child's exaggerated fears and sense of power. "The infant imagines, 'If I threaten or challenge my parents, they will abandon me and I will die,'" Williamson explained. "When the parents are old, people think, 'If I challenge them, my father will have a stroke and die.' The first is grounded in a fear of suicide, the second of homicide."

There are other families that look quite different from Hillary's but are just as lacking in separateness. Therapists call them "conflicted" or "reactive." When parents are too involved, they say, the kids can feel suffocated and push them away. If we're in a family like this, we may look more independent because we're constantly fighting our parents. But we're actually just as lacking in separateness: We're always reacting *against* our parents rather than making independent and reasoned judgments.

That was the state of things in Larry Berman's family. In his early fifties, he was still at war with his old, widowed mother, acting as if he didn't care whether she lived or died. She remained the indestructible shrew of his childhood.

LARRY: IGNORING HIS MOTHER'S VULNERABILITIES

Larry and his brothers grew up in a Baltimore household where each of them (and everyone else for that matter) was valued according to how "smart" they were. Their father, an accountant, encouraged them to compete with one another and compared their report cards. "With Dad, it was his way or the highway, and he could hate," Larry said. Their father and mother were locked in eternal conflict: The boys were either excluded or used as pawns. "Mom was not a warm, generous soul," Larry, now a sixty-one-year-old political consultant, said dryly.

The brothers grew up angry, especially Larry, who exploded easily. This was one reason, he thought, that his first marriage ended. Larry would go months without speaking to his parents. In his forties, after his father died and his mother moved to Florida, Larry would have furious confrontations with her on the phone, then silences for months at a time. That she was eighty, that her health was weakening, that she was on her own, did not trouble him. He did not see her as a lonely, vulnerable old woman nearing the end of her life. She was still the horrible, indomitable force of his childhood. For a long time he was still reacting as he always had, not making judgments as an adult son.

If we grew up in a family with very little separateness, we *can* become more separate and adult. It's just harder for us. Still, life happens. We change and grow in our relationships, our work, by becoming parents ourselves. We experience the first signs of our own aging, see friends pass away. Some of us have therapy or benefit from wise mentors. In the 1990s, in his mid-fifties, Larry was happy in a second marriage, had undergone anger management therapy, and had established his own business, a successful political consultancy in Washington, D.C. When he had the privilege of observing the Middle East peace talks at close range, he was ripe for an epiphany: "If Rabin can talk to Arafat," he realized, "I can talk to my mother."

At this point, his mother was in her late eighties, still living independently but with a myriad of health problems. Something in her age and aloneness moved this polished player with a caustic wit. "I have a responsibility," he told me. "I don't know what it is, but I have it. I have a fifty-six-year history with this woman. And," he added significantly, "I no longer need her approval."

What Larry did, finally, was let go of the parent he'd needed to blame. He began calling her regularly and visiting. He tolerated her complaints and contentiousness without getting angry. This more adult behavior wrought what he saw as a near-miraculous change. At ninety-two, she began expressing gratitude previously unimaginable. "We think it means she's about to die," Larry joked. "If I tell my brother, 'Mother said "Thank you" and "I love you," he'd say, 'Holy shit. Call the cardiologist!'"

If we have not fully grown to seeing our parents adult to adult, we react very powerfully to the idea that their time is running out. "Children have an undying hope," Williamson told me, "that the 'good' mother will show up someday. One of our wishes and hopes is for our parent to wind back the clock and do it all differently. It's painful. Recognizing that Mom is this far gone calls for a mourning process on the part of the children—mourning the mother they did not have and clearly never will have."

Even for the most emotionally healthy of us, our parents' aging poses challenges. Having reached a place where we can finally relate to them as one adult to another, we have to make a new leap; not only do we have to take care of ourselves, but our parents may now need us to take care of them. Some psychologists call this the "filial crisis." It evokes powerful anxiety in us, which we resolve by accepting the reality of their aging and responding to it appropriately.

I WANT MOMMY AND DADDY!

The people I quote sometimes referred to a parent in more than one way, sometimes as Mom or Dad, sometimes as

Mommy or Daddy or some other variation. I have noticed that when my interviewees felt especially vulnerable, they would often call their parents by the names they had called them in childhood, almost as if in that moment they were channeling their childhood selves.

FROM PANIC TO DENIAL: WHY SIBLINGS DIFFER

Although emotional separation is a quality of families, siblings will not be separate to the same degree. In childhood, for example, I am bound to have a different relationship with my parents from my sisters and brothers. Each of us is likely to be treated differently according to our personality, age, gender, or some characteristic that strikes a chord, positive or negative, with a parent. *(She's just like me. . . . Who does he get this trait from? . . . Her brother never did that. . . .)* In adulthood, each of us will have had completely different lives. It's not at all unusual for us to respond differently to our parents' aging.

The contrasting images that Hillary and Larry had of their mothers' vulnerabilities are at opposite ends of a spectrum that runs from panic to denial. Both ends are exaggerations of the reality of their parents in old age. I have heard many such opposing overreactions within the same family. Each of us sees our parent's health through the lens of our own anxiety, which may be minimal, in control, or over-the-top. Let's say my sister sees our mother fairly accurately. I, on the other hand, could be way off. A woman in New England told me how her sister nearly disappeared from their family life after their mother had knee surgery. "I need to withdraw from Mommy," she told her astonished sister. "I need to brace myself for when she dies." A panic reaction.

In another common difference of opinion, let's say I am the one who thinks that my sister is nuts, when really I am the one in denial about what's in front of my nose. A fiftysomething woman in Arkansas told me that she had fought both her sisters for months when they insisted that their ninety-three-year-old mother was "off" and couldn't live alone anymore. She was absolutely convinced her mother was perfectly fine. Total denial. Then one day in her mother's kitchen, she saw her mom light the burner on the stove, then put the frying pan in the oven. Something clicked; she saw her sisters were right. Later, she realized that her own needs were blocking her vision. "Of the three of us," she said, "I had the longest time unpartnered. I'd spend a lot of time at Mom's. She and I would sit outside under the big tree, and I'd talk about my kids and my job. I guess I still needed her to be my *mom.*"

Many adult children struggle to understand the changes they perceive in parents. Are these normal signs of aging or a signal that the end is near? Purdue family studies expert Karen Fingerman found this kind of anxiety common. In interviews with healthy mothers who were over seventy and had a nearby daughter, Fingerman found in these relationships a mix of mutual pleasure, tension, and ambivalence. She also found that some adult daughters had trouble seeing their mothers as women with their own feelings and agendas apart from being mothers. Some middle-aged daughters still wanted their mothers' praise and approval; they felt guilty and ashamed when their mothers criticized them. What particularly interested me was that the daughters often worried more about their mothers' health than the older women felt was warranted. The mothers complained that their daughters hovered too much and made them feel old.

For all of us to work together, for our family to be prepared for the challenges of this new life phase, family theorists King and Wynne said, each of us would need to have made the transition to seeing our parent as a separate person who does not exist only as our parent, to accept that they are just human beings like us, fallible and mortal. Some of the daughters in Fingerman's study still had a way to go.

It is unlikely all of us will have reached the same place in this journey. Our first test will be to see our parents' aging accurately, neither minimized nor exaggerated by our anxiety, and to work together for their benefit.

ACROSS THE MILES: DISTANCE AS SHIELD OR MAGNIFIER

On the most basic level, how often we see our parents affects the kind and quality of information we can glean about their health. If you see your parents every day or once a week, you will probably know more about how they're doing than siblings who can't visit so frequently. Among those I interviewed, usually it was someone close by who raised the first alarm about their parents. A sister had noticed troubling signs of forgetfulness: Mom staring at a row of pill bottles unable to remember whether she'd taken them, Dad having trouble negotiating the stairs, a near fall, vision problems, money lost to lottery scams. On the other hand, if I'm the sibling who sees my mother regularly, I may miss the incremental signs of decline that will shock you if you haven't seen her for a whole year. Even without factoring in our complicated relationships with our parents, it's possible to be too close or too far for accurate perception.

But family dynamics do add a whole layer of complication. I remember one pair of siblings who provide a good illustration. The sister who lived locally saw her father's aging with some clarity, but with some overreaction at the edges. Living alone in his old house, her dad had become forgetful, letting the cellar flood because he forgot to turn off the sprinklers. The neighbors told her they often saw him asleep in odd places, at the wheel of his pickup truck, curled up on his front steps. "There'll be a day," she said dramatically, "that when I check on Dad, I'll find him collapsed in the yard or dead in bed!" Her younger brother, who lived far from home, insisted there was nothing to worry about. "My dad had gray hair when I was in grade school," he said. "I didn't feel he was old. He'd always worked himself till he dropped and he'd sleep on the floor—all my life." This brother was not only a continent away, but he deliberately kept his calls to his father short, infrequent, and uncommunicative, he told me. "After my divorce and losing my job," he said, "I didn't want to upset him." This middle-aged man still saw his father as the occasionally loving tyrant he needed to please, so he stayed far away—in every sense—to preserve the myth of his father's eternal invincibility.

DOWN THE STREET OR ACROSS THE COUNTRY

It can be enlightening to examine the meaning of being close or far. What might our relative locations say about the kind of relationship we have with our parents? Is it just happenstance that one of my brothers lives around the corner, I live three hundred miles away, and my sister lives in Europe? What is the emotional meaning of being far? And what is the effect? The research on these thorny questions is mixed. Some scholarship concludes that we leave home primarily to pursue education or better jobs rather than because of problems with our parents. Other researchers argue that we're likelier as young adults to move away if our relationships with them are troubled. Some say that some distance from our parents can serve a useful purpose, easing tensions.

Although cultural and ethnic differences affect proximity to family, experts have found that parents and children who live near one another may always have had strong ties, especially mothers and daughters. These may be healthy relationships or deeply enmeshed. Either way, one cause and/or effect is this: When researchers ask older people to name a child who is particularly important to them, they tend to name one who lives *near* them.

Clearly, this issue of distance is complex. Family therapists say the more important question is whether we have achieved *emotional* separation from our parents. If family members are too fused, with parents and children seeing one another as an extension of their needs, it is more likely the children will put miles between themselves and their families or put up other barriers to speaking intimately with their parents.

"We take it as a sign of growth," family therapist Michael P. Nichols reflected, "to separate from our parents, and we measure our maturity by independence of family ties. Yet many of us still respond to our families as though they were radioactive and capable of inflicting great pain. Only one thing robs Superman of his extraordinary power: kryptonite, a piece of his home planet. A surprising number of adult men and women are similarly rendered helpless by even a brief visit to or from their parents."

How can we tell whether we are one of these people? Some of us readily confess that we fled from our parents when we were young. That does not mean, however, that in middle age we're still reacting to them the same way. Telltale signs, therapists say, are an aggressive show of independence and denying that family is important to us.

When we are middle-aged adults, the frequency and intimacy of our contact with our parents are probably the most revealing factors, especially because technology has also altered some of the effects of distance. We can call our parents three times a day if we like, no matter where we live. We can email or set up video calls and conferencing to see one another's faces when we talk.

Obviously, it is possible to live next door to our parents and have a terrible relationship with them—or a fabulous relationship. The same is true if we live a thousand miles apart. Still, it's worth considering what distance or closeness means to each of us and our siblings. Understanding the meaning may give us another clue to our own and our siblings' emotions as we react to our parents' aging.

OKAY—OR NOT? WHEN OUR PARENTS
CREATE THE CONFUSION

As long as our parents are competent, they should be deciding their own fate. Some are clear-eyed about their health and prospects and frank with their children. They plan for their own needs, hiring help or moving to a retirement or continuing care community. On the other hand, many cling to their houses and way of life until an incident or accident frightens them or their family. Alas, as research shows, many actively hide health problems from their children.

So, let's say I have a sister and she tells me Mom is starting to have balance issues. I should pay more attention, not dismiss her perception outright because my mom says it isn't so or because my sister tends to exaggerate. I also should not assume that I know what's happening and my sister doesn't. She may be readier to accept Mom's aging, or I may be. Or we may not be operating from the same set of facts.

For any number of reasons, good, bad, or happenstance, our parents often tell us each different things. Mom may feel closer to you and be more open to confiding her worries. She may talk to me more because she sees me more often or I just happen to be there when she's in pain or needs help. My father may be more willing to show me, his daughter, his vulnerability but feel he has to keep up his manly image with my brothers. Or our mother may take some perverse satisfaction in creating trouble between us and tell us each something different.

It's important to acknowledge that parents, whether their behavior is innocent or whether they have conscious or unconscious ulterior motives, can contribute to confused and differing perceptions among siblings. Even something as minor as a routine call home (*Isn't it odd that Mom won't put Dad on the phone when I ask to speak to him?*) or a Sunday dinner (*Why does Dad, who used to be so meticulous, keep wearing that stained, dirty shirt?*) can set off alarm bells in one of their children and cause the first conflicting perceptions among siblings. *(What are you talking about? Dad's fine, I talked to him on Thursday.)*

Gradually everyone will see that a change must be made. Some dramatic health event will occur, diagnosis of a serious illness, a broken hip, a stroke. "Whatever the trauma," writes Mario Tonti in *Siblings in Therapy,* "the impact on the children is powerful; it inevitably and inexorably changes the patterns of interaction between parents and children as well as among the children themselves."

The urgent question now is no longer *Is my mother old?* It becomes *Who will care for her now?* And this is where the real crisis comes for sisters and brothers—and the greatest opportunities for growth.

WHEN SIBLINGS DON'T SEE
THE SAME PARENT: WHAT TO DO

If you are the one in your family who is worried about changes in your parent and believe your sisters and brothers are in denial, what can you do?

Give it time.
Wait and try again, both with your parent and your siblings. A lag between one child and another seeing their parent's aging is typical. And, for all the reasons I have discussed in this chapter, it happens this way in many families. Usually the child who sees the parent frequently will notice something; others will sign on over time. So anticipate the gap and also expect that you and your siblings will close it.

If you feel your parent's long-term safety depends on some change being made, perhaps hiring help or moving them to a different residence, continue to bring it up. Barbara Silverstone's advice on how to discuss this with parents also applies to siblings. The social worker and author of *You and Your Aging*

Parent spoke to me just as the fourth edition of that work was going to press. She suggested an open and candid conversation with your father in which you express your worries and also tell him exactly what you can and cannot do for him if he has an accident and needs care. He may resist the first couple of times. "But after another month," Silverstone predicts, "maybe there is a mishap or two, or a robbery next door. Then bring it up again," she advises. "Let it sink in; don't push it." Time and events did resolve this issue for most people with whom I spoke.

Question your own perception, too.
Whether you are the concerned child or the one who thinks a sibling is overreacting, be willing to question your own version of the truth. Very often, each person understands a piece of it. There is seeing and then there is interpreting. I spoke with two fiftysomething sisters, for example, who lived in different cities from each other and from their eighty-four-year old mother. Whenever one visited, she told the other what she observed about their mother and her apartment. On one visit, the younger sister noticed a terrible smell in her mother's bathroom and spotted a smear of feces on the wall. Her mother refused to talk about this humiliating subject. This daughter believed her mother was losing control and should move to an assisted living apartment. But her sister disagreed. She said she knew about the odor but felt it was a result of their mother's diminished eyesight and failing sense of smell rather than something more serious. Moving her was too extreme, she said. Instead she suggested their mother have someone in a few hours a week to bathe her and do body care. Later, less debatable events occurred; the sisters and their mother agreed she should move. "I still think I was right," the younger one told me, "but it was all about waiting."

If you recall, Dottie Keller held out against her siblings' decision to move their mother through several months of contentious meetings. Later, she told me, "I was wrong. I am so grateful now that [my siblings] bring such different perspectives."

Factor in the possibility of incomplete information.
If you live far away, it is important to be aware that on a visit, you may not see the same behavior that a sibling nearby sees most of the time. Parents can put on a good show for a visit or feel especially enlivened by having a missed child show up. So Mom looks and feels better when you're there, and so you fly home dismissing your sister's observations as exaggerations. Try to find out for yourself.

Get reliable information on normal aging.
Not knowing what is normal aging and what is a symptom of something serious creates anxiety, and anxiety in one sibling can breed anxiety in others. Educate yourself about the aging process through reading, the Internet, or talking to an elder-care organization or doctor. Then, when any of your siblings overreact, someone in the family will have a reality mirror to hold up to the others.

Get a professional assessment.
In many cases, it does not matter who is right and who is wrong because the answer will become clearer with time. But if you feel your parent is in danger, bring in a professional, such as a physician, social worker, or other expert in aging to do an assessment of your parent.

"Very few people come to us to plan," Rona Bartelstone says of her geriatric care management company, Senior Bridge. "They come to us with the third or the tenth crisis." Yet, she says, getting the whole family on the same page early, which outsiders can often accomplish, can avert many of those crises. "Parents will listen to an outsider before they will listen to their children," she says, expressing a sentiment I have heard from other professionals. Elizabeth James, a nurse and geriatric care manager in Florida, is often called upon by families to make an evaluation of an older person living long-distance from their children. "Where the siblings divide," she told me, "my role, be it through telephone counseling or conference calls, is to be a consensus maker. Frequently, an outside professional doing a paper report helps them focus on the report rather than the emotional issues from childhood or wherever. Also, if I can get everyone involved initially, they relate to me, not to each other."

PART 2

RETURN TO THE HOUSE

OF CHILDHOOD:

ADAPTING OLD ROLES

AND RELATIONSHIPS,

CONFRONTING

OLD CONFLICTS

CHAPTER THREE

WHO'S TAKING CARE OF MOM? ADAPTING ROLES AND RELATIONSHIPS TO TAKE ON PARENT CARE

NOT ONE OF THE WAGNER KIDS lived anywhere near Lincoln, Nebraska, as their parents aged. Tammie and Tim, the oldest at sixty-one and fifty-nine, respectively, had moved to California, and Susannah and Stu, fifty-four and fifty-seven, to Portland, Oregon. The parents had said they never wanted to be a "burden" to their kids and had saved money for an assisted living apartment, but well into their eighties—and riddled with health issues that included failing eyesight, memory, and mobility—they resisted leaving the house where they'd raised their kids. Every time one of the children visited, he or she would take their parents to tour senior facilities with no result. The siblings talked to one another with increasing anxiety and to their parents with greater persuasiveness, until finally the family reached a consensus. The couple, now nearing ninety, would relocate to a care residence in Portland near Susannah and Stu. They picked one less than a mile from Susannah's home. And so this daughter became her parents' primary caregiver, supervising her parents' care and being first on call for emergencies. "I was happy to have them close," Susannah said.

None of it was easy, but it all made perfect sense. Susannah, an HMO administrator, worked four days a week, her children were grown, and her husband was supportive. Stu, a newspaper reporter, had lunch with the parents on Tuesdays, Thursdays, and Sundays, days Susannah generally didn't come. They also coordinated their vacations. And Tammie and Tim spent their own vacations in Portland, taking over for their siblings.

Although Susannah had always felt closest to their difficult mother, an insecure woman who often put her children down, being with her now was hard. Her mother's negativity and depression had intensified with age. She railed against the medical system, blaming her macular degeneration on her cataract surgery. She refused all advice. "It's hard for me," Susannah said, "that she can't say, 'That's that. At least, I can still see and recognize people.' I'd spend more time with them if I didn't have to listen to her constant complaining. And my dad, who was always afraid to 'rile' her, hardly says anything anymore."

When her mother's unrelenting misery got her down, Susannah called one of her siblings to vent. They would commiserate. "The boys are willing to call Mom's bullshit," Susannah said with a laugh. "I could never have handled my mother emotionally," Tim told me. "Susannah voices frustration about Mom, and I laugh. It's a way of being in it together. But I do feel guilty." As does Tammie, who calls her younger sister nearly every day and sends her "little girly gifts, like her favorite face cream or some cute, funny pajamas."

"I appreciate the recognition," Susannah acknowledged with a pleased lift in her voice. "It makes a difference to me to feel I have their support."

PLANNING AHEAD FOR CAREGIVING

Experts agree that when it comes to making a decision on the whens, hows, and ifs of caregiving, what works best for the family is for everyone—elderly parents, adult children with spouses and children and other intimates—to get together and make a plan, in advance. But the reality is, few families behave this way.

Care management pioneer Rona Bartelstone has seen many attitude shifts since the 1970s, when an older generation automatically expected their kids would care for them. Now, she says, many old people feel they don't want to be a burden to their kids. Yet they don't go the next step and plan for the care they might need. "My mother," Bartelstone said, "who is demented now, always said to me, 'I don't need to worry about these things because it's not going to happen to me. Or when it does, I'll know what to do.' Well, obviously, when you're demented, you don't know what to do," she said with a laugh, "because your judgment is impaired. This is a pretty typical attitude. So it's often hard for boomers to get their parents to plan."

As adult children, we're not exactly eager to broach this conversation, either, and it doesn't always go well when we do. Research conducted by Home Instead Senior Care found that almost a third of adults have trouble communicating about elder care with their mother or father because of "a continuation of the parent/child role." Another poll found that 60 percent of boomers report that they talk regularly to their parents about health issues. Yet only 32 percent of older people say their children talk to them about this. What does the disparity mean? When we do talk, we're not clear? Our parents don't remember or don't want to remember? Maybe. In my own research, I have found that, typically, as long as one of our parents is healthy enough to care for the other, and even after one dies, we still put off planning for our surviving parent. A great many of us do nothing to address our parents' aging until a crisis strikes and we siblings may suddenly have to act in concert—if we can.

AS GOOD AS IT GETS: FAMILY CAREGIVING DONE RIGHT

No family is perfect, and neither were the Wagners. But they met the tumultuous changes of this transition in a close-to-ideal fashion, separately and together. In some ways, of course, they were lucky. Susannah was relatively available, Stu lived nearby, and money was not a problem. Nor were they plunged suddenly into crisis. But even this was not just luck. From the first signs of their parents' aging, they made good decisions. The parents planned for their future while they still could, and everybody was involved in the discussion. The old couple was able to live in their own space, a practical solution that removes one potential source of tensions, and the situation most older people prefer, as AARP housing specialist Elinor Ginzler explained.

Most important, the right person became the primary caregiver for the right reasons, practically and emotionally. No one assumed, for example, that Susannah would just slip back into being her mom's emotional support, although Susannah, more than the others, had done that as a child. While she took primary responsibility looking after her parents, she also took care of herself. She did what they needed with kindness, but without heaping more on herself than she could handle. She did not, for example, make herself excessively miserable by spending more time with her mother than she could tolerate. She took satisfaction in helping her parents, and she reached out to her siblings for comfort and accepted whatever help they could give. They not only helped but kept a constant stream of appreciation flowing her way. This is nearly as good as it gets. And many families don't get even close.

A host of obstacles make such sharing and mutual support difficult to achieve, including lack of money, lack of options, and perhaps, sometimes, the absence of family goodwill. But as families, we can do this *better*. We need to recognize that caring for an aging parent is not just a job to be done but a new era of family life that involves us all. This is true even if one person does most of the day-to-day work. It is far too easy to think, "I'm off the hook because my sister lives near Mom and will take care of everything." She may very well do everything. But if your sister falls into parent care by default, and ends up alone with total responsibility for Mom, that is not a good thing—for her, for Mom, or, believe it or not, for you. I can attest to this from my own experience.

As siblings, we need to be more conscious about who becomes the primary caregiver. We need to rethink our old roles and not just round up the usual suspects. We often assume that the sister or brother who has always done everything in the family will now shoulder all the caregiving. Obviously there are practical considerations such as location, availability, and competing responsibilities. The usual suspect may turn out to be the logical choice. But we also need to consider which sibling is best-suited to care for Mom or Dad, given the temperaments of parents and children and their relationships with one another. Most of all, we need to consider all this as a family.

I say this with the caution that family dynamics are difficult to change. They alter slowly, if at all. For instance, if I am the sibling who has always been the most responsible one in my family, the great likelihood is that I still am, and that the caregiving load will fall most heavily on me. If you have always been regarded as the successful outsider, admired yet seen as aloof and resented, your family is unlikely to stop thinking of you this way even if you rush back and try to be more involved now. Each person has a stake in seeing you the way you have always been. They'll probably resist your help even as they complain that you're not helping.

If Susannah Wagner's brother Tim had suddenly decided that he needed to be the one to take care of the parents, the others might have resisted, which would have been a shame. A family that remains rigidly static limits the possibility of surprising and healthy changes. Yet the Wagners did adapt successfully, not with a revolution but with adjustments.

BUT WE DO IT DIFFERENTLY! WE'RE LATINO, AFRICAN AMERICAN, ASIAN . . .

Different ethnic groups and nationalities have different customs regarding obligations to family, beliefs about gender roles, elders, and ties with in-laws. Outlooks on life and caring for the elderly may also vary by group. Some scholars have found, for example, that African Americans see caring for the elderly more as a part of life rather than a disruption of life as do many of their white counterparts. Latinos expect more help from their extended families than Anglo-American families, and Native Americans have very strong beliefs about giving back to those who gave to them. But cultural norms go just so far, especially in this fast-paced world of trying to balance work and family. In every culture there are families that may eventually break with tradition, often out of necessity. And within each family, each sibling can interpret these traditions differently, making interactions complicated, whatever the cultural mores.

To take just one example, family therapist Celia Falicov, an expert on Latino families, told me about a middle-class Mexican American family whom she saw in her practice. "They fit the stereotype and reality of Latino families," she observed, "to maintain lifelong connections, to have much less geographic mobility." Nevertheless, Falicov reported, the mother wanted more closeness than her

Americanized children could give her, and there were tensions among the three daughters about what they each did to take care of her, even though they all lived nearby. The daughter who felt closest to Mom, Falicov said, would tell the sister closer to the father to be loyal to Mom and do more, be nicer and not get angry. If you feel that you or other family members are running up against deeply ingrained cultural norms within your own family, perhaps because you aren't willing to have a parent live with you, keep in mind that these issues affect all adult children during this transition. "These dynamics," Falicov concluded, "are pretty universal."

Why Only One?

Look around. It's pretty rare for any of us to share parent care equally with a sibling. After poring over a dozen caregiving studies, Victoria Hilkevitch Bedford, a family gerontologist at the University of Indianapolis, concluded that despite how different families were, nearly all of them had one "exclusive principal caregiver." Among those I interviewed, I found the same thing: Even in warm and cooperative families, one person did most of the care.

On the face of it, this does not seem to make sense and seems terribly unfair. But having one person she knows she can rely on may feel better and safer to Mom. As people grow old and dependent, family therapist Mario Tonti explained in *Siblings in Therapy*, they are suffering many losses—of people they love, their health, what they can control. The kind of care they need becomes increasingly personal. "In order to maintain a sense of value and dignity," Tonti observed, "elders require an intimate relationship with one person who will provide both personal care and reassurance of individual worth." When the family works well in this new phase of the family, he says, it creates one primary caregiver and siblings who support her.

SELECTING THE "RIGHT" ONE: WHY ONE SIBLING CAN BE A BETTER CHOICE THAN ANOTHER

There are invariably reasons beyond the superficial why one sister or brother ends up taking this role. The research on this is only a little helpful. Most of it has focused on demographics, such as the location, career, and family responsibilities of the adult children. A few studies have delved a little deeper, looking, for example, at how memories of favoritism in childhood affect an adult's willingness to help an aging parent. But on the whole, with the exception of Elaine Brody's early studies, scholars have only recently begun to study the interplay between family dynamics and caregiver selection. The jury is still out, for example, on the question of whether the sibling who lives nearest to the parents is likely to be the one with the best relationship to them or the worst. Nor does it tell us which child is the best person to care for a parent. But if we consider what these relationships are like, we can make better choices.

WHO ARE THE CAREGIVERS?

The "typical" caregiver is a working, educated forty-six-year-old woman helping her mother about twenty hours a week due to "old age," diabetes, cancer, or heart disease, according to the National Alliance for Caregiving. Almost a quarter of primary caregivers live an average of more than seven hours from their parent.

Since the 1980s, when the first swell in the elderly population made itself felt, researchers have devoted study after study to understanding how families care for their old people and who does the care. The findings remain remarkably consistent. Cleveland State University sociologist Sarah H. Matthews, for example, found that, overwhelmingly, daughters were more likely than sons to be caregivers and proximity ruled: Even among daughters, the one who lived closest to their parent, even ten minutes closer than a sister, would probably take on the job. Yet who worked and how much, and who was married with kids, also factored in.

But the times they are changing—a little. More of us are caring for our parents long-distance. More of us are men, now at 39 percent, says the National Alliance for Caregiving. And those numbers may be on the rise. When Towson University gerontologist Donna Wagner surveyed employees of three Fortune 500 companies in 2003 for the MetLife Mature Market Institute, she found that men were as likely as women to be primary caregivers, defined as the person who took responsibility for making care decisions for a parent or providing care themselves. They helped their parents with medications, shopping, and transportation, although they rarely did hands-on personal care.

It used to be that most men who took care of their parents relied on their wives to do the actual tasks. While many women still care for their in-laws, too many of us are now working to do elder care full-time. Also, with our high divorce rate and so many of us in second or third marriages, wives are less likely to have had long, intimate relationships with their in-laws. "If I'm in this position," said geriatric care manager Rona Bartelstone, "when my husband's parents start to have health issues, I'm going to say, 'Listen, they're *your* parents. *You* need to be the caregiver.'"

Some men become caregivers because they have no sisters. But that's not the only reason. Some of the men I interviewed had been involved fathers. They saw no gender disconnect in caring for their parents; for them, it was almost a no-brainer. They made the same kinds of sacrifices as women, experiencing stress on their family relationships, friendships, and work lives. Yet, for all these changes, women still do more—more hours, more hands-on care.

Who's Right? Consider the Relationships

One reason the Wagners worked so well as a family is that Susannah had the best relationship with their querulous mother. Probably any of them could have cared for their easygoing father with relatively little angst. In her psychologically probing studies of caregivers from the 1970s through the early 1990s, Elaine Brody found that the caregiver's history with her parent played a critical role in the caregiving experience. This is basic.

Of her siblings, Susannah Wagner had always felt closest to her mother. She could tolerate her insecurities better than anyone else, and having her father's unflappable temperament helped. Her older sister, Tammie, had a much harder time with their mother. Throughout their childhood, Mom reacted to Tammie as if she were her own taller, prettier sister, whom Tammie resembled. As for her sons, Mom had not known how to relate to them. Tim recalled his mother's disapproval. "A couple of times really crushing," he said with a rueful laugh.

Whatever difficulties the Wagner kids had with their mother, each was willing to take some part. For Tim, taking a secondary role was a reasonable and valid choice. Some people are clearly wrong for the top job; recognizing this is important for all of them.

REASONS OR EXCUSES?
WHEN YOU DON'T WANT TO HELP

Why aren't we more involved in our parents' care? We tell ourselves many things; some of them are true, some are half true, and others are distortions. Here's a sampling of some that I've heard: *I have my hands full with other problems. I'm too far away. My sister has it all taken care of. No one has asked me to do anything. It's not my job—my brother is the empathetic one. It's women's work.*

> Whatever we say, our reasons are likely to have deep roots in our family dynamics, some of which I'll talk about more in the following chapters. Whatever reasons we give ourselves, at the least it's worth questioning our logic. We may decide to behave differently; we may not. We may find that we've been right all along and there is little we can do because our siblings won't accept our help. But if we at least try, we'll probably learn something—and be less subject to guilt and regret.

Who's Wrong? Adapting Old Roles to New Times

Within the house of childhood, as I explained earlier, we are each implicitly assigned roles that keep the family running and stable. One of us may carve out a niche as the well-adjusted one, another a troublemaker, another a peacemaker who smoothes things over when we get angry at one another. Let's say that my job is to make sure our emotionally fragile mother doesn't fall apart. If you are my sister, you may be Dad's partner and confidante. Inevitably, some of us will do more of the family work than others: remember that emotional division of labor.

Whatever function these roles served in the past, they may be obsolete and counterproductive when we are middle-aged adults with needy parents. Yet if I were the one who took care of things when I was a child, I may just keep on keeping on no matter how overwhelming my responsibilities and emotions become. My sister and brother are likely to let me carry on, just sticking with the status quo. It's common, it feels natural, and it's a very a bad idea.

University of Miami nursing professor Victoria Mitrani fights this role inertia among the families in her studies of dementia caregiving. When people are in crisis, she told me, they usually fall back on ways of behaving that feel familiar to them, with one person doing everything. The therapists working with Mitrani's families take this tack with them: "Don't go back to acting the way you did when you were kids, and one of you was obviously much more competent than the other because she was older. You now are all competent adults."

Mitrani has found that when the siblings hear this, they often begin to see how tasks can be split up. Without this outside perspective, it often doesn't occur to them. "It's not because you have a bunch of lazy people," Mitrani told me, "but because they're just reverting back to old ways. Even in well-functioning families, when they're hit by a crisis, they tend to adjust by going back to what they know."

MARY-ELIZABETH: ALWAYS IN CHARGE

Of the smart and feisty clan of ten children in one Boston family, Mary-Elizabeth was the wrong choice to care for their mother, but none of her siblings realized this at first. As the first child, she had been thrust very young into a traditional slot in big families: surrogate parent to her sisters and brothers. Although she resented the responsibility, she cherished the special position it gave her in the family. At sixty-three, when their mother needed help, this supercompetent retired auditor took charge with a vengeance.

This felt natural to her sisters and brothers, who were grateful, at first. Mary-Elizabeth hired a full-time aide, wrote out lists of foods and activities for her mother, and strictly enforced her rules. Her style was to get the job done. But it soon became apparent that Mary-Elizabeth had what one brother called an "abrasive" style of care. One of her sisters gave me this example. It was their mother's birthday, and they took her shopping for clothes. "Mom was in Filene's dressing room," she related, "and Mary-Elizabeth was yanking her around like a paper doll. It was horrifying, but my sister was on a mission."

Mary-Elizabeth was devoted to her mother and was convinced she knew what was best for her. She had no idea that she was acting out her old resentments. This beleaguered oldest sister had enjoyed little childhood, her brother explained. "She was a mom figure to all of us, and we looked up to her. But my parents gave her the brunt of the housework when she was just ten. Dad would yell at Mary-Elizabeth, and she'd yell at us. Nowadays, I find her delightful, except when she gets back with the family, which turns her into a crazy person."

Luckily, their mother could still speak for herself, and she whispered to the others, asking if someone else could take care of her. Gingerly, Mary-Elizabeth's siblings, with their mother's encouragement, made new arrangements. Although done as gently as possible, this was not an easy shift, especially for Mary-Elizabeth, who was reluctant to accept a supporting role. But theirs was an example of a family that adapted successfully to the new demands of family life rather than clinging to the parts they had always played.

THE "PERFECT" CHOICE? NOT NECESSARILY

Perfect choices don't exist. We have complicated lives and established family dynamics. Let's say my sister—who's a geriatric nurse—lives right near our mother. Perfect, right? Well, no—not if she can't spend ten minutes with Mom without screaming at her. If, after considering all possible alternatives, she's still our only option, we need to recognize what their relationship is like and find ways to work around it. Could we, for example, minimize contact between them? Maybe we could make sure one of us calls Mom every day so that she's less emotionally needy. Maybe we could pool some money and hire paid help. We need to look at what each of us can do to help. And if we don't want to help, we need to examine what is holding us back.

Whatever else we do, it's important to give emotional support to the sister or brother who's taking the major responsibility. This, more than anything else, a mass of research has found, helps the caregiver. Inevitably, it also helps the whole family. I have spoken to so many people who felt isolated with their parent, caught up in sadness and stress. They were overwhelmed by their emotions and by the mountain of responsibilities they handled for their own families and jobs as well as for their parents. When they cared for a difficult parent, like the Wagners' mom, sharing their frustration and being able to laugh about it gave them comfort and ease. Psychotherapist Judy Zarit, Steven Zarit's wife and early collaborator, has conducted family meetings with caregivers and their siblings for thirty years. She vividly recalls one woman at wit's end caring for her demented mother. When her family asked how they could help, she said, "Just call me once a week and let me vent. You're the only ones who can understand."

ACROSS THE MILES: YOU CAN STILL HELP

With some planning and good communication with your on-site sibling, you can feel connected to the caregiving process (and can alleviate some guilt) if you choose or are given the right tasks.

LEND AN EAR (AND A SHOULDER).

Calling to express appreciation and concern, research shows, and letting your sister or brother simply vent (about a parent, about each other, about anything) is one of the most valuable services you can offer as a long-distance sibling.

LEND A HAND BY PHONE OR INTERNET.

Even when you're far away, there are still things you can do, such as arranging meal deliveries or a car service to take your parent to doctors' appointments. You may be able to pay your parent's bills online, fill out and mail insurance forms, take care of taxes. You can also do research online to find out more about your parent's condition or locate resources such as adult day care or support groups. If you can afford it, pay for an aide to come in part-time or even for special occasions. But also be aware that some things are just too frustrating or complex to try to manage without being there.

OFFER PERSPECTIVE—CAREFULLY.

If you're the sibling who lives far away and visits only a few times a year, you may be the one who notices certain declines (or improvements) in a parent's condition, as opposed to the sibling who sees the parent daily or weekly. In families where siblings really get along, a sister or brother may ask for your input: "How do you think Dad's doing? Do you see a big difference between this summer and last fall? I can't tell if he's getting worse or is just about the same."

Your attitude should be, advises Evan Imber-Black, a family therapist at the Ackerman Institute for the Family and author of *The Secret Life of Families,* "I'm coming to give my sister a break," not "I'm coming to tell you what to do. Be a little humble." Your observations can be valuable if they don't imply criticism of the on-site caregiver. Instead of something accusatory, like "Dad looks awful. Are you sure you're giving him his medications on time?" try something collaborative, like "How does Dad look to you? His color looks a little off to me. Should we go over his medications with him?"

RECOGNIZING OUR NEEDS:
WHAT PARENT CARE EVOKES IN US

All of us, whether women or men, whether caregivers or not, have complicated motivations that we bring to anything we do. When we talk about caregiving, we think of our parents as the ones with needs. But, as adult children, we also have emotional needs, typically unconscious, evoked by the very nature of caring for parents in decline. Gratifying some of these needs helps us get through this difficult time. Satisfying others makes things harder. But either way, uncovering and examining them can help us better navigate the tough transitions ahead.

A Job Worth Doing: The Need for Positive Meaning

The texture of caregiving is different for everyone. Some of us live in the same home with our parent and do hands-on personal care, such as bathing and dressing. Most live nearby and act progressively as chauffeur, shopper, medical adviser, and first responder. Some supervise care from a distance, spending countless hours on the phone and in paperwork with hired staff, nursing home administrators, and insurance adjustors. We all make sacrifices of time with people and things we love; we have lives disrupted, relationships strained, plans put on hold.

People have told me of periods of relative calm when Mom and Dad are doing okay, the health aide has been showing up, the care staff has been attentive. Then these stretches of tranquility are punctuated by heart-stopping trips to the emergency room, waiting for life-and-death outcomes as systems shut down, kidneys fail, lungs fill with fluid. After sleepless nights, exhaustion, and worry, a lucky outcome is back to "normal" for that parent. Suddenly the other parent has a stroke, and it's off to the hospital again and recovery or rehab or a nursing home or hospice or death. Loss is always a near possibility; ambivalence can lurk as a guilty presence; and for some, piercing loneliness is a constant companion.

On the other side, most adult children experience profound satisfactions. Researchers tell us that the vast majority of people caring for their parents see themselves in a very positive light: expressing affection, ensuring good treatment for their mothers and fathers, strengthening their family bonds, and showing their own children a model for responsible and worthy behavior.

Some, like Susannah Wagner, had relatively easy parent care situations. Others I spoke to had it harder but made it look easy. Then there was a small minority who suffered through the experience as an ongoing trial with little reward. What spells the difference? That's a question that has long intrigued researchers. Many years ago, Penn State gerontologist Steven Zarit noticed that some caregivers became demoralized or depressed even when their parent's condition was manageable while others with more strenuous care demands rolled with the punches. Zarit was studying dementia caregivers, but experts say that his results are likely to apply to caregivers generally.

As Zarit and others studied these people over many years, they found that whether they experienced depression or satisfaction, felt exhausted or coped well, did not depend on how much work and sacrifice they put in. It depended on the meaning they gave to the experience. If their cultural or religious beliefs put a high value on caring for the old, for example, or if they thought of parent care as a normal part of life rather than a disruption, they did much better than those who felt trapped in a consuming chore without any choice.

Among those I interviewed, I found that how punishing, how satisfying, or even how joyful people found parent care depended not on how many hours they spent doing it, how much money they had, or where they did it. What mattered more? The complex mix of emotions they brought to their role, their history in their family and especially with the mother or father they were caring for. In other words, what *we* need from parent care—often without realizing it—colors the meanings we give it. It profoundly affects our ability to cope, to set reasonable limits for ourselves, and to get help when we need it.

So Many Balls in the Air: The Need for Control

One of the biggest struggles of adult children is how to take care of parents and also take care of themselves, their families, and careers. Workplace studies show that compared with other employees, caregivers are more likely to be absent, work fewer hours, do less socializing, pursue fewer outside interests, and have higher anxiety levels.

Health-care professionals, support groups, books, websites, and social service organizations offer many suggestions to caregivers. Take care of yourself. Exercise. Talk to friends and family. Read books about your parent's condition. Use respite services. Reduce your workload. Let go of unessential household chores. All of this is good advice, according to a study of "sandwich" generation couples by the Portland State University team of Margaret B. Neal and Leslie B. Hammer. The caregivers they studied who managed best amped up their emotional stores by making time for their spouses, their personal relationships, and themselves. Those who gave up their social lives did worst.

I know caregivers who were near breaking point until they joined a gym, lost weight, or changed or limited their responsibilities. But for many of us, doing such things is not easy. We have to let go of some deeply held convictions before we can allow ourselves to do less and find ways for other people to do more. Whether or not we have sisters or brothers willing to help, caregiving experts say, we need to look at whether we are actually willing to accept help—from any source—and to relinquish any part of our role.

At Rush University Medical Center in Chicago, I got a window onto some of these internal struggles and how professionals can help. I'd spoken to other experts, but Robyn Golden, head of the Older Adults Program here, offered me a chance to brainstorm with her staff of social workers: Debra Markovitz, spirited and insightful; Madeleine Rooney, an earnest midlife woman; and Lauren Petchenik, an eager young recruit.

Every day these professionals work with families of the elderly, from affluent suburbanites to urban working-class minorities, and they see it all: overwhelmed caregivers, families trying to work together, distraught middle-aged children squabbling over their parents.

It was a common cry among their clients, Golden said, that they needed help and no one would help them, but she and her staff had seen many of these same complainers refuse to share their labors with a sister or brother. "Caregivers often deny this," she said, "but they won't *let* the others do it."

Her colleagues nodded agreement. When I asked for an example, several heads turned toward Madeleine Rooney. Someone prompted: "Madeleine?" Rooney hesitated. Then someone else reminded her of the difficulty she herself experienced in sharing elder-care responsibilities before moving to Chicago.

Well, yes, she conceded. Her parents lived in their own home in Maryland; her younger brother lived nearby, and her older brother in California. "Even though my brothers would offer to step in," she said, "it was difficult to tell them what to do." Her older brother, in particular, offered help, to call the doctors or anything else he could do long-distance. "It was very difficult for me to delegate," she said.

"I've often heard caregivers say," Golden interposed, "'I have all the balls in the air, and I can't drop one.'"

When Rooney shopped for her parents, she explained, "I felt no one else would know about the special store Mom liked, the coupons to use, the brands to buy. It was stressful for me, but I continued to do it and my mom encouraged me to do it. She didn't acknowledge my stress."

"It's hard to get people to step back from their role," Markovitz commented. "It's a paradox. They ask, 'Who will help me?' Then they say, 'I'm the caregiver, I know all the routines and subtleties of what my mom needs.'"

"No one understands Mom the way I do." Golden volunteered an oft-heard sentiment.

Markovitz told the group about one client who would not take a night off because his sister wanted to cook chicken instead of fish for their mother. "They had a big fight," she recalled. "I asked him, 'What's the worst thing that can happen if your mother eats chicken instead of fish?' I showed him, 'This is a big deal for *you*, not for your mom. But caregiving is about *her.*'"

The irony, Rooney learned, was that when she had to leave Maryland, she easily found a substitute shopper. "We called the church," she related, "and found five ladies who were willing to do the shopping." The social worker learned something from this that she wished she'd known sooner. "If I'd done this before," she said, "I would have had less stress, and Mom would have had more quality time with me."

"As a professional," Markovitz explained, "I need to preserve the caregiving capability of the person. They experience guilt and they're entrenched in their role. It's become their identity, who they are now. When I ask caregivers how it would feel to let others do this role, it's hard for them to even *imagine* it."

It's My Job as a Daughter: Gender-Based Needs

Caregiving can become a one-man show, but it is likelier to be a one-woman show. This is not only because there are more female caregivers, but because, as caregivers, women generally have different expectations of themselves than men. Women not only do more caregiving, they suffer more from doing it: more anxiety, anger, exhaustion, and depression. Why?

One reason may be that, as women, we do more hands-on, intensive care. But even when we don't, we feel that more is demanded of us. Women are still conditioned to be the ones who make others happy. Even in this postfeminist era, we still experience higher expectations on all fronts: from ourselves, from society, from our sisters and our parents, especially our mothers. When sociologists Jill Suitor and Karl Pillemer asked older women which child they'd want to care for them, they overwhelmingly picked a daughter, usually the one who had helped them most in the past.

These higher expectations of women play a powerful,

sometimes hidden role in our family dynamics. Often, Elaine Brody explained, "they do not differentiate between caring *about* and caring *for* the parent. Care then, is interpreted as doing whatever is necessary *for* the parent; if the caregiver does not do it all, she doesn't care enough *about* the parent."

This cultural bias can make life even harder for a woman whose old role in her family was to be the responsible one and take care of everybody else. These were some of the things driving Bev, a sixty-one-year-old corporate consultant with a regal bearing and decisive manner.

BEV: WORKING TO MAKE MOM "HAPPY"

When I first spoke to Bev, she had just taken charge of her mother. After her father's death, she and her brother, Hank, had been shocked to discover that he had been actively covering up their mother's poor health. Mom could not live alone in her Florida condo. So Bev decided to find her mother an assisted living home near her own home in San Diego. "Connecticut [where Hank lived] is too cold for Mom," she said, "and my brother's relationship with her has always been rocky."

From childhood on, Bev explained, her parents had looked to her to make decisions for herself and for them. On the one hand, she was treated like a "princess." But there was a cost. "I was never really a child," she said, sounding both regretful and proud. Her role in the family, appointed and self-appointed, was to be the fixer of whatever was wrong. "I am overresponsible," she said. "With everything I do, I suffer from the need to do more than I need to do—and everyone benefits—my clients, my friends, my mother. I take care of business. It's who I am, and I do it alone." In her voice I heard pride, resignation, exhaustion, and a hint of resentment.

At her mother's nursing home, she was the same A-plus student her parents had so admired. "I think I can never do enough to take care of her," she said. Despite a seventy-hour workweek, Bev saw her mother at least four times weekly. She bought her a tank of tropical fish, and cleaned and serviced the tank. She took Mom to doctor's appointments, shopping for clothes, and haircuts. She obsessed: "Is she having a good time there?"

"Mom sits at dinner with one friend," Bev told me, "and has stopped doing other activities. I worry constantly, and I've ripped the staff apart. That's who I am."

"I'm exhausted," she added. "But I'm proud of the job I'm doing, and everyone says, 'Your mother is so lucky!'"

A year after this conversation, Bev told me she had made some peace with the limits of what she could do for her mother. Other women I met could not let go of their need to take care of their mothers emotionally; inevitably, they felt anxiety, guilt, and anger. Theirs is an impossible mission, as Elaine Brody observed. "Making people happy," she said, "is an unrealistic and unachievable goal. Given the human condition, given the fact that some older people's life-long personalities preclude their being made happy, and given the unhappiness and depression of older people that often accompany their age-related losses (including loss of functional capacity), the expectation of caregivers that they can make the parent happy is often doomed to failure."

The men I met who were caring for a parent did not speak of their parent's happiness as a goal. They focused on giving them the best care. Nor did they ever feel they were doing too little or that, generally, their efforts were taken for granted. Rather the reverse. One man called it a "sad social commentary" that so many professionals and visitors at his father's nursing home heaped him with praise and seemed astounded that a son would attend so tenderly to his father.

Another difficulty women face is that most are caring for their mothers. As recent feminist scholarship has documented, the mother-daughter caregiving relationship is almost universally fraught with ambivalence. Feeling ambivalent gives us one more thing to feel guilty about and to defend ourselves against, often by getting angry at somebody else.

STUBBORN AND UNCOOPERATIVE: WHEN PARENTS ACT LIKE "CHILDREN"

Your dad won't take his pills, goes out without his oxygen tank, and drives away the aides you hire. Besides wringing your hands, what can you do? Try banding together with your siblings and present a united front. Discuss with him the consequences of his actions. Just as important, be clear with him about the limits of what you and your siblings will do. If he can't keep an aide, for example, he probably won't be able to live at home because none of you are available to help him during the day. If he lives in an independent senior apartment but won't follow his doctor's orders, enlist the staff to explain that he'll have to move to assisted living. Ask someone he'll listen to, such as a medical professional or therapist he respects, or a clergyperson he likes, to talk to him. Sometimes a few clear conversations are all it takes, especially if you are firm and set limits. But if you can't get anywhere with him (and the professionals who work with him can't), all you can do is accept that as long as he is competent, he will make his own decisions, whether they are good for him or not—no matter how much they pain you. Like a parent letting go of a child, here's yet another moment where we may have to let go of our parents, and let them make their own mistakes.

ADAPTING ON THE INSIDE:
THE PUSH-PULL OF THE TWILIGHT

Taking on the actual job of caring for parents doesn't mean we've reached the other side of our developmental challenge as adult children. We may have changed what we're doing, but not necessarily how we feel inside. That's the nature of a developmental crisis. As we push forward to becoming more mature, we're also pulled backward to what's familiar, trying to hold on to what we're losing: the self that is still the child of our parents. That's the push-pull that affects every aspect of this long transition.

Which of us has not had the unsettling experience of visiting our parents and finding ourselves reacting like teenagers? "Put on my jacket? Mom, I'm fifty years old. Don't you think I know how to dress myself?" Perhaps your mother was just looking for a way to mother you, and a more mature response would have been: "Thanks, Mom, that's a good idea." That's a minor example of a childhood struggle resurrected. A sibling's hot buttons will be different from yours. The needs they evoke will be different. You might find yourself reacting defensively to an offhand remark by your father that sounds critical. Your sister might feel hurt that your mom doesn't seem interested in what she's saying.

By the time our parents are in decline, most of us have learned to relate to them, more or less, as one adult to another—although, psychologists say, we will never relate to them as maturely and independently as we do to other people. However, the adult-to-adult relationship we've formed with our parents is thrown off-kilter by their growing dependency and our feelings about their mortality. Now we are taking care of them, doing things that one adult does not usually do for another, especially a child for a parent. We have to interact with them intimately again about their lives, struggle with them over important decisions, eventually even make decisions for them. Ironically, as we take on these mature responsibilities, we also feel pulled backward to our original parent-child dynamic. It's as if an invisible hook from the house of childhood grabs us with a gentle tug—or a yank that knocks us off our ever-so-adult feet. We can find ourselves reenacting some of our childhood patterns of relating to our mother or father: disagreeing, rebelling, obeying, trying to please, or trying to get attention with good (or bad) behavior.

In her studies of caregiving daughters, Brody observed that they fell into certain psychological categories: the favored child; the rejected child; the exceptionally close daughter who has not fully separated from her mother; the daughter who finds self-esteem and a worthwhile role in caregiving. One of her more crowded categories was that of the "burden bearer," the daughter who, from childhood on, had assumed the major share of family responsibilities. "These women may present themselves as long-suffering, patient, martyred, self-sacrificing, and even oppressed," Brody observed in *Women in the Middle: Their Parent Care Years*. Still others, she noted, might feel envious and resentful. "Although the behavior of such women may be viewed as admirable," Brody speculated, "one wonders what gratification they may be obtaining from the very burdens that ostensibly weigh so heavily."

The categories Brody observed are useful, but they also overlap. Bev, for example, was both a "burden bearer" and a favored child. I think it's more helpful to think of ourselves as operating out of a complex mix of psychological needs, some mature, some less mature. Taking satisfaction in being able to do a good thing for someone we care about is mature and healthy. So too is feeling competent and responsible. Can you feel these satisfactions but also take a tiny bit of less mature gratification in feeling superior to your sister or brother? Yup.

When I interviewed people about caring for their parents, needs like these usually emerged from between the lines. Most wanted to express their love for their parents; some were yearning for their mother or father to finally show *them* love. Some needed to prove something: that they were the only ones in their family who knew how to do things right, for example, or that, no matter what they did, nobody would appreciate them. Many felt a subtle—or not so subtle—wish to think of themselves as a better child or a more caring person than their sister or brother. Some needed to feel worthwhile, to have a cause, to be right. Others were trying to atone for having hurt or disappointed their parents.

Very few of us are fully aware of all our motivations. In my interviews, people might have a sudden insight about their motivations. Once they understood themselves better, they found it easier to cope with their parents and siblings. Some people figured this out on their own. Maria, for example, had been trying very hard to take care of her mother in a responsible and mature way and usually succeeded. But until she figured out what was happening, she sometimes found herself drawn into childish interactions with her mother that reduced her to tears.

MARIA: DARING TO DISPLEASE MA

Maria seemed the kind of good-hearted, affectionate woman who would hug a stranger who looked sad. The fifty-four-year-old business owner and mother in Queens, New York, was solid, sensible, and empathic. When her mother's hypertension and diabetes made her too weak to work or grow tomatoes or take long walks, Maria said, "Ma, move in with us." "It wasn't an obligation," she said. "You do it because you want to."

On a practical level, this made sense for the Herrera siblings. Maria's children were grown, and she ran her carpentry business from her home. Her older sister, Luisa, and their mother did not get along, and her brothers lived out of town. Maria's becoming caregiver also computed on an emotional level. Maria had always been closest to their mother. She never clashed with the strong-willed older woman the way her fiercely independent sister did. "I knew all Ma's secrets,"

Maria said, "and she knew all of mine." When Maria got married, she bought a house around the corner from her mother.

Maria's was no picture-perfect childhood. She was a little girl when her mother brought her, Luisa, and Carlos, children of three fathers, from Mexico to New York. Shortly afterward, her mother married and gave birth to Ricardo. Even in adulthood, Maria recoiled from the memories of her stepfather's harsh treatment. At nights, while their mother worked, he "disciplined" them with beatings. "At four o'clock every day," Maria recalled, "my stomach would start to hurt because he was going to come home from work. Sometimes he hit me with his belt. Once he kicked me." Maria left home right after high school, and only later did Ma divorce this abusive man.

As a child, Maria felt safest being close to her mother. She adored her, was obedient, tried to make her happy—and never dared risk her displeasure. Then, when Maria was in her thirties and had kids of her own, she felt the first doubts about her mother. "How could you have done that to your kids?" she challenged her. Ma would not explain. After her own divorce and remarriage, Maria came to an answer that she could live with. "She just loved him," she told me. "Women do dumb things when they're in love. And my mother was a really good person. She had four kids. Where was she to go?"

Maria had learned to see her mother, woman to woman. But living with her again, caring for her, she sometimes found herself feeling like a little girl even while behaving like a grown-up. She knew, for example, that it was bad for her mother to have sugar or alcohol. So Maria refused to buy them for her, effectively exercising power over her increasingly dependent and childlike parent. Maria also resisted waiting on her, making her breakfast, or doing anything for her that she could do herself. "That was healthier for her," Maria said.

But her mother did not make this internal battle easy for Maria. She fought back, and she knew just which buttons to push. "Oh, you'll miss me when I'm gone," she would prophesy, regularly reducing Maria to tears, after which this middle-aged daughter would beg her old mother's forgiveness. Over and over, her mother punished her by manipulating Maria's fear of the inevitable reality: that she would die, and that Maria would miss her. Her mother was also reviving Maria's childhood fear of abandonment. In this no longer adult-to-adult interaction, Maria reacted as if she were a child who could not survive without her mother.

But Maria grew in the caregiving experience. Just as she'd learned to see her mother as a fallible woman like herself, she now saw her mother's manipulative side and Maria drew on her own resources as a grown-up. "One day I just got it," Maria told me. "I said, 'Ma, don't do that anymore. It makes me feel really bad.'" Once Maria's mother saw that this ploy would no longer work, she stopped.

When her mother's physical demands increased after a stroke, Maria felt overwhelmed. One need she did not feel was to have her mother all to herself. So when her brother Carlos moved back to town and offered his help, Maria instantly agreed. "I could breathe again," she said.

The push-pull of this life passage, being pulled backward while pushing forward, can affect even the healthiest of us, but the more emotionally separate we are, the easier it is to recover and return to more adult relating. If we've had a troubled relationship with the parent we're caring for, if we're prey to unsatisfied yearning, anger, or other needs, the childhood hook is even stronger. Emily-Jane, an accomplished woman in her own life, was reduced to misery when she took on full-time care of her mother. She was so driven to fight her childhood battles again that she could not extricate herself.

EMILY-JANE: NEEDING TO BE A VICTIM AGAIN

Emily-Jane was one of the saddest caregivers I encountered. I see her as a dramatic example of an overcommitment to caregiving with which many people struggle in less extreme forms. A nurturing mother and devoted daughter, Emily-Jane wore herself down with the choices she made in caring for her mother and the tortured meanings with which she invested her efforts. A museum curator in New Mexico, she was a widow in her late fifties when her eighty-eight-year-old mother had a stroke. Although her mother regained partial mobility, she lapsed into a mental fog. The family (Mother, Emily-Jane, and Emily-Jane's older brother) agreed that she could not live by herself.

The brother, a celebrated heart surgeon, offered to supplement their mother's savings to pay for a luxurious care center in Houston, where he and his family lived. This plan was fine with their mother, who said she didn't want to be a burden and would do whatever was best for her children. But everything about it was abhorrent to Emily-Jane. Her brother would move their mother far away, and he would "put her in a home."

Emily-Jane had battled her brother all her life. "He was controlling and tyrannical," she said, "and he bullied me every day. I could not let him take control now." As a child, her mother had rarely intervened when her brother went after her. Emily-Jane had felt hurt and angered by her mother's passivity and longed to be closer to her. This need for a connection reemerged around caring for her mother, who now, increasingly dependent, let her daughter make all the important decisions. Though their relationship did not have a healthy emotional basis, Emily-Jane finally had a close bond with her mother that she did not want to relinquish.

This professional woman reduced her work schedule by half, closed up her own house, and moved in with her mother. "Apart from dressing herself," Emily-Jane explained, "she

needs me for everything—bathing, cooking, cleaning, tele-
phoning, bills, driving, yard work, scheduling appointments."
Emily-Jane told me she was exhausted, her health was suffering, and she had sacrificed much of her life. She rarely saw
friends or even her new grandson, on whom she doted.
"When I took my mother to Florida for a family reunion," she
related, "everyone said, 'Why are you doing this? It's not good
for you or your mother.'" In a voice tight with desperation,
she said, "I put her—and everyone—before myself. I know it's
not healthy."

Emily-Jane yearned for her mother's love and hoped somehow that in devoting herself selflessly to her, she would find it.
But her mother's gratitude and thanks were not enough.
Emily-Jane would see her mother's eyes light up whenever her
brother's name was mentioned. "He's still her golden boy,"
she told me bitterly.

The needs she imposed on her wish to provide good care
for her mother were tortuous and complex: among them, to
gain the love she felt she missed as a child, to keep herself the
victim she'd always been, and to win the battle for control with
her brother. She was also driven by unexpressed anger at her
mother. It was not until her mother died that she emerged
from this self-destructive morass. "That's when I finally forgave her," she said, "for turning a blind eye to what my
brother did to me."

LEARNING TO DECIPHER OUR HIDDEN NEEDS: WHY BECOMING AWARE IS THE SOLUTION

When we are swept up in the turbulent emotions and immedi-
ate needs of our family, it may be hard to recognize what internal forces are prodding us into misery. Perhaps few of us are

as driven as Emily-Jane, but if we are honest with ourselves we might find that some of her motives, to some degree, however subtle, play a role in how we relate to caregiving: the need to win love, to act out resentment, or to retain the satisfactions of being the family workhorse. Sometimes our motives come less from our family history than from our current lives. Identifying these hidden drives, whatever their origin, is an important goal for Steven Barlam, the founder of LivHome, a geriatric care management company in California. This is especially true when he sees his clients locked into self-defeating behavior in caring for their parents. "I ask myself," Barlam explained, "Why are they holding on with white knuckles to these miserable situations? What psychological or practical functions does it serve?"

Barlam recalls one woman who was so obsessively involved with her mother's care that she actually interfered with it, visiting the nursing home two or three times a day, insisting her mother be bathed more frequently than was good for her, and pushing her doctor to try medicines that were not indicated. As Barlam got to know this daughter, he realized that her consuming involvement with her mother was preventing her from having a last-chance round of fertility treatments. When Barlam talked to her about it, it became clear to both of them that she was ambivalent about having a child. She was using her obsession with her mother's care to avoid confronting her ambivalence. Once she realized what she was doing, she understood she was being less "selfless" than she liked to think, and she was able to be more reasonable about her mother.

Some of us become overinvolved in parent care to avoid dealing with marital or career problems. When we recognize what we're doing, we can redirect our energies. In my interviews, I found that when caregivers were willing to take a hard look inside, they often could identify what was really driving them and how they were contributing to their own unhappiness. Those who could own their behavior, in other words, could change it.

There are many ways this can happen. Self-reflection, talking to friends, support groups, counseling, or therapy can all help. So can reading books like this one. The important thing is to be willing to look at our own part in a very complicated family picture that involves us all.

WORKING TOGETHER TO TAKE ON CAREGIVING

IF YOU ARE THE PRIMARY CAREGIVER . . .

Don't assume it has to be you—or *all* you.
Call everyone together, including your parent, and look at the options. If you think you need help, have a social worker or family therapist call your siblings and run the meeting. Introduce the idea that this is a *family* responsibility.

Ask yourself: What's the worst thing that can happen if your sibling takes over for a spell?
If you are resisting your sister's or brother's offer to stay with Mom for a few days, think about your reluctance. How much harm can your brother really do? Is he so irresponsible that he'll endanger your mother? Or are you worried he'll cover her with the pink blanket even though she hates pink? Or order chocolate pudding for her instead of tapioca? Think about it.

Don't confuse good care with happiness.
If your mother was never a happy person, you will not make her happy now, but you can make yourself miserable trying. If her health and her losses have made her sad, you can be there for her. But remind yourself that she is an adult and responsible for her own happiness. Contrary to popular belief, we are not supposed to take care of our parents the way they took care of us; that's what we do for our *children*. And aging and death are things we just cannot fix, no matter how perfectly we care for our parents.

Take a hard look at what you're getting from caring—the good, the problematic, and the ugly.

- Look at the positive things you get from caring for your parents—deep satisfaction, pride, healing, and more. When things get really hard, bring these things to mind.

- Ask yourself whether the less healthy satisfactions you're getting are really worth the cost. Is thinking of yourself as better than your brother really worth more than having his help? Is showing everyone how exhausted you are really better than taking advantage of resources for help?

Be alert to the hook from childhood.

- It's easy to fall into childlike behavior with our parents when we spend a lot of time with them. Think about whether you are behaving like an adult and what's holding you back. Be *conscious*.

- Try to identify your most vulnerable points with your parents, the stresses that make you regress. If possible, strategize ahead of time to defend your adult functioning.

IF YOUR SIBLING IS THE PRIMARY CAREGIVER . . .

Don't think that you're off the hook.
Your sister may live closer to your mother. She may feel closer, too. Or not. That does not mean she should do everything. Ask what you can do. If she says she's got it covered, keep checking back. Remember that caregiving can start small but avalanche later.

Contribute time or money to give your sibling a break.
If you can afford to pay something, consider paying for a part-time aide or any service that will make life easier for the caregiver. Whether or not you can afford paid help, try to visit when you can. Giving your sibling even a few days off, where you are the one dealing with everything, can help.

Don't underestimate emotional support.
What your sister or brother most wants is not to feel alone. Your brother may just want to hear that you care. Your sister may need to chew your ear off for an hour about how Mom is driving her crazy. Just call and listen.

If your sister is driving herself into the ground, factor in the stresses of being on the spot.
You may feel that your sister is making life harder for herself than it needs to be. She may be, and you may not be able to change her behavior. Try to be sympathetic. She is not only dealing with the practical burdens of parent care on a regular basis. She is also thrust into prolonged and intense contact with a declining, perhaps unpleasant, parent in ways that you are not.

CHAPTER FOUR

DAD STILL LOVES YOU MORE: REVIVED RIVALRIES, CHANCES FOR RESOLUTION

BEV AND HANK WERE DRIVING along a San Diego highway after visiting their mother in the assisted living complex. Bev, you may recall, is the self-described "fixer" in her family who had chosen to move her mother near her San Diego home. Hank had done everything he could think of to support his sister. He called her once a week, emailed frequently, and flew in twice a year from Connecticut to visit and to give her a break.

Bev's becoming the caregiver had gone smoothly between them. They'd agreed that Hank harbored too much resentment against his mother, and he lived in too cold a climate to suit her. A few months before this drive down the highway, Bev had told me that she and Hank were working well as a team; they were open and honest about their feelings. Yet on the second day of this trip, they got into a fight.

"A turn came up and I didn't get in the lane quickly enough—for her," Hank reported. "Bev started giving me a hard time, and I said, 'I can't do anything right for you, can I?' And she said, 'No, you can't!'"

"I always felt," Hank explained, "that I was the little brother and whatever I did wasn't right. Bev could not accept that I was an adult, grown up with a family. We had this big blow up and didn't speak for a couple of months."

"The fight was about everything," Bev agreed, "all the old stuff."

There, in a car on a California highway, the two middle-aged siblings had reentered the house of childhood. To Hank, Bev was still, partly, the prom queen who'd let him tag along with her cool friends. To Bev, her brother was still, in part, the intrusive, bumbling ten-year-old she'd had to share a room with until she was twelve. These designations, the star and the screw-up, the responsible and the irresponsible ones, were accepted truths in the world of their family.

Think of this period as a classic horror move. *It's back!* Just when we think we're safe as grown-ups . . . we are dragged back into this metaphorical haunted house that contains the memories of what we learned in our family: each person's identity, worth, and role, and our scripts for interacting with one another. But, as siblings, we now have serious business to do together, important decisions to make. To do it optimally, we need to deal with one another as the grown-ups we are now and get past how we saw one another as children.

This is not so easy. For one thing, many siblings are unlikely to know one another well as adults. Yet even siblings who remain close into middle age and beyond may never fully let go of their childhood perceptions of one another. You may recognize that you've each developed separate, adult lives with their attendant complications and joys. But still, you see your adult sister or brother through a layer of perceptions and memories from when you were both children living together every day, playing your defined roles. And old family dynamics die hard.

On top of that, we're all painfully aware that time with our parents is growing short. If there's anything any of us need from them—love, approval, forgiveness—now is the moment.

It's all too easy for those old competitive feelings (*Mom loved you more, Dad gave you all the good stuff*) to fuel our interactions over caring for them. Although these rivalries sometimes develop into pitched battles, they often play out in more subtle ways. Much of the time we don't even realize they are influencing our behavior. For instance, you tell yourself that you're trying to do what's best for Mom, and you are. But it's also possible you're trying to shut out your brother or show up your sister.

If we have worked through our old rivalries, we'll be better positioned to resist the draw to compete with one another now. Even if we haven't, we can catch ourselves at it. We have a huge advantage over our childhood selves. We can look back on our rivalries and our feelings about favoritism from a grown-up's perspective, understanding that our parents do not have a finite store of love and anything they give to you means less for me. Now we can learn to recognize when we're being competitive and disentangle ourselves from the childish side of our dealings with one another. We can also reevaluate some of the ways we hurt one another as children, apply our adult understanding, and get past old wounds.

EVERYTHING'S DIFFERENT
BUT MY BROTHER'S STILL THE SAME:
UPDATING OUR CHILD'S-EYE VIEWS

What Bev and Hank experienced on that California highway was a collision between their childhood perceptions of each other and who they were in the present. Why didn't they see each other as the adults they were? One reason is that they'd lived thousands of miles apart most of their lives. They had seen each other only a few times a year and caught up on major news over the phone. There were occasional exceptions, such as the time ten years before when Bev had surgery for breast cancer. Hank had volunteered to stay with her and help out during her recovery. This was mature behavior for both of them: his offering help, her accepting it. Yet during Hank's stay, they sometimes reacted to each other in ways that drew on Bev's experience of Hank as the little brother who crowded her, and Hank's memories of Bev as the princess whose wishes were always considered more important than his. For the most part, they did not act on these feelings. But they were together only for a week.

After their father died, working together became a constant necessity, especially after moving their mother to assisted living. These changes brought them into more frequent and intense contact than they'd had since living together as children, with their mother once more a major presence in their relationship.

Until our parents need care, many siblings know one another the way Bev and Hank did, as adults, yet not in the way we relate to other adults. Even when we maintain intimate friendships with our sisters and brothers throughout our grown-up lives, we will still, at some deep level, remain the children we once were to one another. During the twilight, even the best-adjusted siblings can feel this backward pull.

The pull will be even stronger for those of us who really don't know our siblings well in adulthood. After we leave home, we tend to lead separate lives. It's part of the normal process of emotional growth. Just as we need to make a life that's ours, not our parents, we also create some distance from our siblings, and that often occurs in a distant city.

"Ours is a 'neolocal' society that encourages young people to seek jobs regardless of where one's family of origin is located," Stephen P. Bank and Michael D. Kahn point out in *The Sibling Bond.* We can use this geographic distance, they say, as a "helpful safety valve"; it can help us work out separate identities. But when we come together in a crisis . . . well, many of us have some pretty outdated notions about one another.

It's unlikely you think of yourself as the same person you were when you were eight or eighteen. But, if we have not spent much time together since then, we tend to remember one another the way we were or, at least, to layer our present knowledge with our ingrained memories. As your sibling, I may hold on to my old image of you out of fondness, your absentmindedness, your mania for dogs, your weird taste in music. These are memories from when we were most connected. If you are not still that person, then who are you? Do I still know you? So, no matter how many times you tell me, with exasperation, that you're not like that anymore, it may not stick. On the other hand, you may slip into being the person I remember when you're with me, the bumbler, perhaps, or the clown, because that's easier for you, too.

There's also a less benign side to this. If you always thought of a particular sibling as selfish, or as taking advantage of you, you may be quick to interpret what this brother or sister does now through this child's-eye lens and to react to it that way. If your mother always treated you as more competent than another sibling, you may now resent the way she looks to this sister or brother to manage her care.

These ideas about one another originated when we were children with limited understanding, when our beliefs were shaped by our needs and level of development. If we stood back and looked at them now, we might well see them differently. But even if you were right about a brother back then, you may not know who he has become as an adult. Like you, he will have had profound experiences with relationships, parenting, work, illness, maybe even tragedy. Surely you are no longer the same people. Yet, exhausted with worry or anxious about our parents, many of us slip into our default settings, our earliest beliefs and reactions.

"We haven't negotiated anything of great importance since childhood," explained geropsychologist Sara Hohn Qualls. "Our experience is coded at the emotional level from earlier in our life, and our reactions come from then. I see myself as a midlife woman. My siblings filter the roles through who I was thirty years ago."

WHY OUR OLD RIVALRIES REEMERGE—OR INTENSIFY

As we try to work with one another as adults to do what our parents need, the shifting structure of our family and the lack of clarity about our roles now often affect our sibling interactions, spurring competitions to be most important to our parents. Let's say, for example, that I always felt that our parents treated you as smarter and more able than I. My alarm bells will sound when I see signs of this now. If Mom has become fearful and childlike about her illness, she may look to you to calm her. I notice that nothing I say seems to have an effect on her; then you walk in the room and she is instantly calm. I may throw a temper tantrum about something apparently unrelated. I may insist that the doctor she's going to, whom you feel fine about, isn't any good.

If I'm the main contact with Dad's doctor, I may confide in you that he thinks Dad could have cancer but won't know for sure until the tests are back. Mom's already a basket case and we don't want to worry her unnecessarily, but I may not think to warn you not to say anything to her yet. Competing to be the one in charge, you may rush to tell her. Old sibling rivalry, but it's unlikely you realize that's what you're doing.

Rivalries also reemerge because we no longer know who is who in our family, or at least, who does what. If your father always gave you advice in a crisis, well, he can't now: He's dead or in crisis himself. If your mother always moderated disputes among her children, she can't do that anymore because she has dementia. The missing or disabled people may have served any number of functions in making our family run. I have had people describe their mother or father as a "buffer" between them and their other parent or the "glue" that held them and their siblings together. When this parent could no longer act the part, the rest of them were suddenly thrust up against one another without familiar ways to relate.

"When the strong parent becomes more dependent," said therapist and grief scholar Therese Rando, "when one or more people in the family system changes, it destabilizes the system. I have seen adults jockeying for position in a new system."

What positions are up for grabs? Well, if my dad relied totally on my mother for emotional support, my sister and I may compete to be the person he relies on now that Mom is gone. If we are daughters who always competed with Mother for Father, as Freud would have it, that rivalry could now become pretty intense. Any adjustment to our family system could potentially revive rivalries between us. If Mom always directed her anxiety and solicitude at Dad, for example, I may resent that you are now the one she constantly worries over. Or if my sister takes charge of Dad's care after Mom dies, she may try to one-up me by taking on many of Mom's old roles, including guilt-tripping me about not visiting my father more often. So who's on first now?

Many of the rivalries we act out over our parents' care are subtle, yet seriously counterproductive. At their worst, they can compromise or even endanger our parents' well-being.

FOR BETTER OR FOR WORSE: A SPOUSE'S ROLE

A husband or wife can be the greatest source of support and help with your parent and your siblings, or he can fan the flames of sibling conflict. What makes the difference? His long history with your family and his even longer history with his own. Chances are, you will be dealing with his parents and siblings at some point even as he is dealing with yours. Best case: Your spouse is on your side in any sibling dispute but he's also objective enough to give you valuable insight about how to deal with your siblings. Worst case: Your spouse is angry, maybe on your behalf, maybe on his own. He thinks you are being badly treated by your siblings and he stokes up your anger, escalating the conflict. He may even feel guilty because he is not doing as much for his mother as you are doing for yours. The possibilities for bias are endless. And this is true for other family members who become involved.

You two need to talk. Try to separate your marital issues from your family issues. This is not easy, especially if you are the primary caregiver. He may be resentful about how much you are doing for your parent and may feel that your own family and marriage are suffering. If this is the case, you should discuss, among other issues: making regular time for each other; modifying the care arrangements for your mother; moving her into a senior apartment or hiring help; negotiating vacations with a sibling; using adult day care or other respite resources; getting marital counseling, if necessary; getting family therapy to work out more equitable caregiving with your siblings.

Competing to Care More

I have heard wonderful stories of siblings lovingly sharing parent care, as well as stories of sisters and brothers fighting because one person did everything without help. I also heard accounts of siblings competing to see who could do more for their parents, which of them would become most important to them. Sometimes they even disagreed about which of them was the primary caregiver. In these latter families, caring for Mom or Dad—or controlling a parent's destiny—became a longed-for and fought-for prize.

Most families I met were in the middle range; sibling rivalry played a role but without high drama. One fifty-nine-year-old woman in Nevada, for example, told me that she'd always imagined she and her older sister would care for their parents together. But she didn't count on their old rivalry, intense in adolescence, reappearing. After she sold her business, she began spending more time with her parents, becoming their driver and helper. Her sister suddenly disappeared. "She's bowed out," this woman told me, sounding surprised and hurt. "My other sister says I won the prize—recognition from our parents and brothers. But instead of being grateful to me, she's jealous!"

This vanishing sister had a not uncommon reaction, feeling she was on the outside, excluded. When a brother or sister becomes our parent's primary caregiver, we may find ourselves envying the special relationship we see developing or deepening. We may not be imagining it. Despite the many hardships of caring for a parent, people have told me of its immense rewards, of feeling trusted, valued, needed, and depended upon by their parent. They spoke of feeling worthy, competent, a good daughter or son. Some considered it a gift to be able to "give back."

People have told me how their parents shared things about their lives with them for the first time. There was a father who finally answered his son's questions about why he had treated him so harshly as a child. There were mothers who expressed regret for their mistakes and asked forgiveness. There were intimacies of soul and of body, of mothers and daughters, laughing together over an episode of incontinence or memory loss, talking about beliefs in an afterlife, imagining what a daughter's future might hold.

If you are the one enjoying this special relationship, your brother may feel shut out, especially if he lives far away. He may feel that you have become more important to Mom. He might feel, at some level, that this is his last chance to be Mom's "special" one, to have her finally see what a terrific person he is. "It's not a conscious thing," said sibling researcher Victoria Hilkevitch Bedford, "but the siblings feel, 'It's got to be *now*.' They become needy children not getting enough of the goods, the parents' love, and the things they have. You feel these feelings surging, and you don't stop to ask yourself why, but you act on them. The fighting happens before people become conscious of these feelings."

Fly-ins and White Knights: Competing Across the Miles

Geographic distance factors into our relationships now in many complex ways. Let's say, for example, that I am my mother's caregiver. It is likely that I live closest to her and have the most regular and intimate contact with her. If you live across the country, you may look for ways to be just as important, just as smart and helpful. Unfortunately, this can take the form of second-guessing the way I am taking care of Mom.

Your criticisms may be minor, motivated partly by your anxiety about Mom, maybe a little by guilt, maybe by rivalry with me. "Mom and Dad need to get out more and exercise," one sixty-year-old brother reprimanded his sister on a rare trip to see his parents in their assisted living apartment. Her reaction? She felt helpless, guilty, and unappreciated. "I took his criticism personally," she told me. "I can't *make* Mom and Dad take a walk. I was really tired and burnt out. I have a job. I have a husband and family."

"The same things for which you congratulate yourself, becoming an individual in your own right, which could have been hampered or delayed by remaining too connected to whatever issues are going on in the family," psychoanalyst Michael Kahn told me, "can make reentry at a point of crisis and reorganization in the family very, very difficult. Now you are being treated as the outsider."

If we've been away a long time, Kahn suggested, we may not be familiar with the subtleties of communication that the remaining family has developed. "The outsider," he said, "can come tromping back in and be repelled in a day. Or one can come up with a perfectly logical set of recommendations from afar only to find that others have taken leadership positions and initiatives, and you didn't know what was going on."

I have heard of such disagreements flaring into skirmishes, with the distant child trying to change doctors, treatments, or nursing homes. So common are these near-and-far dramas that professionals who work with families of the elderly have labeled the players. Sisters and brothers who show up to "rescue" their parents are called "white knights" or "fly-ins." They see themselves as saving their parents from "neglectful" or "incompetent" siblings. I don't doubt that some "saves" are genuine, but health-care professionals see them primarily as ill advised, overemotional, and sometimes downright dangerous for the parent. These professionals are not infallible, and they do have a stake in the established treatment, but they are likelier to understand the full picture better than an adult child newly arrived on the scene with incomplete knowledge and perhaps runaway emotions.

Rona Bartelstone recalled working with a family where a daughter was caring for her hospitalized father. Her brother, a physician who lived in another city, tried to wrest away control of their father's treatment. This son, Bartelstone said, despite his success, had never been able to get his father's approval and was jealous of his sister. No matter what she said, he would contradict her. "He tried to get the doctors to do things that were not in his father's best interests," Bartelstone said, "even advocating for surgery that might have killed him."

That's an extreme example. In general, family visits are important even though they may sometimes be a nuisance for medical staff. Still, interference by fly-ins can be the bane of an on-site caregiver's existence, said Minneapolis social worker Lynn Cibuzar. "White knights are so irritating to caregivers," she said, "especially because of their lack of appreciation for what their sister is doing."

These competitions don't occur only long-distance. One of the most dramatic, saddest, and destructive battles I saw occurred between sisters Debbie and Leila, who lived within a mile of each other and their parents in their small Virginia town. More important than where they lived was that their mother incited and fed their rivalry, perpetuating a lifelong family dynamic. These sisters were among the most damaged and least emotionally separate adult children I met. They became entrenched in a bitter contest over what they imagined they could get from their mother—finally.

DEBBIE AND LEILA: A LAST-CHANCE BATTLE FOR LOVE

Debbie, a thirty-three-year-old nursery school teacher, was sweet and vulnerable, pretty but self-conscious about being overweight. She had begun "caring" for her mother when she was in high school and Mom developed kidney disease. As her helper, she found a way to feel loved. "Mom was not a nurturing person," Debbie said. "I can count on one hand the times she said 'I love you' or hugged or kissed me."

By all accounts, Debbie's mother was a charming but troubled woman who kept her husband and children in a perpetual state of longing for her crumbs of praise or affection. It was a family in which it was unsafe for any of them to become separate; if they moved in that direction, they would be cast out and punished with coldness or anger.

After Debbie's mother broke her hip, the eighty-six-year-old woman spent months in a nursing home. She cried and begged to leave. Her doctors advised against it, but Debbie could not bear to see her mother cry. Her solution was to move her parents into her own home with her husband and young children. Her sister-in-law, Christine, sometimes helped, but her brother was rarely involved. His work took him on the road regularly, and when it didn't, his strategy for dealing with the family dramas was to stay out of them as much as possible.

The actual care was difficult: bathing her mother's ulcerated feet, taking her to dialysis, transporting her in a wheelchair. But Debbie's hunger for her mother's love turned the experience into a nightmare for her. Mom screamed when Debbie bathed her feet, and she often refused to take her medications. Even worse, she began berating Debbie to anyone who would listen. Debbie wept as she told me about overhearing one of her mother's phone conversations with her sister. "She runs around in a towel after she takes a shower," her mother said, "and it is not a pretty sight."

At the age of forty-six, Leila, a store manager, felt the first light of her mother's favor and confidence, and she saw a chink in the tight relationship between her mother and younger sister. Leila, who prided herself on her toughness and lack of sentimentality, conceived of herself as her mother's champion, rescuing her from a miserable and inadequate situation. But, like her sister, her wish to care for her mother was complicated by many of her own emotional needs.

"Leila and Debbie *were* treated differently," Christine told me, giving the background to Leila's wounded feelings and sense of injustice. Leila declined to speak to me, but Christine felt some empathy for her. Christine had once tried to explain the differential treatment to Leila.

" 'Remember,' I said, 'when Debbie was little, all the other kids were out of the house, and your parents had more money and patience.' "

But Leila retorted bitterly. "It was always like that."

"She couldn't get past it," Christine said.

Leila began taking her mother out for lunch and other outings. When they returned, her mother loudly sang Leila's praises, crowing to everyone, "Oh, we had *such* a good time!" Soon the two were whispering together. On their outings, they secretly toured nursing homes. Enjoying the attention, the old woman chose one. "Things around here will change," Mom predicted mysteriously at home. Finally, she made a grand announcement: She was moving out! After some shock and tears, Debbie's father agreed it would be best, and Debbie, drained and defeated, gave in.

On the night before moving day, however, the old woman burst into sobs, begging not to go. Like King Lear bouncing from one daughter to another in hope of better treatment, she implored Debbie not to let Leila put her away. The family, minus Leila, had long, emotional meetings. "I told Mom she had to stop bashing me," Debbie said. "She had to take her pills and not yell at me." Frightened into compliance, their mother agreed. Leila, disgusted and disheartened, made herself scarce.

Leila's behavior, though roundly vilified by the rest of the family, was sadly understandable. She'd been the family scapegoat all her life, especially after an "angelic" older sister died. For Leila, a battle-scarred veteran of life at forty-six, this was her last chance. As Donald Williamson told me, some less-favored children may feel at such a moment, "She's vulnerable now. She *needs* me."

It is improbable that Leila voiced these thoughts to herself. I think it unlikely she would have been willing to stand back from her rivalry and examine it. She was too deeply committed to it. But most of us suffer from far less virulent rivalries. As adults, we have usually grown past our most intense rivalries; when these competitions become reactivated over our aging parents, we have a shot at understanding them differently and learning to defuse them.

PLAYING FAVORITES: THE GROWN-UP'S LOOK BACK AT CHILDHOOD RIVALRIES

You may have put it behind you, or think you have, but if your father had a favorite, you would certainly know who it was. Or would you? As children, we often get this wrong. When Duke University professor Deborah T. Gold studied pairs of adult siblings, she found in many cases that each thought the *other* was the favorite. Clearly, during our childhood we may misinterpret our parents' messages. When rivalry and favoritism raise their hoary heads over the beds of our aging parents, it pays to reexamine our assumptions from our more mature perspective and to learn what sibling rivalry is really about.

Sibling Rivalry: Not All Cain and Abel
First off, childhood sibling rivalry is not only normal; it's not all bad. By measuring ourselves against our sisters and brothers, we develop our own identities, strengths, and talents. We learn how to compete, cooperate, and resolve conflict, critical

skills for living in the world as adults. The problem comes when the rivalry becomes central in our lives, and it's especially painful when we feel on the losing side of a competition for our parents' love. As grown-ups, we can understand that our parents are fallible, just like us. They're neither calculating machines nor weighing scales. Maybe Mom seems more relaxed with me because we have the same energy level and need for downtime. Maybe Dad has an easier time with you because you're more like him temperamentally. Maybe you were born during a calm period in their lives while I came along when they were struggling.

"Achieving a feeling of overall fairness is the best that a parent can hope for," Bank and Kahn observed in *The Sibling Bond.* If our family were relatively healthy, they suggested, our parents would value each of us for different qualities. Or they might favor me at one point and you at another. Or they might achieve a balance in some other way. The important thing is that parents can have different kinds of relationships with each of us without loving one more than another.

DOES BIRTH ORDER TRIGGER FAVORITISM?

Although the research on the birth order effect is inconsistent, experts agree there is something to this. It can be comforting to realize that your father probably treated your big brother and you the way that older and younger children usually get treated. If Dad let you "get away with" more, for example, it wasn't because he favored you but because, inevitably, parents are less strict with their younger kids.

Let's say that I'm the older child and you're the younger. It's likely that Mom and Dad saw me as more mature and responsible than you, then treated me and nudged me toward actually becoming that way, a common self-fulfilling prophecy. On the other hand, I am probably more anxious and insecure than you because I had the shock of losing Mom and Dad's exclusive attention when you were born.

If you are the youngest of a large brood, you may develop better social and emotional antennae because you were born needing to fit into an existing group. To make a place for yourself, you may create some special role: the helper, the peacemaker, the clown. As the last one left at home, you may also get more attention and affection from our parents than the rest of us.

Research has not uncovered any special advantages to being a middle child, but some middle children say they feel freer of parental pressures than their older or younger siblings. Relationships between parents and children are endlessly complex, and birth order can add yet another dimension.

Favoritism: Not Your Sister's Fault

Suppose your parents really did play favorites in ways you found crushing. The most important thing to understand as an adult is that none of it is your sister's or brother's fault. Hard as this may be to accept, our sisters and brothers are not responsible. Our *parents* are.

Not that shifting blame is the answer. The ways in which our parents create conflict between us have deep roots in their own family histories. It doesn't help us to blame our parents, but it does clarify things to see them as *responsible,* and certainly more responsible than a little sister or big brother.

Blatantly favoring one of us is the most obvious way our parents can set us against one another. But there are other ways parents can fuel sibling conflict. If they're always fighting with each other, for example, observed Karen Gail Lewis, author of *Removing Ghosts from Your Past: Understanding Sibling Conflict,* we may imitate them. Lewis, a family therapist who conducts workshops for adult siblings, has identified a number of ways parents cause sibling conflict, none of them intentional. Let's say, for example, that my mother competed with *her* older sister; she may go harder on *my* older sister and easier on me. Our parents also tend to assign labels to each of us: Bev was the "star," for example, and Hank the "screw-up." These labels stick and become the way we see one another. And there are other parental dynamics that also result in sibling conflict.

What's important to realize is that whatever our parents have done to turn us against one another, as Bank and Kahn maintained, you and I are both victims, not perpetrators. As kids, we get angry with one another because we need our parents too much to risk getting angry with them. As adults we probably have outgrown this fear. Yet, about to lose our parents forever, we may once again resist seeing their faults and direct our anger at one another.

Favoritism in the Twilight

If your mother played favorites when you were a child, she may still favor your brother in her old age. Or she may now show partiality to you or your sister. But don't be too quick to assume that favoritism is what's at work now. These relationships may simply reflect her changing needs as she grows more dependent.

When sociologists Jill Suitor and Karl Pillemer asked women ages sixty-five to seventy-five which of their children they felt most "emotionally close" to, most of the mothers named a younger child. But when they were asked which child they would turn to with a problem or crisis, most chose an older child. So who, then, is the "favorite"? This research supports our adult understanding that our parent's relationship with each of us is different, rather than a reflection of how much we are loved.

Even in middle age, many of us misperceive our parents' feelings about us. When Suitor and Pillemer asked adult children which of them their mother felt closest to, two thirds of them gave a different answer than their mothers gave. So even as grown-ups, we can get this wrong.

This is important to understand because our perceptions about favoritism can be especially hurtful when we are caring for our failing parents. Elaine Brody's research found that 40 percent of caregiving daughters believed that a sister or brother was her mother's favorite, and this was often a source of pain. There's a classic version of this scenario that experts see often: the devoted daughter versus the adored but often absent son.

Whatever the dynamics in a particular family, it's important to acknowledge that gender bias runs strong in the World War II generation of parents, and many do see their sons as more important. "This older generation usually has a soft spot for one son who's successful and lives out of town," said Denise M. Brown, founder of Caregiving.com, a website offering caregiving support and other resources. "If the son steps up to the plate once, the parents make a big deal of it," University of Miami professor Mitrani explained, "even though the daughter is doing all the work. Our therapists have to work with the parents on this as well as the kid."

If you are this daughter, you're bound to react to this behavior. But you don't have to conclude that your mother loves you less than she loves your brother. Really, who is your mother's "favorite"? The daughter who talks to her every day, shops for her, and goes to the doctor with her? Or the son she's proud of and misses? Overwhelmingly, research shows that mothers want to be cared for by someone to whom they feel emotionally close, and they usually identify this person as a daughter.

So why does Mom make such a big deal about *him*? Well, if he's successful in the world, his success reassures her that she's done a good job as a parent. A child's success validates parents just as they are looking back and facing their own judgments and regrets about what kind of parent they were.

Or sometimes it's just a matter of birth order, similarity of temperament, or gender bias.

Some parents may be clear-sighted about the limits of their relationships with the kids who don't have much time for them. Others may rationalize their disappointment at not seeing them often, care manager Rona Bartelstone suggested to me, by focusing on their success or some other positive quality. They may also feel less secure with their absent sons and be on their best behavior when they visit for fear of driving them away. You, on the other hand, she can count on, maybe take for granted. She trusts that you will always be there for her. "Often," Bartelstone said, "the local caregiver gets *all* of the behavior, whereas the distant child gets only the best behavior and, therefore, can't understand the 'burden' on the local one."

Divide and Conquer: How Failing Parents Foment Rivalry

Feeling increasingly helpless and afraid in old age, some parents may unwittingly feed into our rivalries with one another. Because frail parents depend on us so completely, psychologists say, they may anxiously ask all of us for the same things as a kind of insurance policy in case one of us doesn't come through. Take this hypothetical example. A mother in a nursing home asks all three of her children to buy her a bathrobe. All of them do, and each one ends up feeling unappreciated, with two of them irritated because they have to return the robe they so carefully picked out to please their mother. They may also be left wondering whether she kept the red robe Susie gave her because she likes red better or because she likes Susie better.

In a less benign example, a mother may make sure someone is always there for her by setting up a competition for her approval. When her son comes to see her after a month, she might exclaim enthusiastically, "Do you know your sister came to see me *twice* last week?" Understanding his mother's need for companionship may prevent this brother from resenting his sister.

In one family Bartelstone worked with, an elderly mother fueled her daughters' competition with a strategic silence. When one daughter, who believed in alternative medicine, came to town, she stocked her mother's shelves with organic meals and supplements. When her sister showed up, she cleared the shelves and insisted her mother have medical tests and "real" food. "The mother never said what she wanted," Bartelstone noted. "She got more attention this way."

Luckily many of our parents work to promote closeness between us; they'd like to feel that after they die, their children will have one another. One of my interviewees confessed that she would sometimes complain to her father, who lived with her, that her brother was neglecting him. Wisely, her dad refused to take the bait. Instead he encouraged small signs of rapprochement between his kids. "You and your brother are getting along!" he would sing out whenever her brother called and asked to speak to her.

If any of us are tempted to badmouth (however subtly) our siblings to our parents, we should think about what we are accomplishing, and we should examine our own motivations. Still, we need to be alert to signs that maybe our parent is the one stirring up competition. If we catch on to what's happening, we have a shot at aligning ourselves to circumvent it.

TALKING OUT OLD RIVALRIES—INSTEAD OF ACTING THEM OUT

Our sibling rivalries and resentments have long histories. The best way to resolve them is to address some of this old stuff earlier rather than later. "Before Mom or Dad has a problem," sibling therapist Lewis advised, "clean up your relationship with your siblings. Or at least read about the causes of sibling problems. Because when you're in the midst of a crisis, everything gets worse. If you have some preparation now, it helps you understand."

"Of course," Lewis added, "nobody ever takes this suggestion."

Well, not many people. Most of us are too busy dealing with what's pressing in our lives—our marriages, our kids, careers, finances, even our own health issues. Until we start butting heads again with our siblings, we rarely look back at our relationships with them. Maybe we've moved on and just don't feel the need. Or maybe the tensions are still there, but nothing is forcing us to confront them. "In our fifties and sixties," therapist Donald Williamson told me, "the most sharp competitive stuff has worn itself out. But if it's still alive, it needs acknowledgment and addressing."

A few people I met made this effort. Generally, they were women who felt troubled about the strains in their relationships with their sisters. Those who tried to clear the air early, I found, were better able to defuse potentially destructive competitiveness later. But early or late, talking through this old stuff calmly—with a mature perspective and an open mind—can make a huge difference in the twilight. The Miller sisters, for example, not only resolved their old grudges with each other, they also were able to foil their mother's attempts to divide them.

THE MILLER SISTERS: FIXING WHAT'S BROKEN BEFORE IT GETS WORSE

Each of the three Miller girls felt she had to fight for her own identity and a share of their parents' attention. Marcy, a tall, striking, fifty-three-year-old computer scientist, defended her place in the spotlight against her irresistible younger twin sisters by bossing them around. "Staying the older sister," she said, "that's how I maintained who I was."

When I met Judith, a family-law attorney, and Pennie, a violin maker, sisters who live in different cities, I was struck by the resemblance of the fifty-year-old fraternal twins: the same trim build, toothy smile, and deep-set brown eyes. Although she loved both her sisters, as a girl Pennie felt suffocated by her togetherness with Judith and her mother's possessiveness. "I could not wait to get away and be my own person," she said.

Judith saw herself as a family loser on two fronts. Their father, a crusading civil rights lawyer, gave special attention to Marcy so that she would not feel displaced by the adorable twins. Their mother, a law professor, needy and depressive, identified with Pennie as the music prodigy she herself always hoped to be. Judith felt as if she were no one's favorite and had to fight for an identity separate from her twin. "Everyone lavished attention on Marcy so she wouldn't feel left out," Judith recalled. "If she got fifty cents, we each got a quarter. Being Marcy's sister was like being half a person."

As adults, the sisters lived in different cities in the West and Northwest, married, had kids, had lives. Their parents divorced. While Judith went into family law, and Marcy became a computer scientist, Pennie rebelled against her "bourgeois" background and, with her husband, joined a farming commune in Northern California. Her mother lost interest in her and began following Judith's career instead; she had a new favorite. Pennie's reaction? "Ouch!" she recalled with a rueful laugh.

Years passed and the sisters held grudges, rarely gathering in one room. When Marcy had a life-threatening illness in her early forties, though, Judith realized how much her sisters meant to her. Shortly afterward, she wrote Pennie a letter, pointing out that they hadn't seen each other for nearly ten years. "Let's get to know each other," Judith proposed, "this time as adults."

This conversation continued in fits and starts for years until their mother, retired and alone in Manhattan, started losing memory and mobility. Phone calls and emails among the sisters began to fly as they tried to figure out how to help her.

But their mother put obstacles in their way—as she had always done, they realized. But this time it didn't work. "As we talked to each other more," Pennie said, "we realized that Mom was fomenting conflict by talking about us to each other, praising one of us to make the other one jealous. And we wouldn't let her divide us anymore."

The sisters helped their mother find a retirement apartment with care services, and agreed that one of them would visit her every month. Whoever went emailed the others detailed reports. When possible, they tried to overlap their visits. Sometimes the old competitiveness came up, but they never let it go too far. "Marcy would sometimes 'joke,'" Judith related, "'I'm the oldest, prettiest, smartest.' It got to me, and I said, 'Marcy, you don't have to do that anymore. We're *grown-ups*.' She got it."

One day, Judith and Pennie, sitting on a bench on upper Broadway outside their mother's care complex, finally talked through how their mother's favoritism had affected them. Judith tried to convey her sense of being shortchanged. Pennie talked about the double-edged sword of her mother's favor: affection, yes, but possessiveness and interference, and then the painful switch in adulthood. As a fifty-year-old with a dying mother, Judith, surveying the big picture, finally realized something. She said, "There was plenty of love in our family for all of us."

BEAT-UP OR ABANDONED: UNDERSTANDING AND HEALING OLD SIBLING WOUNDS

Our old grudges against our siblings don't always seem to be related to rivalry. As children, we can hurt one another in ways that can reemerge when we come together to care for our parents. A forty-nine-year-old teacher, for example, told me how her older sister, whom she idolized, had mistreated her as a child. "She used me as her whipping boy," she said. This hurt her a lot. Yet as an adult, she understood why her sister had done it. Their mother treated her cruelly, and she, in turn, inflicted her pain on her little sister. "On the outside, my sister was like an iceberg," the younger one said, "but now I understand that she was suffering inside. And I know she felt really guilty for the way she treated me."

How did she know? When they reached their forties, they were finally able to talk about what happened in their childhood. They could now see their mother and father as people trying to parent out of their own strengths and weaknesses. By opening this subject up, the sisters figured out how they'd both been hurt by their mother's detachment and their father's disapproval.

Feeling abandoned by a sister or brother, usually an older one, is a common childhood wound. When a child is young, he doesn't understand that it's normal for his adored older brother to hang out with his own friends when he moves into his teens or to go off to college and become immersed in his own world. This is so natural and normal that an older sibling may have no idea that a younger one feels hurt. But abandonment is a theme that runs deep in sibling relationships. Early in her career, sibling researcher Bedford did a study in which she showed subjects drawings of adult siblings and asked them to make up stories to go with them. One showed a young person leaving with a suitcase and stack of books. In the stories people told, Bedford related, "There were very few instances where it was *okay* for a sibling to leave. The one left behind is angry; the one leaving feels guilty."

In my interviews, I have found that some younger siblings felt the hurt of this "abandonment" throughout their lives, especially if they grew up in emotionally troubled homes. The older one's leaving may also have upset the emotional balance at home, leaving the younger one even more exposed and alone when the family started to fall apart.

As your younger sibling, if I have looked to you to take care of me because Mom and Dad didn't do this very well, I may be devastated when you leave home. As a kid, I can't understand that it's not your job to take care of me. That's our parents' responsibility. Your job is to go out and make a life for yourself.

Even in adulthood, we don't always see this clearly. I met a few middle-aged people who still blamed the sister or brother who "left" them. These are deep wounds that can be rubbed raw when we get together again over our parents' care. But we also have an opportunity to mend these breaches. The three Kristal sisters managed the healing route, although it was clear when I met them that the old wounds had not been forgotten.

THE KRISTAL SISTERS: HEALING ABANDONMENT IN THE TWILIGHT

Abbie, fifty-six, a leather-booted folksinger with graying ringlets, had a nagging feeling that her sisters felt she'd abandoned them. While she moved around and traveled the world, her sisters rarely left their small Missouri town. According to their parents, the world outside it wasn't safe. Their father had a phobia about crossing bridges and rarely left their town. Their mother's only friends were her relatives. "No one fought," Abbie said, "because anger or conflict were not permitted. But when I was eighteen, I wanted to escape."

When I met the three of them together near their hometown, Abbie's sisters—Ginny, fifty-eight and a smartly dressed homemaker, and Diane, fifty-six and a teacher—made affectionate jibes about Abbie's flight from the family troubles. "I *did* think you ran away," Ginny confirmed, a knife glint of pain in her smile.

"I felt Abbie deserted me," Diane added, looking pointedly at her sister from behind her oversized neon-framed glasses. "As kids, we shared a room and played Monopoly on the floor between our beds," she recalled fondly. "Abbie was always there. Then I was left without my partner to deal with stuff at home."

"Stuff" at home was a *lot*. Ginny had gotten pregnant at seventeen and married. At twenty-two, she had moved back with her two kids while fending off a gambling, alcoholic husband in flight from loan sharks. Diane went to college but dropped out, came home, and got married, too. They both subscribed to the family belief that their parents were a loving, happy couple, and family was everything.

Abbie struggled for many years to extricate herself from her family. She had panic attacks and spent years in therapy. She argued with her sisters about her parents and their views, but she always loved them. In her forties, she reopened a dialogue with Ginny and Diane. "We agreed to disagree," Ginny said, looking fond but unconvinced.

"I understood," Diane said, "that Abbie needed to go away in order to grow up, but it still wasn't easy for me. She was the only person I could talk to."

We spoke together a few months after their father's death from Parkinson's. Although Abbie lived three hours away, she tried to be "there" for them in ways that salved the old hurts. She phoned often and came as often as she could to give her sisters a break. "She knew when we needed a rest," Diane said. "She just knew."

This story might have had a very different ending. Although Abbie, Ginny, and Diane disagreed about many things, they still managed to be family to one another.

STRATEGIES FOR TAMING SIBLING RIVALRIES

Look again: You're not sharing a bedroom anymore.

Don't assume your siblings are grown-up versions of their childhood selves, even if you slip into your old relationships when you are together. Give them the benefit of the doubt. Assume that they have grown and developed; if you talk to them adult to adult, they may just respond that way.

Be ready: Rivalries can erupt after decades of dormancy.

If this happens, try to put a new grown-up spin on your childhood relationships. Start a conversation but don't attack. Explain how things felt to you as a kid, what hurt you, what comforted you.

Near or far, imagine yourself inside your sibling's skin.

There are some predictable traps here that you may be able to sidestep. Whichever side you are on, think about what it's like to be in the other position. If you are the primary caregiver, have some empathy for your sister or brother who feels left out. If you are living far away, consider that your sister has a really tough job. If you need to play a part, you're likelier to be included if you show appreciation and don't couch your suggestions as criticism.

Be alert: Is your dad fanning the flames?

If your father is crowing to you about how great your sister is, he rather than your sister may be setting up the competition. Your sister may even be an innocent victim, hearing the same kind of stuff about you. Try talking to each *other*. You might find out that you can extricate yourself from your rivalry.

Call a truce: Agree to cooperate on the concrete tasks at hand.

Negotiate to focus only on concrete issues concerning your parent. If you can recognize that your parents' needs are primary, and you keep the discussion on the practical decisions and tasks that must be done, you and your siblings may be able to care for your parents without rancor. "Sometimes this can work," sibling therapist Lewis suggests. It can help the siblings realize, she also notes, "the primary caregiver is not *loved* more, but *each* of us has a part to play."

CHAPTER FIVE

"WE WEREN'T YOUR NORMAN ROCKWELL FAMILY": HOLDING THE IDEAL UP TO REALITY

NO SIBLINGS I SPOKE TO ever claimed their family had been the real-life incarnation of the painter's dreamy portraits of adorable and adoring children, watched over by perfect parents. Yet the Norman Rockwell reference often came up. This domestic ideal, the flawless fantasy family that exists only in the imagination, somehow remains the standard against which so many adults measure the less than perfect family in which they grew up.

Even the four Wagner siblings, who cooperated so seamlessly and affectionately over their parents' care, had a few wistful moments. They saw themselves as a reasonably healthy, happy family, reflecting what they'd learned around their parents' kitchen table. "We were brought up to value kindness, to be unselfish, and to think about others," out-of-town sibling Tim said. Yet they all recognized that kindness was not always achieved, and some more than others suffered from their mother's occasionally harsh tongue. Overall, though, they accepted this ideal as one they should strive for, and, to different degrees, they all did.

In other families, siblings did not agree on a family ideal. Listening to so many from within the same family, I repeatedly heard comments like "When my sister and I talk about our upbringing, you'd think we were talking about two different families." Really, this is not so surprising. As psychoanalysts like to observe, no two people ever have the same parents, even identical twins. When siblings seriously differ about their family ideal, it can be very hard for them to agree on what they're supposed to do now that their parents are failing.

Although the norms of our culture color this ideal, it is in the house of childhood that our definition of family is stamped on each of us in different ways. It is shaped by what our parents say about family and how they back it up (or not) with their behavior, by the roles that we are assigned and our relationships with each parent. If you and I are siblings, the idea each of us takes away is likely to be a simplification and an exaggeration of the complex reality that is our family. We create an image based on our experiences growing up: feeling favored or rejected, valued and encouraged to pursue our dreams or not. I may idealize our upbringing while you devalue it. Maybe I see our tightly knit family as a safe haven while you experience it as smothering. Or, perhaps, like the Wagners, we share a basic ideal, one that comes pretty close to how our family really lived. Each of these visions comes with a set of beliefs about how we should feel and act toward one another, what rights and obligations each person has.

Among the families I interviewed, I found that siblings could differ about their perceptions and still get along if they did not insist there was one "right" way to see and do things. The ones who demanded an absolute standard of behavior—how a "good" daughter or a "decent" brother should behave—were invariably frustrated. Reality just wouldn't conform to their standards. When we're unrealistic about our family, our expectations are bound to be unreasonable. We demand impossible things of ourselves and then feel guilty or discouraged when we fall short. We expect things from our siblings that they can't live up to, and when they don't deliver, we feel let down, hurt, or angry. Our reactions can bounce off one another, setting off a destructive cycle of guilt and anger. The siblings I met who got along well, or at least found a way to cooperate, recognized that their sister's or brother's vision of the family, however different from their own, deserved to be taken into consideration.

THE IDEAL FAMILY:
INFLUENCED BY CULTURE AND SOCIETY

Since ancient times, we have been surrounded by images of the "good" family—in mass culture from Renaissance portraits of the Holy Family to television shows such as *The Waltons;* in our religious institutions, which teach us to respect and obey our parents and exhibit brotherly (and sisterly) love; in education, where experts deem family stability a must for success; in government and politics, where "family values" stir many a debate; and in various ethnic cultures, where family life is often the centerpiece of one's very existence. But these cultural ideals and social dicta play only a small part in our deepest ideas of family. Certain notions, such as the commandment to honor one's mother and father, are expressed in most cultures in some way. But exactly what that means can vary from culture to culture and from one era to another.

In Shakespeare's time in England, for example, family virtue was based on hierarchy, with a strong slant toward patriarchy. Just as God ruled the universe and the king ruled the nation, so a father stood at the head of his household. His wife and children belonged to him and owed him strict obedience in all things. Not that disobedient children and henpecked husbands (and strong women) didn't exist. They did. Shakespeare's Juliet defied her parents to follow Romeo; Lady Macbeth dictated strategy to her lord. But, you may recall, these characters met rather bad endings. They were examples of what happened when families did not work the way they "should." They went against the family ideal.

Standards for today's families are very different, not just from sixteenth-century England but even from twentieth-century America. Most boomers' parents grew up in Depression-era families consisting not just of parents and siblings but also grandparents, aunts and uncles, and cousins. Big extended families lived close to one another and were often economically interdependent. This is still the case for many minority or less affluent communities. But by the 1950s geographic distance and affluence contributed to the nuclear family becoming the new mainstream cultural standard of how families should be: the Ozzie and Harriet family.

Writing about this shift, family studies expert Karen Fingerman described a fifties-era scholarly tool to measure subjects' sense of family obligation. The test included such questions as "A person should always support his aunts and uncles if they are in need" and "A person should always help his parents with support of his younger brothers and sisters if necessary." In those days, as social worker Barbara Silverstone told me, children were expected personally to take care of their aged parents, if they had any—no buts! And, as mentioned previously, this was the premise of many state laws, some still on the books, requiring adult children to support their impecunious old parents.

Today, divorce, single parenthood, and gay marriage have altered the Ozzie and Harriet family almost beyond recognition—even where it really existed. But, however much cultural images change, these external standards ultimately have very little bearing on what really exists or what we really believe. Our deepest beliefs about families come from our own parents.

THE REAL FAMILY:
SHAPED BY THE HOUSE OF CHILDHOOD

The ideal of family that our parents promote usually draws on their own upbringing, whether they are imitating it or rebelling against it. It is bound to reflect the standards of their cultural or religious background and the era in which they came of age. But the core of it derives from the family in which they themselves were raised, what their parents told them and showed them, colored by their own reactions and fantasies.

In our family, parents may teach us, we siblings can love one another deeply even though we have our differences; after all, we are blood. Or we may be told that in a "good" family, we must all get along and never express anger or ambivalence toward a sibling, period. Our parents may tell us that we're all responsible for one another or, conversely, that it's good for each person to be independent and stand on his or her own two feet. We may be told that our family is the only safe place in a hostile world or that the outside world is an exciting place in which to find fulfillment. Our parents may espouse the idea that everyone in the family should be treated the same or that people should get special treatment based on gender or merit or something else. We may learn that family members should share the same beliefs and feelings or that a family is enriched by a multitude of viewpoints.

Here's the tricky part. Whatever our parents say to us or believe themselves, the vision of family they promote may or may not reflect the way our family actually works. For instance, a mother who's read "Dear Abby" on the importance of avoiding favoritism may proclaim at Christmas, "I treat all of you equally; I spent exactly the same amount of money on presents for each of you." Maybe she did. Yet her kids, looking up at her, know that she dotes on her youngest daughter, never cuts her eldest any slack, and lets her son get away with murder.

To take a more extreme example, let's say a father talks up the ideal of a strong father who leads and protects his family, takes pride in his home, and encourages his well-disciplined kids to be successful at school. This is what he says and perhaps believes. In reality, he is a tyrant who berates his wife for not living up to his high standards and punishes his children for the slightest infraction of his rules. Rather than a strong and wise man, he is a bully who loves his family but is traumatizing them.

How likely is it that his children will all grow up with the same idea of family? One of his kids may identify with him and believe in this myth of the strong and beneficent father (and he may go on to treat his own wife and kids the same domineering way). Another may understand the family more realistically, as bound by affection but deeply flawed. A third may see the family as a place of unmitigated torment and injustice from which escape is the only answer. When this father gets old and needs care, these siblings will have very different ideas of what their family should be, what each "owes" their parents and one another, what they feel or ought to feel about one another.

Most of the people I interviewed did not come from such extreme families. Nevertheless, in some families siblings had strikingly different ideas of how family should work and how children should relate to their parents and one another, especially about caregiving. The best-working families were clear-eyed about their strengths and weaknesses: They accepted reality.

NOSES AGAINST THE GLASS: WHY CAN'T WE BE LIKE THE MONROES?

When we're kids, sometimes we look longingly at the family down the street and wish we could be more like them. The mom and dad are smiling and fun, the kids never argue, and their family life seems idyllic. Yet all may not be as it looks. There are happy families and unhappy families, but there are no perfect families.

I have talked to these mythical "Monroes" . . . well, to siblings in families that were universally admired—from the outside. "Everyone thought we had the perfect parents," a pair of sisters told me. Their mom volunteered for all the neighborhood projects; their dad would always give a hand to someone in trouble. But under this superficially shiny surface, these sisters explained, was simmering anger between their parents that never found release and terrible feelings of inadequacy among the kids. How could they ever be as perfect as people expected? When these sisters each made terrible early marriages, they wondered what was wrong with them and why their marriages weren't "perfect" like that of their parents. So your family may not be perfect, but then again, what family is?

THE TRAP OF THE ABSOLUTE STANDARD

"You should do this for Mom, for our family."
 "I wish you would be there for me the way a brother should."
 "You're doing too much for Dad."

I have heard many people passionately assert that there is a "right" way to behave toward one's old parents, an obligation that is absolute. Their conviction did not always reflect the way their family really worked, and their siblings did not necessarily buy in. That was true in Russell's family. The sixty-one-year-old CEO in St. Louis had always been fond of his little sister. But as caregiving took its toll, he found himself fuming because she did not show the same sense of obligation to their parents that he felt.

Growing up, Russell had witnessed the solicitous way his parents treated his grandparents and heard their little asides about duty to family. So did his sister, Maureen, who felt far less obligation than her brother. Why? Russell was taught that as the male child, he should look after his sister as well as his parents. Maureen was not groomed to be the "patriarch" as Russell was, but rather the reverse.

RUSSELL AND MAUREEN: A BROTHER WITH HIGH EXPECTATIONS, A SISTER WITH LOW OBLIGATIONS

Russell had been his father's caregiver until his death and was now coordinating care for his mother, hiring and supervising around-the-clock aides, dealing with emergencies, and visiting often. A dignified, deeply introspective man with lustrous silver hair, he had high standards for himself and for his younger sister, Maureen. He believed that in a family, people should take care of others and put their own needs aside. He assumed Maureen felt that as well.

When I first spoke with him, he told me how angry he had been with his sister for not helping out more during his father's illness. Maureen generally did what Russell asked her to do, but it ate at him that she obviously wasn't enthusiastic about it. "I had expectations of her," Russell said, "that she would react the way I did." All these feelings he kept to himself until after their father's death. Then one day Russell ripped into her, reducing her to tears. "I said to her," he recounted, "'These are your parents! How could you not be *willing*?'"

His anger toward Maureen cooled, but he remained disappointed with her. Not that he minded caring for his mom. His relationship to his father had been tense, but his mother—this was different. "I had a special relationship with Mom," he said fondly, leaning back in his executive chair. "We could always talk about anything: sex, drugs, rock and roll."

Russell told me how special his parents made him feel as "the son and firstborn." As a kid, he'd resented their high expectations of him, but as an adult he felt successful, fulfilled. In caring for his father, Russell said, "I felt the mantle of the patriarch drop on my shoulders."

Although Russell thought Maureen was as smart as he was, maybe smarter, their parents had no ambitions for her. She'd fought with their father and was not close to their mother. She'd gone on to have a decent family life, but she'd also drifted from one pursuit to another without finding much satisfaction. "If my mother and father had reacted the same way to her as to me," Russell later reflected, "she might have become different. She's an unhappy woman, and it all came out of growing up in our family."

As we talked, Russell realized that he and Maureen had a different idea of family and what was "owed" to their parents. He felt comfortable in his role as patriarch, with its obligations and rights. But Maureen had no such vision or role. Maybe, Russell reflected, it was not reasonable to get angry at her for not feeling what he felt.

Whatever the messages we hear, as siblings you and I will respond differently to our family's stated and unstated rules and beliefs. "If the family belief is that achievement is next to godliness," said Peggy Papp, a leading family therapist recently retired from the Ackerman Institute for the Family, "one child goes to Harvard, one drops out, and a third becomes a revolutionary." It is the same with family responsibility, she said, with each of us carving out our own relationship to the family value. "If one is very responsible," she posited, "why should the others be? I bet there is hardly a family in which all of them take the same position."

Russell was willing to consider that Maureen's idea of the family had some legitimacy, and their relationship grew warmer. But I met other siblings who remained inflexible. The more a sister or brother refused to see it their way, the angrier and more accusatory they got, invariably sabotaging their chances of winning either cooperation or emotional support.

The Family We Wish We Had: Insisting on a Fantasy

What should a brother be? A sister? In our culture, perhaps in most cultures, brotherly love is glorified as an ideal. Sisterhood is seen as a warm and wonderful connection. These are relationships to which people aspire. If I call you my "brother" or "sister," I honor you and pledge my loyalty as if you were a member of my family, of my blood or clan.

On a more intimate level, parents often idealize the relationship they imagine for their children. Whether or not these parents got along with their own siblings, they imagine that their children will be close. Some even decide to have a second child partly to give the first the "gift" of a sibling; they express the hope that when they are old or after they die, their children can look to one another for love and support.

Many siblings are loving and supportive. Others are not and never have been. Yet some expect that now, as the family goes through this stressful passage, they will somehow become close. This is magical thinking. We don't want to feel alone as our parents fade. We don't want to care for them on our own. So we conjure up a sibling who will be a partner we can rely upon, who will share our feelings about Mom and Dad, and support us.

The idea of the fantasy sibling crystallized for me when I met Christian Beels, a pioneer in the family therapy world, much honored for his early work with families of schizophrenics. Dr. Beels, looking very much the picture of a distinguished psychiatrist with his mane of white hair and silver beard, talked about his own long-ago experience of caring for his widowed mother. An only child with an ambivalent relationship with her, he was totally responsible for her over her long years in nursing homes with dementia. The experience, he said, evoked in him a persistent longing: "If only I had a sister to help."

I asked what his imagined sister (I noted that he didn't wish for a brother) would have been like, and he immediately elaborated. "If I had a sister," he spun it out, "I would have done less but with more grace. In my fantasy, my sister and I would have split responsibilities. And if my sister lived far away, at least we could have talked about it. I felt quite alone and short of options, and thought, 'If only I had someone to talk to about this.'"

The irony here is that an only child's longing for an idealized sibling in the twilight is often equally matched by the yearning of people who have flesh-and-blood siblings. They feel a void that their real sibling does not fill. "At this time, people often long for closeness with a sibling," said geropsychologist Qualls, "even though historically they have not had this relationship."

We run into problems when we don't recognize who our sister or brother really is—or ever was. If we try to force-fit our fantasy on the sibling we've got, insisting he or she be the way we need them to be, we are likely to feel frustrated, angry, and probably even more alone than we have to be. If I am in this position, I see my sister not as she is, with strengths and limitations, but as the awful person who isn't what I want. In my disappointment, I may end up pushing her away, along with anything good she might have given me.

Laurie, a speech therapist in Georgia, wanted to see her family as the place where she belonged and was accepted. But, in fact, this was not the family in which she grew up. To ease her isolation as a closeted gay woman in a small town, she longed for her brother to be her partner in caring for her father. However, he was not the brother she pictured. Although he lived right across town, she described him as "absent." In fact, her "ideal" brother was absent. He had never existed and did not exist now. Fighting this reality nearly cost Laurie her health as well as any possibility of a bond with her brother. But over four very difficult years, she came to grips with the unreality of her vision and taught herself some critical lessons.

LAURIE AND JIMMY: A SISTER YEARNING FOR THE IDEAL, A BROTHER REJECTING HER FANTASY

As Laurie's mother was dying, she spoke to her tenderly, making Laurie feel, for the first time, truly loved and accepted. After her mother's funeral, she made a sudden, emotional decision—to move back home to care for her grieving father. She easily found consulting work as a speech therapist, but the sacrifices she made were huge. None of her friends could understand why she did it, and Laurie was at a loss to explain it to herself. At fifty-two, she'd had a great job in Austin, Texas, a serious girlfriend, and a wide circle of friends, gay and straight. At home she lived a life of social isolation. Her parents, who lived for and feared the spotlight in their small Georgia town (this was especially true of her mother), had begged Laurie to keep her lesbianism secret. Even after her mother's death, Laurie felt obliged by her father and brother to maintain this secrecy.

Much of the time, Laurie said, she felt "invisible." She expected that her brother, Jimmy, whom she called "homophobic," would at least become her partner in looking after their dad. As their father grew more frail, this wish grew into an insistent yearning. Laurie was full of ideas for making this ideal partnership happen. She suggested insistently that her brother and his wife meet with her to plan a regular schedule for visiting their father, but Jimmy evaded her. Over the first months, Laurie made other suggestions. "Why don't we take Dad out on his wedding anniversary?" she proposed once, thinking that would be a hard day for him. Jimmy responded sarcastically. She expected he'd volunteer to fix things around the house or at least come by more often. But Sunday breakfast a couple of times a month and an occasional call to dissect the latest football game was her brother's contribution. "I needed a sibling," she reflected later, "but my brother is not nearly the ideal sibling you have in your mind."

Over nearly two years, Laurie's anger at his "absence" grew.

She reached the breaking point one day when Jimmy canceled a date with her dad at the last minute. "What is your *problem?*" he asked acerbically as she screamed into the phone.

"I have never been so enraged with anyone," Laurie told me. "He got to have his life, and I had given up mine to do this." She hung up the kitchen phone, picked up an iron frying pan, and hurled it at the wall, where it ricocheted and struck her in the leg. Sitting on the kitchen floor, she cried and cried. When she finally calmed down, she related, "I realized I did have a problem. I was engaged in a fruitless struggle, and I had to accept reality. I had to save my own life."

She started taking care of herself. She cut back on her work hours. She joined a gym. She took yoga. She reflected and talked to friends. She realized that she had chosen to care for her father, and that she was getting a lot out of it: making up for lost time and feeling her father's love, assuring herself that she was a good daughter despite not having given her parents grandchildren.

She recognized that these reasons were her own, not her brother's. She forced herself to stop making demands on Jimmy. After a while, he began calling and dropping by. She noticed that he was nicer, his humor more gentle and less biting. When their father was briefly hospitalized, Jimmy responded to Laurie's distress about an unpleasant nurse by calling the right people, fixing the problem. She realized that his strengths were administrative and managerial. Emotional support was not what he could give. "I let go of 'how a brother should act,'" she told me. Not long after, he gave her a present: an easel and a set of watercolors. "He remembered that I used to paint when I was a kid," she said. "It's his way of being a brother, and it's really neat."

What Laurie discovered is that when you accept the reality of your sibling, setting aside both your idealized version and its flip side, the horrible sibling, you have a better chance of working with him and getting at least a little of what you want.

CAN FAMILIES EVER BE FAIR? THE REALITY OF BEING A SIBLING IN THE TWILIGHT

"It's not fair!" This is the eternal cry of a child with siblings. And this protest comes from the child's powerful belief that a family is a place where each person *should* be treated fairly. Well, it often doesn't turn out that way. Even in the happiest families, each person will be born with different assets, be assigned a different role, and have different relationships with each parent and sibling. Life in families is not always "fair." Mom may have lavished attention on you but treated me like a virtual outsider. How can these feelings not come into play when caring for Mom requires work and sacrifice?

When parents need care, complete fairness may be even less possible than when we were children. Certainly siblings rarely care for their parents equally. What *is* essential for getting along well, sociologist Sarah Matthews found, is that we believe that each of us does what is appropriate and possible given our circumstances, understanding, for example, that someone who lived two hours away and also had small children would naturally be able to do less than a sister who lived down the block and whose children were grown.

But what is appropriate and possible may also depend on differences in the relationship each sibling had with the parent who needs care. After analyzing thousands of interviews with caregivers and their siblings, Brody concluded that the quality of each person's relationship with that parent significantly influenced their experience of caregiving. If you felt like your mother's least-favored child as a kid, sibling researcher Bedford found, as an adult you may feel less willing to help her.

Seems obvious, right? Yet many of us do not consider that different relationships with our parents should factor into how willing we are to care for them and with what degree of enthusiasm. The siblings who seem to do best accept this reality and work within it. I recall one woman who took total responsibility for her sick mother and did not resent her sister's doing nothing. "I wouldn't even ask her," she told me. "Mom was horrible to her, and I don't blame her for wanting to stay away." Few differences are this stark or acknowledged as such. At some level, I might understand that Mom wasn't the same with you, but I don't really get what the difference was. Yet this difference may be critical to our getting along now. If, for example, Russell had considered his sister's relationship with his parents from the start, he probably would have been less angry and may even have received more help from her.

EMOTIONAL STALEMATES: THE SPIRAL OF ANGER AND GUILT

Fighting reality, as we have seen, inevitably leads to frustration and anger. We get angry for other reasons, too, some legitimate and realistic, others not. Maybe your sister repeatedly offers to do things but rarely follows through. Maybe your brother does something hurtful that dismays and saddens the whole family. It's even possible we're angry about a decades-old childhood slight, or something else entirely, but we end up directing our anger at a sibling. Whatever its source, acting from anger is invariably counterproductive.

It's Not Just What You Ask, It's How You Ask

Many of us are unaware of the emotions we communicate when we talk to one another. Take Laurie, whose frustration with her brother made her throw a frying pan. She insisted to me at first that she had made her requests to her brother "pleasantly." When she looked back, though, she realized that she must have been conveying anger and disapproval, exactly what she felt. His responses were telling. The more aggressively she demanded his help, the more he withdrew.

Russell attributed his sister's seeming lack of enthusiasm to her being "self-involved," and others have described their siblings to me as "selfish," "immature," and "irresponsible." Maybe they are, and it's hopeless to expect anything from them. But, as we have seen, these issues are usually far more complicated, and these labels are rarely helpful. I talked to many people who saw their siblings—incorrectly, as it turned out—as less willing to help than they really were. That may be because, like Laurie, they asked for help in a way that almost guaranteed they would not get it.

There's an old joke about a man whose car gets a flat in the middle of the night on a dark country road. He can't change the tire because he has no jack. So he starts walking toward a farmhouse in the distance, which was dark except for a small outside light. As he trudges on, he imagines waking up a suspicious, angry farmer. "These country folks dislike city people," he thinks. "They keep shotguns. I bet this guy will be so pissed-off, he'll take a shot at me. And the last thing he'd do is open his door and lend me his tools." By the time he gets to the doorstep, he is furious. He knocks on the door, and upstairs, a window opens. A gray-haired man looks out and says mildly, "Yes? Can I help you?" and the traveler yells up at him, "You can keep your damned jack!"

I've found that we often operate out of the keep-your-damned-jack principle when dealing with our siblings. Some of us may even want to be refused, although we'd never admit it. I recall one sister who told me she found it difficult to ask her brother for help. So she usually waited until she was really angry and then she "demanded" it. Not an ideal strategy.

None of us can hear the way we sound to others, making it difficult to assess the impact on the person we're asking. "The single greatest impediment to understanding one another," family therapist Michael P. Nichols wrote, "is our tendency to become emotionally reactive and respond defensively instead of listening and hearing each other. Like all things about relationships, this emotionality is a two-way street. Some speakers express themselves with such emotional pressure that listeners inevitably react to that pressure rather than hear what the speaker is trying to say."

"I SHOULDN'T HAVE TO ASK" AND OTHER FANTASIES ABOUT GETTING HELP

Asking for what we need from one another can be complicated, especially now when there are so many needs to reconcile: our parent's, our own, and our siblings'. Communicating can be even harder when we speak indirectly and assume that our siblings will know what we mean. How can they know what we want? Sometimes even we're not sure what we want. We may have learned things growing up that get in the way of asking our siblings for help or hearing them when they do ask. Maybe in your family expressing need was considered weak or selfish. Maybe in my family it was a sign of strength. Or maybe it was okay for children to express need but not parents, or women but not men. It's possible I grew up learning that my needs were fine but that yours were excessive or irrelevant. Or maybe I learned that people should anticipate one another's needs and automatically respond. These internal rules probably affect how we express need in all our relationships, but they are especially charged when we are once again negotiating within our family. We may end up asking for what we want indirectly or maybe we don't ask at all. The result? Often nothing at all except frustration and anger. If you're acting on any of these fantasies, take a hard look at your logic.

"I SHOULDN'T HAVE TO ASK."

This all-too-common belief implies that other people should read our minds. Let's say that I am caring for Mom, and I talk about how hard it is. I may just be letting off steam and just need you to listen. On the other hand, maybe I want you to do something, but I don't say what. Maybe I don't even know what I want. This ambiguity makes it hard for you to respond.

There is often another destructive dynamic lurking when we think, "I shouldn't have to ask." Our premise may be: *If you were a good person, good son, good . . .* —fill in the blank—*you would automatically know the right thing to do.* As we have seen, siblings often do not agree about what's right, and many things can interfere with their perception of what may be needed. Still, many will respond if asked to help in some concrete way.

"HELP IS *WORTH* LESS IF I ASK FOR IT."

"When she volunteers," one woman said of her sister, "it means more to me. It's worth more." Why is a sister's help worth less if you've requested it? "I don't want to *force* her to do anything," one brother said in answer to this question. Really? Can one adult force another to do something against her will? Or will your sister be choosing to respond to you even though what you're asking is inconvenient or not what she wants? How is what she does *less* valuable when she puts your needs ahead of her own?

"IF I ASK, HE MIGHT SAY NO."

Let's say that your brother refuses when you ask him to do something. How are you worse off than if you didn't ask?

Maybe you're afraid, as some people told me they were, that his "no" will mean something hurtful, that he doesn't care about you, for example, or doesn't care about your parent. But that's not necessarily a reasonable interpretation. He might be having a crisis in his life. He might have difficulty doing this particular thing but be willing to do other things. And suppose he is angry at your father. That's something you could talk about. Maybe he'd agree if you asked him to do it as a favor to you.

"I CAN'T ASK FOR MYSELF."

People rarely said this out loud, but this premise was a frequent basis for miscommunication. People would tell their siblings, "Mom needs more attention from you," when what they really meant was, "I need you to be more in touch because I'm lonely." Maybe you learned in your family that it was selfish or wrong to ask anything for yourself. But think again. In this new era, everything is changing, and the old assumptions may not apply.

The Guilt Gridlock

Guilt is hardly a necessary part of being the child of an aging parent. Many conscientious, loving adult children feel good about how they care for their parents. Unless we are mistreating or stealing from them, we probably have no reason to feel guilty. Yet too many adult children experience this painful and unproductive emotion.

As Brody found with caregivers in the late 1980s and again with baby boomers, guilt often goes along with being the child of a failing parent, especially for women. Many of the women Brody studied felt they should "give back" what their mothers gave them, a goal that defies reality. These women suffered the guilt of never being able to do enough. Their sisters reported that the one doing the caregiving had tried to make them feel guilty for not helping more or by complaining about how hard they had it. Invariably, they did feel guilty. When they lived far away, they felt triply culpable—for not helping their mother, for not helping their sister, and for living far away. "I interviewed working women and nonworking women," Brody told me, "and there were no differences in their guilt and anxiety."

It's helpful to bear this in mind. If I am your sister and you ask me to do something to help you with Mom, it's all too easy for guilt to infect our interaction. If you are the primary caregiver, I am likely to feel guilty. It's even possible you may feel a little guilty.

When researcher Berit Ingersoll-Dayton and her colleagues at Portland State University and the University of Michigan analyzed focus groups comprised of caregivers, they found that some caregivers were angry at having to do everything but felt guilty for harboring negative thoughts toward a sibling. Still other caregivers communicated badly about what they wanted because they felt ambivalent about accepting help. Some who were not primary caregivers felt guilty for not helping but defended themselves against this feeling by being critical of the person doing the care.

There seems to be a common misperception among siblings that if the "slacker" among them is made to feel guilty, pressured to live up to an idea of what a family member *should* do, then that person will do more. In virtually all my interviews, I have found this strategy to produce conflict or gridlock.

Stan and Leslie provide a perfect illustration. Stan, a fifty-year-old contractor in Los Angeles, was caring for his father in a local nursing home. His sister, Leslie, a fifty-four-year-old dental insurance manager, was living in Tennessee. Stan quite liked his sister, but after several years of total responsibility, he was feeling increasingly resentful and hurt that she was so rarely in touch. He assumed that as a daughter, as a sister, she would *want* to be involved. He interpreted her silence as meaning she did not care about him or their father.

When Leslie finally made it to L.A. after their father broke a hip, Stan took her aside. Yanking open his file drawers bulging with bills and documents for his father, he yelled, "Look, *look* at what we deal with on a monthly basis."

Leslie felt terrible. "It hit me like a ton of bricks," she told me, "how much time he had to spend and what a sacrifice he was making." She was overwhelmed with guilt. She felt selfish. But apart from calling her father more regularly, she never offered to help. "Why not?" I asked her. "I guess it didn't occur to me," she said. "I didn't know what I *could* do from so far away. But I'd do anything for Stan if he asked me." Suddenly an idea occurred to her: "I could fly in more frequently and give him some time off." The night she and I talked, Leslie called Stan to ask what she could do to help and thanked him for everything he was doing.

Guilt can make us hide out and try to avoid seeing what is happening. Leslie felt useless until, with my prompting, she thought of asking Stan what he needed. She was elated when she came up with the idea of giving him a weekend off. Knowing what to do not only lifts the oppression of guilt, it also makes it easier to give the caregiver the most valuable thing we can, the feeling we are in this together.

Sharing an Ideal . . . Imperfectly

Certainly not all the siblings I met were in conflict, but even those who held the same basic idea of family, like the Kellers, faced challenges.

THE KELLER FAMILY: A FLEXIBLE UNION

Once the Keller siblings had recovered from the trauma of moving their mom from the farm to the assisted living home, Dottie and Arlene, their two sisters, and their brother, Donny, settled into a peaceful routine of calling and visiting their mother.

Growing up, they had learned to value both togetherness and being different. "Our family strengths," Arlene said, "are that we all bring different perspectives and angles, and we have a lot of love and respect for each other." All five believed it was right to help their mother and to make life easier for her in her new situation, but they interpreted this belief in their own ways. Occasionally tensions arose that might have led them into the guilt/anger spiral, but they sidestepped the trap.

For example, there was the question of how often one "should" visit Mom. Donny, who most of his life had lived and worked across the road from the homestead, swung by every day for a quick visit with his mother, a custom some sisters described as "unnecessary." "I'm reading it as guilt," Arlene remarked, "because my sisters don't want to or don't care to. I feel like telling them to get off his back! But I don't say that. I just explain that seeing Mom every day has been a part of his routine all his life."

Arlene may well have been right about her sisters' feelings. Maybe they did feel a little guilty; maybe they judged their brother by some standard of their own: not too much, not too little. It's probable they each visited according to some internal calculation: what they could do for their mother, what they needed to do for themselves, what it felt like to be with her: pleasurable, difficult, sweet, unsettling, or some combination of all these and more.

Now ninety-four, their mother was getting around in a wheelchair, occasionally confused but still feisty, and inspiring in her cheerful acceptance of aging. Arlene and Dottie described their visits with her as bittersweet. When they came, they always made sure to push her outside into the sunny garden "to surround her with the things she loved," Dottie related, "and see her look of joy. We know it's not going to be forever, and every once in a while, my sister and I will take a deep breath and look at each other and say, 'These are precious moments.'"

REALITY, WHAT A CONCEPT!
STRATEGIES FOR REAL FAMILIES

Ask for what you think you can get—realistically.

One no-nonsense sister in Wisconsin told me, "I never expected my brother to be much help to me or my mother. My mom is a piece of work, and my brother can't stand her. So I said, 'Listen, Mom needs help. I'm willing to do everything, but I can't afford to pay for everything. Are you willing to send me a check every month?'" Her brother said he would. Over time, he started calling his sister more often, offering to help out. "I was really surprised at our becoming friends," she said. What did she do to make this magic? It's probably what she didn't do. She didn't start from a fantasy, and she didn't try to make her brother feel guilty.

Try to see the family that your siblings see.

Imagine what it was like for *them* to grow up in your family. This helped Laurie. When she stopped demanding her brother's help, she found herself better able to *see* him. She noticed how his conversations with their dad lapsed after discussing the latest sports scores, and that her father used her as a "cushion" to make it easier to spend time with his son. While she had lived as the "black sheep," Jimmy followed the prescribed family path from football hero to their father's business—but never with the same success as his father. "I see that my brother has perhaps felt as unaccepted as I have," Laurie concluded, "although his outer world conforms more to parental desires. I truly feel for him."

Don't attempt the impossible: You can't fix other people's relationships.

When we have an idealized notion of what a family should be, it's tempting to try to "improve" a sibling's relationship with a parent. One woman told me that her sister was missing out on "forming a wonderful, warm, and sometimes delicious relationship with my mother." Maybe she meant to say "our" mother, but, in fact, the relationship she was describing was her own. It was unrealistic to expect her sister would ever have that relationship no matter how many weekends she spent with their mother. Laurie had also been engaged in a similarly futile mission to make her brother and father as close as she wished they were. When she stopped insisting on this dream, she began to feel better. "I learned that I can't fix my father and brother's relationship," she told me, "and I can't fix my dad's loneliness." Accepting this reality brought her peace.

Examine your own role in your sibling dynamic.

As the primary caregiver, do you ask for what you need? Demand? Accuse? Whether or not you are the caregiver, do you minimize or criticize whatever your sibling does? Because it's not enough? Or because if you admit how much she really does, you'll feel guilty? Answering these questions honestly can help you improve your interactions with your siblings. Often a subtle change in one person can work positive changes in the other.

Remember: Guilt is cheap.

I recall having myself fallen into the fallacy that I must be a good person because at least I felt guilty about the things I didn't do, such as writing a check to a charity. But by itself, feeling guilty accomplishes nothing, helps no one, is not a virtue. Instead, make an effort to do something useful. You don't have to buy into your sibling's vision of the family to do it. If your sister thinks you should fly in five times a year to see your father, you don't have to feel guilty about flying in twice. Do what you feel is right. Don't get paralyzed by guilt.

Trapped in the anger/guilt spiral? An objective outsider can help defuse your dialogue.

Sometimes we are so caught up in our old rivalries that we cannot step outside our emotions and talk in a constructive way. If you have a friend who can be objective (a hard thing to find), rehearse what you plan to say and listen to the feedback you get. A trusted clergyperson or counselor may be even more helpful. A family therapist, social worker, or geriatric care manager can also sometimes act as a go-between. Rona Bartelstone, for example, coaches some clients on how to talk to their siblings. In really hard cases, she drafts emails for them, keeping the language objective and nonemotional. This way, she says, the sister or brother receiving it "can hear the information without the drama, anger, or guilt that's part of the old communication."

CHAPTER SIX

WHO PUT YOU IN CHARGE? ADJUSTING TO NEW DECISION MAKERS

"**I KNEW MOM AND DAD** before you were born!" Agnes protested, on the verge of tears. "This is not *right!*"

Six of the eight Moynihan siblings—everybody who could get there—sat tensely around Cath's dining room table in Milwaukee. The four sisters and two brothers, aged fifty to sixty-two, were professionals, business owners, parents, and grandparents. Two years before, they had, one by one, reached a consensus that their mother was too frail and their father too demented to live independently. Agnes, the oldest, had seen their problems first, and then everyone worked together to persuade their parents to move to assisted living. Stephen, one of the middle kids, had been instrumental. A high school principal, he was respected by everyone in the family as a leader and a good communicator. Since then, their mother had died, their father's dementia had progressed, and he needed surgery. Stephen and Celia had consulted a lawyer, then called this meeting to activate the powers of attorney their parents had signed ten years before. Along with making a living will, they had appointed Stephen as their power of attorney for finance and Celia their health-care proxy. Christopher, who'd flown in from Phoenix for this meeting, and Cath, who lived in town, had been appointed alternates. Until this moment, only the four of them had known about the documents. Stephen had just told the others, and Agnes, who considered herself a surrogate mother to all of them, was devastated.

"We don't know why Mom and Dad picked us," Stephen said carefully. "They wouldn't explain. But it is what they wanted—what Dad said he wanted when his mind was okay."

He held out a sheaf of papers. "Here are the documents they signed."

Agnes stared at them in disbelief but did not take them.

Several of the others told her how great she had been to Mom and Dad. And how important she was to all of them.

"Of course, we want your input on the important decisions," Stephen said.

"Absolutely," Celia seconded.

But Agnes just wept and wept.

The transfer of power, literal power, over money and life-and-death decisions marks a watershed in a family's life. Until this happens, our roles—as caregiver, helper, or something else—have been negotiated and assumed informally. Up to now, in most families caregiving has been about responding to our parents' medical or practical needs, but becoming a legal agent for our parents' finances or health means assuming real control. This can be unsettling, no matter which of us our parents have drafted, and this position, whether one is tapped for it or not, can be fraught with emotional significance.

In her intense reaction to not being appointed, Agnes Moynihan was not unusual. Many people find it "crushing," psychoanalyst Michael Kahn told me. "They may have felt they were thought of as capable and smart, and sometimes they are shocked by the parents saying, 'No, I don't think you are.'"

Often, our parents do not say this—or anything at all. We have to draw our own conclusions. As with any important family interaction, if our parents have handled this well, we'll all have an easier time of it. If they have chosen wisely, they increase the probability of having their affairs and their health decisions handled the way they'd like. If they've made uninformed or naïve choices, or don't have good options, they reduce their odds. Yet whomever they choose, there's always a chance that those people may act out of their own conscious or unconscious agendas. Still, the very fact of our parents choosing one or another of us can touch on old hurts and doubts about their love or confidence in us. Any choice has the potential to upset old power relationships and sharpen already revived rivalries.

If we are the ones appointed, we need to understand the legal and moral responsibilities that come with this power, to administer it for Mom and Dad's benefit. This demands that we be especially careful not to take advantage of our new control to settle old scores or for any other needs of our own, emotional or otherwise.

If we are not given these powers, we may need to reframe our thinking about the appointment in ways we can accept. We also must be careful not to impose our needs and distortions on our siblings. They may have been chosen for logical reasons; they may be doing a burdensome job; they may have good reasons for making the decisions they have. On the other hand, if we have cause to think they're behaving dishonestly or incompetently, we'll probably have to look outside the family for help.

THE TRANSFER OF LEGAL POWERS:
PLANNING AND RESISTANCE

Many of our parents have not put in place advance directives for either finances or health. One AARP study found that barely half of adults over fifty had created a financial power-of-attorney document and another AARP survey showed that a mere 51 percent of adults over sixty had a durable power of attorney for health-care decisions. Many parents won't even talk about their wishes for end-of-life care. "Most believe their family will be there to make these decisions," said Stanford University gerontologist Dolores Gallagher-Thompson. "This is just unrealistic, especially when there is family conflict. You see it in spades with end-of-life decisions."

Still, there are ways of persuading them. Elder-care lawyers told me that sometimes old people will plan when they hear the parade of horrible consequences that can result when they don't. If your parents are private and close with their money, for example, you can warn them about what the courts can do. "Without my having a POA," Colorado elder-care attorney Mark D. Masters explained, "they put my assets and income, my health history and prognosis on the public record. And to add insult to injury, protective proceedings are intentionally cumbersome, time-consuming, and expensive."

Another argument you can use is that if they don't make a choice, someone else will, and maybe it will not be the person they would want. With health-care directives, sometimes you can appeal to your parents' love for you. "Mom, please think about us and how upset we will be if we have to make these decisions. It will be one of the most stressful moments of our lives. We will all want to do the right thing, but we may have different ideas about what you want. It would be a gift to us to take this terrible burden off us and help us be together and comfort one another instead of fighting."

Pennsylvania elder-care attorney Jeffrey Marshall advises parents to discuss their health care and end-of-life views with all of their children. "You still can't tell them exactly when to pinch-hit for you (or pull the plug)," he tells elderly clients, "but the more your family and caregivers know about your preferences, the less they will have to guess and disagree and argue." There are some exceptions, however. "Silence is sometimes a better approach if the children do not get along," noted Larry Frolik, an elder-law professor at the University of Pittsburgh Law School.

Noted family therapist Froma Walsh, author of *Strengthening*

Family Resilience, urged that families who have trouble discussing these issues consult a family mediator and make the decision open. "If all the kids are in the room, then each child will hear what the parents want," she said, "not filtered through sibling rivalry."

Delaying these conversations, warned veteran Chicago-area mediator Brigitte Bell, does not make them easier. "Putting them off only makes them later and more difficult," she said. "Mediators and facilitators really are a great resource for at least getting these conversations started in a way that can be productive." Bell admitted that she and her sisters, one of whom is also a mediator, could themselves have used an outside professional when their mother was failing. "It was painful to realize," she said, "that we really were as stuck as we were and had as much difficulty acknowledging and talking about our problems as we did."

Almost any professional who becomes involved with your parents, such as doctors, social workers, and geriatric care managers, will try to get them to sign health-care directives; professionals often prevail on them when we cannot. Health-care directives are especially pressing in the early stages of dementia when patients can still express their wishes, urged Dr. George Bartzokis, a physician at the UCLA Alzheimer's Disease Center. "If someone needs to get guardianship later," he warned, "it can get really crazy, with people called to testify about whether the parent needs a guardian and which child should get it."

LEGAL POWERS FOR WHAT? AND WHEN?

When I talk about powers of attorney, I'm using this as an umbrella term for any kind of legal instrument that lets us act for our parents. A durable power of attorney, often called a POA, is one of the most common. It is written authority to act on someone's behalf for purposes he or she specifies, and it can be written to be broad or specific. It can be designed to go into effect immediately or when the signer is disabled, usually as verified by doctors. Some parents create a trust and make some of us trustees. Others just put one of us on their joint checking account, not a strategy lawyers recommend. Getting legal advice is a good idea when making these arrangements.

A guardianship (of the person) or a conservatorship (of their assets) can be required if a parent is unable to act for themselves and has not put powers of attorney in place. If a mother or father is obviously incapacitated, this may be simply a formality, although it takes more time, trouble, and money than having a power of attorney in place. If the parent resists, seeking these protections can involve protracted court proceedings as well as emotional upheaval. In either case, becoming a guardian or a conservator means asking a court to let us act *for* them. Courts oversee what we do, and we usually need to post a bond.

Health-care powers include living wills, which spell out what measures may be taken to prolong or sustain life. In addition, parents can appoint one or more people as their durable medical power of attorney, also called a health-care proxy or surrogate. Doctors prefer that there be one person legally appointed to answer questions and make decisions about specifics of treatment in case the parent is unconscious or has dementia. Questions about treatment tend to be most intense when our parents are facing death. I will explore family dynamics over end-of-life treatment in a later chapter.

Understanding Our Parents' Selections

Being appointed a parent's POA for finances or health can be seen as an honor or a burden. Actually, it's both. One of the burdens is dealing with siblings who are upset that it's not them. Lawyers see this all the time. "It is not unusual after the documents have been signed," said Russell Haddleton, a Massachusetts attorney who chairs the Surrogate Decision-Making Committee of the American Bar Association, "for one of the children to call me up and ask *why* they haven't been chosen. When possible, I talk to the family together and tell them, 'Your mom can't choose all of you. She's chosen the most qualified.'"

Who *is* the most qualified? If you are POA for finances (and have to deal with the insurance bureaucracies such as Medicare), you should be responsible, well organized, and have time to do the job. "A child who does not pay her taxes on time," Haddleton pointed out, "is not the right one for the financial POA." Your parents must also trust your integrity and judgment. This is the consensus among the elder-care attorneys I queried.

Being health-care proxy requires different qualities. If you are POA for health, you should be sensitive to your parents' wishes and be prepared to make tough decisions with love and empathy. You must also be decisive in a crisis. "By definition," attorney Masters said, "you're not going to be called on unless we're in a crisis, and some people become indecisive when the heat is on." If you're angry with your mom or deeply dependent on her, you're probably not the best candidate for making life-and-death decisions about her in one of your— and her—most vulnerable moments.

Some parents instinctively choose the most qualified child for each job. Others don't, either because they don't understand what each responsibility entails or they don't want to hurt anyone's feelings, or both. Lawyers wring their hands over the way some parents choose by gender or birth order, regardless of whether the person has the aptitude or time for the job. Why can't our parents just appoint all of us? Legally, they can. But then we'd have to agree about everything. When we're under stress, our differences can become magnified. Worst-case scenario? We end up doing nothing while our parents' affairs fall apart. Or we each hire a lawyer, spend lots of money, and the court ends up appointing a professional, at more cost, to make decisions for our parents.

Sometimes none of us is the best choice, or our parents don't want to burden us, so they appoint someone else they trust. Research by Rutgers University sociologist Deborah Carr found that some parents chose other people as health-care proxies to spare their children the agony of having to make a life-or-death decision about them. She also found that if one child was appointed, there might be dissension among the siblings. There was less trouble when another relative or friend had this responsibility. "If the parent named a distant relative, not a spouse or child," Carr told me, "that was associated with an improvement in quality of sibling relationships."

THE USE OF POWER: A RESPONSIBILITY, NOT A WEAPON

As our legal system tries to keep pace with the changes in society and medicine, there is lots of fuzziness about decision making for elders. New York City elder-care attorney David Dorfman described powers of attorney as the "Wild West" of elder-law practice. Even when our parents have created POAs, they may not have drafted them to offer enough guidance or restraint. The typical POA is all-encompassing and contains no requirements that the person disclose what they are doing, or why, to anybody else, inside the family or out. Most states don't require this, either, so POAs, like joint checking accounts and other devices, are subject to abuse.

Do adult children steal from their parents and siblings? Clearly some do. I would bet, though, that most do not think of it as theft. Rationalizations are endemic to having financial control of a parent's assets: "Mom would want me to fix up the house—she always loved this house"; "I spent so much money on gas and tolls going to see her that I'm just reimbursing myself"; "I would work more hours if I weren't helping Dad out, so I need to make up for that." What looks like misappropriation to you may not be so clear-cut to the POA.

Even when our intentions are good, we may not realize that we have legal obligations as powers of attorney. But we do. If you are a POA for your mom or dad, you are a legal fiduciary. You have an obligation to keep accurate records of how you spend the money and to keep receipts. Although people are rarely prosecuted when they break these rules, some states allow family members to bring an action to force you to account for the money.

If your sister is overwhelmed caring for your dad, she may not realize she has to keep records. She may not have time, and she may not have good accounting skills. "It's easy to get sloppy in keeping Mom and Dad's finances separate," noted Charles Sabatino, assistant director of the American Bar Association Commission on Legal Problems of the Elderly. "POAs may already have a joint checking account with their parent and don't realize what it is to be a fiduciary."

Whatever your difficulties, it's crucial to share financial information with your sisters and brothers. Not sharing it can feed distorted perceptions and power struggles rooted in the house of childhood. If you are the one appointed, I'm likely to see what you are doing through my biases. "One sibling may make the accusation to settle old scores," observed family therapist Walsh, "if there was rivalry before and now one gets to be special, more competent."

In the Moynihan family, Stephen made a point of disclosing everything to everybody to the extent practical. He sent annual reports to all seven of his siblings, detailing the amount spent on his father's care for assisted living and other expenses, information about investments, pensions, Social Security, and whether there would be enough to cover expenses if Dad needed to be moved to a nursing home. On the health side, his sister Celia sent everyone regular updates on their dad's condition and how much longer he could remain in assisted living. She also involved them in any big decisions while taking care of the day-to-day details herself. When her oldest sister, Agnes, made suggestions or offered to take care of something for their father, Celia usually told her to go ahead. "She often didn't follow up," Celia said, "and over time the battles for control have died down."

CREATING A NEW ORDER: FROM PARENT TO CHILD IN THE EVOLVING FAMILY STRUCTURE

For most of us, making decisions for our *parents* runs counter to our deepest feelings as children. It moves us one step further in the ongoing restructuring of our family. Who gets the power may confirm the direction in which we have already been moving, with certain people assuming more responsibility. Or it may upset our old assumptions. Either way, it is a profound shift for everyone. If we have been given this authority, we may ask ourselves, "Am I parent to my parent?" If we are not given the power, we question, at some level, "What does it mean that my brother is making decisions that my parents used to make, decisions that affect all of us? And why *him*? Why not *me*?"

In some families this shift occurs so gradually that it seems natural when it happens. Your siblings see that it's practical for you to pay Mom's bills because you're caring for her. As your long-distance sister who visits two or three times a year, I don't question your decisions; I'm grateful you're doing this. Maybe. Or, if I'm uncomfortable with this shift, we may get into power struggles. "I heard comments from my siblings," one newly appointed trustee related, "like, 'Who do you think you are?' But I also felt, *Who did I think I was, signing for Mom?*"

Our relationship to power over our parents, and indirectly over our siblings, is complicated. We may want it, yet feel uncomfortable with it. We may feel we need to do a good job and to be a good son or daughter. But we can get caught up in other less-conscious longings and resentments: to finally become the favored child, to get revenge for past wrongs, to maintain some feeling or role that feels familiar. If I have always had power in the family, I may use this new authority to perpetuate it. If I have not had power, I may seize this opportunity to flex my muscles.

Enid and Jake, in their fifties and living in Spokane, Washington, show how this transfer of power can trip us up even when our intentions are good. Both wanted to do what was right for their mother. Yet the choice of Enid to be her mother's financial agent, the way Enid used her authority, and her brother's reactions provoked conflict, distress, and legal bills. Their story shows just how many threads wind backward to the house of childhood as we take on power that used to belong to our parents.

ENID AND JAKE: ACTING OUT OLD POWER STRUGGLES WITH MOM'S POA

Enid, a sales rep for designer jewelry, trim and tanned, had been appointed her parents' POA over a decade before she had to use it. With her father dead two years and her mother suffering from early-stage Alzheimer's, Enid was now caregiver and financial manager for her mom, whom she called her "best friend."

The finances should have been straightforward. Her mom had a small pension, owned the house she lived in, and the weekend cabin their father had built. She wanted to stay in her house, but after a seizure, she needed full-time care. Enid was afraid her mother would run out of money. She talked to her younger brother about buying the cabin, which he and his family used. Jake had spent his closest times there with his father, fishing and talking, and to him the cabin represented that bond. "My parents always told me," he related, "'When we go, this cabin is yours, and the house is your sister's.'"

Jake, who ran a scuba instruction school, was not as affluent as his sister. He protested at first that he didn't have the money, but after some discussion, he agreed to the purchase. The deal was that he would receive half the cabin as his inheritance and buy the other half. In a spirit of cooperation, Enid and Jake consulted a lawyer together and hired an appraiser. According to the appraisal, Jake's half was worth $125,000. He offered $103,000. Enid was furious. When he called back with another offer to discuss with their attorney, she spat, "This is *my* lawyer. Go find your own."

"I got angry he offered so little," she told me. "It seemed he was trying to cheat my mom. I thought we lost sight of caring for Mom, and my brother was making it about *him*." No doubt he was—in part. But, as I learned from talking to them, so was she, acting out her old rivalry with him and her new part in their family's changing power dynamic. "I was making sure my mom had adequate care," Enid insisted, then admitted, "but I was probably spiting my brother, too."

"My sister told me they made her POA because Dad didn't trust me," Jake said. "What kind of thing is *that* to say? When I was younger, yeah, I used to fly by the seat of my pants more. Now I'm a grandpa. I think Dad didn't see the long-term ramifications when he did this."

Their anger and sorrow had been building since their father's death two years before. That's when the balance of power in their family became unstable. In their house of childhood, the men were valued and had the power. Dad was in charge; they all feared his temper and valued his approbation. To get what she wanted, Mom applied pressure and nagged him. She also waged a perpetual struggle with Jake, trying to get him to live up to her expectations. Even now, she'd get furious with him and sometimes hang up on him.

Enid was the "good girl." Jake was the "wild kid." As siblings they went through many stages: affectionate, competitive, detached. After their father died, Enid, like Laurie with Jimmy, yearned for her brother to be closer. She nagged him to do more for their mother and got furious when he didn't do what she thought was right.

When we talked one day over coffee, Enid realized that

along with her mother's POA, she had taken on her mother's lifelong struggle with her brother, berating him unfairly. "Whatever you do, Jake," she said, imagining how she sounded to him, "it's not good enough." She began to cry. "I think that is really sad."

She and Jake had just resolved the sale of the cabin. In the end, he'd agreed to the full price—but not before they'd said a lot of harsh words and paid a lot of money to lawyers. "I was upset with my brother because I thought he should have picked up the expenses on the cabin a long time ago," Enid told me, tears in her eyes. "But I'm angriest at my folks for giving me this power of attorney. I'm a control freak, but this is more than I want to take on. I don't *want* to be in charge of my mom. I don't want to be in charge of my brother. It's a thankless job."

Like many people who get their parent's power of attorney, Enid felt complimented by it, at least at first. As a "control freak," she liked the idea that she could take charge. As a woman with less power in her family, she relished having it. But, like all of us, she could not control the fact that her father was dead and she was losing her mother. Having to assume financial authority for her mother brought her face-to-face with this inescapable reality in a new way.

Power over our parent's affairs takes us one step closer toward losing not just our parent, but our idea of our parent. When we start making decisions for them, psychoanalyst Kahn explained to me, "We're dealing with the universal fear, projected onto the parents, that one has to deal with life's demands on one's own, that the parents no longer, in a mythological sense, exert power in a beneficent way. This can be a fantasy of the parent by the adult child, the idea that there is someone over me who controls my destiny somehow and is fair and wise and loving and kind and will always look out for me. The realization that now I have the power over them can be sobering and saddening and frightening, depending on who we are."

Jake was also mourning his fantasy parent. Why did he try to get the cabin for less than the appraised value? Of course, he'd rather pay less than more. But he was also having difficulty with the idea that he had to buy what his parents had said they would give him. His fantasy father had the power to give him the cherished cabin; his real father did not anticipate that the couple might need their resources for themselves. Jake's father could not keep his promise. And his sister, like his mother, had expectations of him that raised his defenses.

SHOULD SHE GET PAID FOR CARING FOR MOM?

While many people think that caring for a parent should be a labor of love, sometimes it is both necessary and appropriate for the caregiver to be financially compensated, most clearly when that child has to give up some paid employment in order to do it.

According to Denise M. Brown of Caregiving.com, compensation should be calculated based on the hourly rate for a home health aide, even if the caregiver is a doctor or other highly paid professional. You can determine this rate by calling several local home-care agencies in your area. Brown also recommends that if a parent is not legally competent, a trusted third party, such as a bank trust officer or financial planner, administer the assets and pay the caregiver. That should cut down on the potential for sibling mistrust or conflict.

GETTING THE POWER—ALONG WITH
DAD'S UNFINISHED BUSINESS

When Enid's parents gave her their POA, they may not have intended for her to take over their emotional battles with their son. Yet parents sometimes do hand over their unfinished business as parents along with their legal powers. This is especially the case when they don't disclose their choice. While they may have a good reason, parents who don't tell everyone may just be avoiding uncomfortable discussions and evading their responsibilities. Did the Moynihan parents do this? It's unclear, but they certainly left their kids with the tricky job of telling Agnes and coping with her wounded feelings.

In another family, a forty-five-year-old insurance broker in Nevada told me that her father, currently alive and well, was trying to put her in this position. He'd appointed her executor of his will but hadn't told her three brothers, and he insisted she keep his confidence. "They'll get upset," he told her. "They don't need to know now. And there won't be a problem because I split everything equally."

At best he was being naïve. At worst he was leaving her a tempest to deal with because he couldn't face up to his responsibilities and mistakes as a father. One of his sons had borrowed large sums from him, another a smaller amount, and a third son was perpetually angry at his brothers. This daughter foresaw a storm unless her dad required that the borrowed money be repaid from each son's inheritance. "Don't you realize you're going to cause pain for me?" she appealed to him.

"At first I felt it as a compliment," she told me, "but, yikes, this is a big responsibility." When I last spoke to her, she was still working on her father to tell her brothers. If he would not, she had resigned herself to doing what he wanted. "When I was younger and my mother died," she said, "I was crushed to see that he wasn't the strong daddy I always thought he was.

He did not step up to his responsibility as a father. It was very hard for me. But now I feel he's doing the best he can and he's too old to change. If I can't get him to tell them, I'll have to handle it when the time comes. The reality is that it causes him more pain to deal with this—and the way he's taught them all to live beyond their means—than the pain it will cause me."

Is taking on her father's responsibility the right thing for her to do? I can't say, but at least she is aware of these dynamics. Not everyone who is entrusted with these powers is so conscious of the baggage that comes with them. Being alert to our parent's role can help us think more clearly and separate ourselves from their agenda, something Enid had trouble doing.

WRESTING POWER FROM THE PARENT: WHEN GUARDIANSHIP IS THE ONLY WAY

Becoming a parent's guardian or conservator when that parent is unwilling challenges our sense of separateness to the max. It can suck us into feelings from our earliest days, when we submitted obediently to our parent's authority or raged against it. It can be very hard to think clearly about taking this step.

One family of three sisters in Wisconsin agonized for three years over suing for guardianship. They could hardly imagine taking charge of their formidable mother. "Why, at sixty, would you be afraid of your mother?" the oldest and the eventual guardian told me. "But I was."

By the time the sisters all agreed, their mother had been picked up by the police a dozen times and was living in a house without food and with the gas turned off. When she was finally subdued, she was diagnosed with paranoid dementia and Alzheimer's disease. Her daughters placed her in the Alzheimer's unit of an assisted living home. "Making the decision was the hardest time," said her guardian daughter. "We all had such strong emotions about not wanting it to be this way."

She was certainly right to try to get her sisters on board, attorneys have told me. The nightmare could have been even worse if the sisters had not agreed, adding a protracted legal battle to the emotional upheaval. "These can be cases where at the end of the day the only people who win are the lawyers," attorney Mark Masters told me, "because through their fees, they've sucked up tens or hundreds of thousands of dollars. On the other hand, these can be cases where the lawyers refuse to allow their clients to play petty games and to wrangle over baggage from childhood and force them to a workable solution or practical compromise."

A good elder-care attorney, people have told me, can be a godsend, both practically and emotionally. They can help us see more clearly and resist our own less mature impulses when we are, understandably, wanting to be our parents' children, not their guardians.

AVOIDING THE TRAPS, RIGHTING THE WRONGS

IF YOU HAVE THE POWER . . .

Don't wait for your siblings to ask. Even if they seem distant and uninvolved, send them quarterly or annual reports of what you have spent. Show them where the money actually goes and for what. If you pay bills by check, keep your check registers and bank statements. Try to cultivate patience. You understand both the big picture and the details, but they may need to have everything explained and justified. And withholding information promotes distrust and fantasy about motivations.

It may not make sense to involve your sisters or brothers in day-to-day dealings, but try to include them, whenever feasible, in important decisions. This goes double for any health decisions. The buck may stop with you, but you don't have to throw your weight around. When you seek consensus out of a genuine concern for your parent, you may also get support from your siblings and a sense of sharing the burden.

Take stock of your feelings about having the power—*all* your feelings—and try not to act out the negative ones against a sister or brother.

IF YOU'RE NOT THE ONE . . .

Try to make peace with your parents' decision. We can start by assuming their decision was made for a logical reason, that it doesn't call into question their love for us or their feelings about our competence. Or we can choose to feel rejected. In this emotional climate, this may be the quickest place for us to go, but it is not the happiest, and we may be dead wrong. These are actual jobs, not popularity contests or tests of our worth. We do have a choice about how to frame our conclusions.

It's easiest for us to accept a decision when it has some objective basis: an accountant daughter to handle the finances, a nurse to have the health-care proxy. A choice by birth order may also avoid hurt, although lawyers advise against such arbitrary designations. Even if the reasons are not obvious, many of the possible ones have nothing to do with your parents' love for you. They may have chosen your sister because she lived closer and saw them more frequently. They may have had an easier time explaining to her what they wanted done and how. Or they may have signed the papers ten years ago when you were distracted with a divorce or were living in China.

Even if you are sure you were passed over because of who you are, you still have a choice. You can consider your parents' love for you apart from their realistic appraisal of your ability to get paperwork done; recall the late taxes, the insurance claims you never filed for your kids. Your parents may feel strongly about not having life-extending technology and worry about your anguish at having to carry out their wishes.

It's hard to be reasonable about these appointments, and it's possible that at the end of their lives, your parents were playing favorites. But we should not be too quick to jump to this conclusion.

Think about the burdens of the appointment. Being a POA can mean cleaning out boxes filled with scraps of paper and chewing gum wrappers. It may involve hours of filling out forms every month and difficult, complicated conversations with doctors or nursing home administrators. A POA may have to oversee the sale of a family home, complete with cleaning it out, preparing it for sale, and dealing with real estate brokers and potential buyers. These are the burdens of administration. Siblings can sometimes help out or they can make the job harder.

WHEN YOU CAN'T AGREE . . .

If honest communication is of no avail, round up a family mediator, geriatric care manager, social worker, or elder-care lawyer. It is possible that an outside mediator can clear up suspicions and quiet unreasonable demands.

If you suspect wrongdoing . . .
If a sister or brother who is acting for your parent refuses to share information and won't meet with a mediator or other professional, you still have options. You can hire a lawyer to write to your sister or brother, requesting access to the records. A lawyer's letter may make them take your request more seriously, suggests Pennsylvania elder-law attorney Jeffrey Marshall. You can also call the local agency handling adult protective services and ask them to investigate a suspected case of financial abuse. This will cost you nothing, but the agency will not report back to you. They'll take whatever action they feel is appropriate.

In many states, according to Marshall, you can hire a lawyer to go into court to "seek an accounting." This obviously costs money, but it is not a very expensive action to bring, he said. Another legal solution is suing for guardianship of your mother or father. This is expensive, but if you suspect that your mother is being neglected or abused, or her money misappropriated, you may need to consider it. Horrible things do happen, but perhaps your suspicions are unfounded.

If you fear your parent is not competent . . .

If there is no other way to keep your parent safe, you may have to consider guardianship. As soon as you see danger signs, bring in a social worker or geriatric care manager. Professionals can assess your parent's situation far better than you can, and they will not be influenced by your father's displeasure or your mother's anger. Consulting an elder-care attorney early is essential. Professionals like these can also help get all the siblings to understand the need, although achieving sibling consensus on such an emotionally charged step may not always be possible.

PART 3

SLIPPING AWAY:

MAKING PEACE WITH

CHANGE AND LOSS

CHAPTER SEVEN

HERE YET NOT HERE: THE DYNAMICS OF DEMENTIA

SOME DAYS ninety-year-old Ronald Donovan recognizes his children. Some days he doesn't. Sometimes he confuses one with another. He is happy to see his tall, broad-chested son "Peter" even though his second son, Frank, a paunchy civil servant with thinning hair, is actually standing in front of him.

Of Ronald's nine children, five still live nearby in Cleveland, Ohio, and most see him fairly often, except for Bobby, the youngest. A dapper insurance executive of forty-five, he'd been closest to his father. "Bobby is a loving, caring guy," his sister Fiona said, "funny like my dad was before he faded out. Dad keeps asking for him, but Bobby told me, 'I can't handle seeing him like this.'"

The Donovan siblings were, for the most part, compassionate to one another, especially those who remembered their own journeys toward accepting their father's dementia. "I'm not as sad as I was at first," Theresa said. "It's hard for everyone, but it's hard differently." Their strength as a family, several told me, is that they come together in a crisis. They did this time, too, but their father's dementia made it harder to get on the same page. The out-of-towners took longer. When their brother Peter, for example, drove up from Georgia, his father knew him—he was having a good day—and Peter left after an hour, assuring Frank and Fiona that Dad was really not so bad off. "We didn't argue with him," Frank told me, sighing as he wiped off his glasses and replaced them. "Each person needs to believe what they need to believe."

Of all the demographic changes that have brought this new developmental passage into being, the onslaught of dementia among our parents has the greatest potential to exacerbate troubled family dynamics, and even the healthiest families will be stressed. With 5.3 million Americans, nearly half of all people over eighty-five, suffering from dementia, the most common of which is Alzheimer's, the likelihood that any of us will have a parent with dementia is growing. Unfortunately, this condition creates the greatest need for families to work together even while it tests and stresses our relationships more than any other affliction of old age.

What makes dementia so threatening to our emotional dynamics? On the most basic level, caring for a parent with dementia is longer, harder, and different from caregiving for most other conditions, averaging eight years and ultimately demanding our parents be helped with the most basic functions of life. It takes a heavier toll on our health and family life; many dementia caregivers, the Alzheimer's Association reports, suffer from depression, anxiety, and anger. We experience the pain of losing our mother or father day by day, year after year, as their memory and personality—what one of my interviewees called "the juiciness of the person"—diminishes and disappears. Also, we may be coping with a parent we now hardly know, whose personality has changed, whose behavior has become aggressive or frightening.

If I am the one taking care of Mom, I will be intensely stressed. Like other caregivers the Alzheimer's Association has polled, I will need help. I cannot do this job alone. The support of my siblings isn't just desirable, it's critical. So we'll work together, right? No matter what else is going on, you'll understand that you have to help. Right?

Sadly, dementia often makes it harder for us to pull together. The ambiguity of Mom's condition (she's here yet not here) inflicts a special kind of trauma on us. It exacerbates all the typical psychological challenges of our twilight family: adapting our roles, coping with revived rivalries, accepting change and loss. If our family's communication style has been less than ideal, this ambiguity is likely to make it worse.

To come through this together, we'll need all the help we can get—with the disease, with our own emotions and our family dynamics. Knowing what to expect can help on all fronts. Early and thorough education about the disease for all family members can also facilitate communicating and understanding one another. Some of us will need professional mediation, counseling, or family therapy. Outside help can spell the difference between a family's breaking apart and being able to heal and move on.

IF IT'S DEMENTIA, DOES THAT MEAN IT'S ALZHEIMER'S?

The term *dementia* describes any condition caused by changes in the brain that produce loss of memory and other mental functions severe enough to interfere with daily life. According to the Alzheimer's Association, which provides services for all types of dementia, Alzheimer's is the most common, accounting for more than half of all dementias. Others include mild cognitive impairment; vascular dementia; mixed dementia; dementia with Lewy bodies; Parkinson's disease; frontotemporal dementia; Creutzfeldt-Jacob disease; normal pressure hydrocephalus; Huntington's disease; and Wernicke-Karsakoff syndrome.

DEMENTIA CAN RAVAGE THE FAMILY, TOO: HOW "AMBIGUOUS LOSS" UNDERMINES FAMILY DYNAMICS

Uncertainty is hard for us. So is feeling out of control. Alzheimer's subjects us to years of feeling both, years in which our parents are still here and yet gone, what family therapist Pauline Boss has named "ambiguous loss." Boss, an emeritus professor at the University of Minnesota, has made a lifetime study of how people react psychologically when a loved one— a missing soldier, for example—is physically gone but psychologically present. Or when the person we love is physically present but psychologically absent, such as a parent with Alzheimer's. *Ambiguous loss* has entered the therapy lexicon with Boss's teaching and her book *Ambiguous Loss: Learning to Live with Unresolved Grief.* The term describes a specific psychological condition with special challenges, a different kind of loss where the "normal" rules for coping don't apply.

When a person dies, she observed, our culture recognizes our loss and provides rituals, such as funerals and mourning periods to support us. We feel the finality of the loss and begin to grieve. But losing a parent slowly to Alzheimer's, Boss explained, can freeze our grief; we can feel guilty if we begin to grieve while our mother or father is still alive.

This ambiguity is especially hard, she noted, for those of us who have grown up in a culture that values getting answers and solving problems. Ambiguity makes us feel helpless and stresses us. "In more traditional cultures," said family therapist Celia Falicov, editor of *Cultural Perspectives in Family Therapy,* "people are more realistic about the limits of life. Those raised in Latin America, for example, would have seen lots of tragedy."

How does this ambiguity affect our sibling relationships and our bonds with our parents? Boss has found that ambiguous loss provokes a confusion of family roles, difficulties in making important decisions, and a lapse of the rituals and celebrations that hold families together. Anxiety is ever present and many of us hold on to denial. Since we have trouble with ambiguity, we resolve it for ourselves with our own truth. I decide that Mom is just fine or that she's just "getting up there" and that her memory loss is a normal part of old age. You decide that she's not there anymore.

Many of us feel guilt and shame about our parents' dementia, Boss told me. The ambiguity can intensify disagreements among adult children. Some feel torn by ambivalence, wishing a suffering parent dead, then feeling guilty for the wish. We get confused, we withdraw, sometimes we fight with one another.

Ambiguity Can Wreak Havoc on the House of Childhood

Even when our parents face less devastating illnesses than Alzheimer's, we have to work through any old stuff that comes with reentering the house of childhood. The ambiguity of dementia only compounds the difficulty.

The Hoyt family, a lively and varied group, shows just how the emotional dynamics of Alzheimer's can intensify the usual struggles. These sisters and brothers had the usual challenges. Their old rivalries grew sharper. They had to adapt their old roles in a family where their parents had been strong leaders but could no longer lead. And, unlike the Donovans, with their open communication styles, the Hoyts had to handle all this with entrenched prohibitions about what could and could not be said, and how. They also had many advantages as a family. They liked one another more than they didn't. They all wanted to help their parents when their mother got Alzheimer's, each in his or her own way. But the dynamics of dementia—ambiguity, denial, anxiety, sadness, anger, fear, and shame—divided them. Confusion ruled, and compassion and understanding were lost for a long time. Their difficulties show how important it is to prepare for the emotional and physical toll of dementia on the entire family.

THE HOYTS: TORN APART BY MOM'S DEMENTIA

The six Hoyt children had grown up in the shadow of Alzheimer's. When the youngest children, Danny, Julie, and Bett, were preteens and teens, their mother's mother lived with them for a time before being moved to the county home in their North Carolina mill town. The three oldest, Harriett, Ray, and Chuck, were already out of the house. The youngest kids said they had the most powerful memories of the frightening mental ward where the few dementia elders of that era were sent—the bad smells, the ugly walls. Julie made a pact with herself that if her mother ever got Alzheimer's, she would never let her go to a place like that.

Bett described them as children "scrambling to survive in a too-big family in a too-small house and get out as soon as they could." Despite the stresses, theirs was a childhood of boisterous backyard barbecues and family poker nights presided over by their extroverted, popular dad, who made the rules. They also recalled special moments of unburdening themselves to their sweet, accepting mother, who held the clan together. And there was pride in being a Hoyt; they felt they were members of a very special club.

By the time of their mother's diagnosis, all six had indeed gotten out. They'd gone to college, found different religious and political paths, from Julie's Buddhism to Ray's fundamentalist Christianity, from Bett's ultraliberal politics to Chuck's conservative Republicanism. They were grouped by age. Danny, forty-four, and Julie, fifty, were the young ones. Bett, fifty-five, was a "bridge" child; Harriett, sixty, Chuck, fifty-eight, and Ray, fifty-seven, were the older contingent. The three oldest lived in their hometown; Danny and Julie lived in Atlanta, and Bett in Dallas. Family Christmases in their old home continued to be big family parties with kids underfoot and everyone on good behavior, as they'd been brought up. "We left our baggage at the door," Bett said. That was the good side of their family's communication style, which one Hoyt sibling described to me as "polite but indirect" and another as "avoid and deny." The negative side of this style became apparent in crisis.

As they saw the mom they knew recede, each of them dealt with her decline internally. They rarely talked openly about their fear of Alzheimer's, although they felt it; Harriett made grim jokes to her daughter that reflected the fear they all felt of getting the disease themselves. The Hoyt siblings could no longer seek solace from their mother, who was the person they had always relied on for comfort. Whenever they had disagreed, Mom would tell them they were each different but special. She was the one who "cooled the embers," one told me. "She was the glue that held us together," another said.

As Mom went downhill, the family gradually became unglued, starting with their father. An ultratraditional husband, he depended on his wife utterly for his physical and emotional support. He responded to her diminished capacity with disbelief and anger, shouting at her when she left a frying pan on the couch or forgot the stew was cooking. His behavior shocked his kids, but according to Boss, is a typical reaction to Alzheimer's from someone who rigidly resists change and is losing the person they leaned on. His inflexible view of gender roles also contributed to the family's troubles; he refused to step up to what needed doing, refused to see the reality in which he was living.

The hometown kids all helped. Harriett, financially the most successful, paid off their mortgage for them. Chuck did house repairs, and Chuck's wife stopped by to check on Mom. Ray mowed the lawn and helped with chores. The out-of-towners visited several times a year and kept in close touch. Then Julie came to stay with her parents for a visit and made a discovery that shocked her. Her mother, who slept in a separate room from her husband, was soiling her bed, making it, and sleeping in it again. Horrified, Julie talked to her father and called a family meeting in their parents' living room. It was attended by her local siblings, their spouses, and Harriett's forty-year-old daughter, Anna.

Julie told them what she'd found. She deliberately kept her words, she thought, nonaccusatory. She said, "We have a problem we have to solve; Dad needs help." What she felt, she said, was "pissed off." She was thinking, "Look what Mom's living in!" She cannot recall whether she said those words out loud, but, either way, her siblings heard her message.

"You have no idea how much we do!" Ray defended himself. "How could I know about the sheets? I wouldn't go into Mom's personal space."

"I bought them their house!" Harriett protested.

"I'm over here all the time checking on your mom," Chuck's wife put in.

"This is what I heard," Chuck said. "'You guys dropped the ball.' Those weren't my sister's words, but it's what her body language and tone of voice said. I felt angry and accused of not caring, not loving Mom. And I felt angry with Dad for not telling me."

"The sad part," Harriett's daughter, Anna, said, "is that it was easier to fight than to deal with Grandma sleeping in soiled sheets."

Shame. Fear. Denial. Sadness. Anger. Ambiguity. A confusion of roles. When I talked to them later, they all acknowledged their own denial and ambivalence. Danny, back in Atlanta, sided with Julie, but he said that when he had lived nearby, until two years before, the gradual changes in his mother were less noticeable. Maybe, he said, he should be more forgiving toward those who lived there and didn't see what Julie saw. And why should they have seen it? Their father was still living there, and several of the siblings stopped by each week for a few minutes. As for Bett, she accused herself. Living far away, she had let the others take care of it, perhaps had not wanted to know.

But mutual forgiveness was a long time coming. After a

short stay in the hospital wing of the dreaded county home (now updated) because of a fall, their mother had a succession of paid helpers. Julie argued with the hometown siblings about which was the right aide, and they all argued about who should help pay for her. While the bickering went on, Julie and Danny (who had always been Dad's favorite) were whispering in their father's ear that he and Mom should move in with Julie in Atlanta. Eight months after the meeting, Dad agreed. Then he told the other kids. Julie and Danny's siblings were devastated. They felt their parents were being snatched away. And they mourned the loss of their parents' home, where they could gather as a family. Although Julie told them they were welcome at her home, they didn't feel welcome. The family broke into factions.

Although Bett didn't live in their old hometown, she was just as devastated by the sudden and secret decision. "I thought the family meetings would keep on and would be part of a process," Bett said, "that we would keep talking as a *family*."

Julie quit her job to take care of her mother full-time. With help and respite from her husband and son, from Danny, occasionally from Bett, and several public agencies, she diapered her mother, bathed her, dressed her, brushed her hair and teeth; she patiently responded to her endless repetitive questions. She did this for a year until a slot opened in an upscale nursing home and she moved her mother there for the last four months of her life.

By the end, Julie was physically and emotionally exhausted. Yet she felt she had made the right decision. She had only her parents' welfare at heart, she swore to me. But her siblings felt she had needs of her own. She did. They all did. They were human and afraid.

"I feel like we abandoned each other," Bett said sadly, "or maybe got lost in the dark."

Julie was shocked at the rift that she had created in their family, and after their mother's death she was still trying to repair the rupture. If she could do one thing differently, Julie told me, "I would have had an outside person like a family therapist or social worker conduct our meeting."

"We needed someone objective, outside the family," Bett agreed. "It was too hard to have to face ourselves, our mortality, Alzheimer's, losing our family home. Our feelings pinballed off each other. It was too much!"

"JUST LIKE ONE OF THE FAMILY"—BUT DON'T PUT THE HOME HEALTH AIDE IN THE MIDDLE

It's a blessing to find a good home health aide for your parent. But if there is tension among siblings, you need to be careful about drawing the aide into it. It's far too easy for this hired person to become either a pawn or a player in the family drama. Aides are generally low-paid women who are only human. They may like or dislike particular siblings based on how that person treats them, what other family members say about them, and the aide's own personal prejudices and family history. If you vent to your parent's aide about your siblings, what you say will feed into the sibling dynamic. And if you hear stories about your siblings from the aide, be aware that they may not be objective. Siblings need to talk directly to one another. However well-meaning the aide, it's not constructive to suck her into your family's emotional vortex.

USING CONFLICT AS A SHIELD: WHEN ARGUING IS EASIER THAN FACING THE TRUTH

In the Hoyt family, no one was in doubt about Mom's diagnosis. She had Alzheimer's, just like Gram. Yet despite this knowledge, none of them was really prepared for what the disease would bring. They had accepted that she was somewhat absent and that she could not do everything she used to do. They were *helping*, as they so poignantly defended themselves. Despite their grandmother's experience with Alzheimer's, no one was anticipating the inevitable, when their mother would begin to lose control of her bodily functions and lack the capacity to recognize it. So when Julie came upon the evidence, they were struck by shame in an avalanche of confused feelings. Shame led to blame. And blame led to an ongoing fight that spiraled over every aspect of their mother's care. They divided into factions and poured their passions into who was right. Their disagreement absorbed and distracted them.

This is one way that families deal with the awfulness of Alzheimer's. Geriatric-care specialist Steven Barlam has seen many families of dementia patients embroiled in just such purposeful fighting. "People hold on to the conflict," he told me. "It allows them not to have to look at the reality of the situation." Harriett's daughter got it right: It *was* easier to fight than to think about their mother sleeping in her feces.

LATE-LIFE STEPFAMILIES, PAY HEED

Did you breathe a sigh of relief when your seventy-five-year-old father remarried? Did you think his new wife would take care of him and let you off the hook? Or did you get suspicious and possessive, resenting your stepmother and worrying about your inheritance? Be very careful about either of these assumptions. Any new stepparent may also have children with their own intense feelings. On either side of this newly forged family, things may not turn out as people hope or fear.

Have you seen the movie *The Savages*, in which Laura

Linney and Philip Seymour Hoffman play siblings whose old father gets suddenly dumped on them after his new wife dies and her kids kick him out of her house? I've heard worse stories, and they are not fiction. So has LivHome's Steven Barlam. He told me he's seen about a dozen cases in which a late-life spouse divorces a husband or wife with an illness like Parkinson's or Alzheimer's at the urging of their own children, who are determined to protect their parent, their inheritance, or both.

What accounts for this heartbreaking scenario? Barlam proposes three possible causes: the marriage is not so great or just not what the new spouse signed on for; the well spouse is burnt-out from caregiving and relieved when her kids push her to get free; the well spouse needs the money to survive for more years or doesn't want to strip the kids of their inheritance.

What to do? After it happens, there's very little you can do. Legal options are scarce and cumbersome. So start thinking about this when the marriage is announced and take these steps:

- Make a real effort to establish good relationships with your parent's new spouse and children.

- Urge your parent to consult an estate planner to deal with contingencies of long-term care and inheritance.

- Help your stepparent avoid burnout by contributing time or money for caregiving.

For better or worse, you're not your father's keeper when he gets married, but you may end up that way if he gets a disease like Alzheimer's, then gets dumped by his spouse.

No One in Charge: A Confusion of Roles
Intensifies Old Rivalries

It is a given that our old family structure and our old ways will require adaptation as we lose our parents suddenly or over time. Typically, though, as long as one of our parents is well enough to take care of the other, we don't expect to become primary caregivers.

With Alzheimer's, the expected doesn't always happen. The fissures in our family structure may be so underground that we don't pick up the cues until the ground gives way. Mary Mittelman, a New York University epidemiologist who has studied Alzheimer's caregivers for twenty years, pointed out some of the things we often miss when one of our parents has dementia. In a traditionally gendered marriage like that of many of our parents, for example, the well parent may be rendered helpless in a variety of ways when the other parent has dementia. In couples where Mom made all the social arrangements, Dad may feel isolated and cut off from his usual social network. If Dad did all the driving and now has Alzheimer's, Mom may have trouble getting around and taking care of life's business. "My children expect me to be self-sufficient," Mittelman explained the thinking, "so if my husband has dementia, they don't think to substitute."

This confusion of roles was part of what derailed the Hoyts. Their father was still healthy and living right there with their mother. For years he'd slept in a separate room because his snoring disturbed her. How were they to know he never went into her room? He'd depended on his wife to take care of everything—feeding him, doing his laundry and her own, and sustaining him emotionally. He was so upended by her loss of capacity that he refused to accept it. He bullied, he yelled, he insisted she be who and what she'd been to him. His kids were distressed by his behavior, but they had no idea that he'd abdicated as head of the family. No one was in charge.

As we've seen, rivalries often rise up in a power vacuum. The confusion of dementia can intensify these competitions. Melody Pearson, who oversees support groups for the Greater

Illinois Chapter of the Alzheimer's Association, says that many of the caregivers in her groups have to fend off criticism by their siblings. "The out-of-town siblings think," Pearson related, "if my sister only did x, y, or z, Mom would get better."

Share What? Ambiguity Complicates Sharing Care

Our relationship to our parents, as I have said before, should be considered when we think about who is making a "fair" contribution to taking care of them. If you are the favorite or have always been close to your mother, you will probably be willing to do more. If you have always felt your mother rejected you, you will probably want to do less. That's reasonable.

But dementia adds a whole new variable to the equation. Whatever happened in the past, we may have different, even opposite, relationships to who our parents are now, whether, in fact, they are still here at all. As Boss pointed out, ambiguity is hard for us. So we tend to resolve it one way or the other.

As psychiatrist John Rolland, an expert on illness and family systems at the University of Chicago Pritzker School of Medicine, wrote in *Individuals, Families, and the New Era of Genetics,* "Family members may be torn between their wishes to sustain intimacy and their need to prepare to let go emotionally of a member they expect to develop a progressive condition that involves dementia or extensive suffering." In other words, you may need to detach emotionally from a parent with Alzheimer's, but I may feel the urge to hold on tighter.

If we have these opposite reactions, we may look like we're arguing about issues of fairness or obligation. But this is different. Sibling therapist Karen Gail Lewis saw this confusion with a pair of sisters with whom she worked. The younger sister was angry with the older one, who, she asserted, was doing the bare minimum for their demented father. "You don't do enough," she fumed. But Lewis discovered that the younger daughter saw her father as still there, still alive. To the older sister, her father was already dead. "When they heard that,"

Lewis explained, "so much of their argument shifted. They realized that their fighting was about their different experience of their father's dementia." Lewis helped them balance the fairness equation by getting the older daughter to agree to handle their father's financial matters, an impersonal task that did not mean regularly facing her "dead" father.

Pauline Boss has taught that families can heal when they understand that it is "normal" for family members to hold different "truths" in the face of ambiguous loss. The Donovans were able to do this and it helped them get along. Boss urges us to have compassion for one another as we struggle with dementia's devastation.

RICH SIB, POOR SIB . . . DON'T LET DOLLARS DIVIDE YOU

It's not unusual for sisters and brothers to have very different levels of education, income, or lifestyle. Depending on our history with one another, these differences can easily spawn resentments and distortions about how much should be spent for a parent's care and, if there is not enough, who can contribute what.

Try to defuse this charged subject by making the discussion as concrete as possible. Draw up a list of Mom's assets, expenses, and potential expenditures. Make sure everyone has a copy and hold a meeting or phone conference to discuss the pros and cons of various expenditures, and how much will be needed. Ask people what they can contribute. Don't attach interpretations to the amount they contribute: He doesn't care about Mom; she wants to lord it over us; he's always been stingy. And don't make assumptions about how well off anyone is. Someone may look "rich" because they have a nice house. But you don't know what debts or other expenses they have—your brother may have mortgaged his house to pay for his kids' college; your sister's child may need expensive therapy.

Money is often a taboo subject in families, so it may be nearly impossible to discuss it. If that's the case, suggests family therapist Evan Imber-Black, talk about the taboo. Ask whether you've been allowed to know your parents' income or talk about their will. Discussing your discomfort with the subject can ease you into talking about the actual dollars and cents. If that doesn't work, a geriatric care manager or family therapist can often help siblings work out an arrangement you see as equitable.

MAKING DECISIONS AMID AMBIGUITY: CARING FOR MOM AT HOME—OR PUTTING HER "AWAY"

The ambiguity of dementia makes family decisions harder. Probably the hardest decision we make now is whether to move Mom or Dad to a care facility. Despite an explosion of new and even luxurious care options, some of us feel guilty "institutionalizing" our parents, especially if we've made a promise never to put them "away."

Others believe they have no option but to care for the parent at home. Experts caution that this solution has an emotional cost. "To bring her mother into a household with her husband and children restructures the whole family," warns Leonard Pearlin, University of Maryland graduate professor of sociology. "It can result in emotional chaos, which doesn't ease the burden but creates a new set of tensions and conflicts."

Julie Hoyt eventually had to put her mother in a nursing home. Julie was physically exhausted, and the toll on her family also weighed heavily. "My father just got more tired, more angry at her for leaving him all alone," she explained. "It was not a good emotional environment for my son, for my mom, for my dad, for my husband, or for me." After Julie's mother died, her father failed quickly and also died in a nursing home.

When we place our parent in a care facility, experts say, that may relieve only our physical stress. If you are living far away and I am the primary caregiver, you may think my life is so much easier now that Dad is not living with me. I may have fewer physical demands. I may or may not have more free time. But research shows that the emotional stress continues. I still feel responsible. I may go to the nursing home every day, which is not necessarily the wrong thing to do; there is evidence that the frequent presence of family members leads to better care for the patient. But if your sister was depressed when Dad lived with her, institutionalizing him may not change her level of depression. We all need to understand that the caregiver is still stressed, and siblings need to keep their support coming.

The More We Know, the Better We Deal—Together

The ambiguity of Mom's or Dad's condition affects every aspect of sibling relationships. How can we communicate effectively with one another if we don't know what is actually happening to Mom—and what will happen? If I'm not there, how can I even begin to grasp what you see every day?

Luckily, in the last twenty years a wealth of resources have poured into studying and helping dementia patients and their families. We know more about Alzheimer's, and the medical and social service establishments, along with groups like the Alzheimer's Association, are poised to educate and help us.

Whatever the complex roots of your fantasy or mine in the face of ambiguous loss, our fantasies feed on ignorance about the disease. Experts urge families, first of all, to get a probable diagnosis, because what looks like Alzheimer's could actually be other things, such as depression or even a B-12 deficiency. If Alzheimer's is the diagnosis, all of us should educate ourselves about the disease as early as possible.

A common misconception is that Alzheimer's is primarily a disease of memory. It is actually a complex disease of the brain, with many ramifications for behavior and physical function. "The brain is being disassembled in a backward manner from the way it was assembled," explained Dr. Bartzokis of UCLA Alzheimer's Disease Center. "You lose high-level functioning first, and at the very end, you can't even walk. Like little children, patients don't have much impulse control."

It's critical to family functioning that all of us understand the nature and the trajectory of the disease, what symptoms are a result of the disease, and what we can expect in the future. Knowing that my father's swearing or aggressiveness, for example, is a result of the disease can forestall my natural impulse to get angry at him. If you know that your mother's disease is not constant, that she will have brief periods of seeming normal sandwiched between hours of profound disorientation, you are likelier to believe what your sister tells you about her condition, rather than dismissing it when you hear it described on a long-distance call.

"Mom may sound fine on the phone," explained Alzheimer's caregiving researcher Steven Zarit, describing a patient's behavior even after a diagnosis. "We educate all the siblings about the variability in the demented person. People with good social skills can cover for themselves for a time." Zarit stresses that family members should educate themselves as soon as possible. The Alzheimer's Association is a good resource, he suggests, lamenting that most people wait too long to get educated, and then they're in trouble.

For the sake of family relations, it's essential for all the adult children, their spouses, and other close family members to understand what to expect as the illness progresses. But how do you educate sisters and brothers who live far away or don't want to know? Let the professionals help. Dr. Bartzokis, for example, typically gets all the siblings on the phone for conference calls. Doctors aren't the only resource, either. There are also independent consultants one can call on. Cindy Keith, a former nurse with dementia patients in College Park, Pennsylvania, is one. She often meets with entire families for a one-time educational session. She not only explains the disease but how to keep the patient safe at home, what behavior to expect, and how to react.

Geriatric care managers can also provide this kind of help as well as practical tips that doctors may not have time to give. They can also send objective written reports to everyone and will get them all on conference calls. This kind of education might have tempered the shock the Hoyts experienced in suddenly learning their mother had been sleeping in soiled sheets for who knew how long. If any of the siblings who lived nearby had known what to look for, maybe they could have caught the problem and dealt with it earlier. "Family members have to be Sherlock Holmes and start snooping," Senior Bridge care manager Rona Bartelstone told me. "If there are slippers in the refrigerator, you know there is a problem."

Education about Alzheimer's can also help us deal with our fear and sense of helplessness. Having a parent with the disease increases the probability that we will get it someday. Surveys have documented our fears. Nearly a third of Americans over fifty-five, a MetLife survey found, were more afraid of getting Alzheimer's than any other disease. Although current medications offer limited help, some Alzheimer's experts insist that there are things we can do to help our parents live better longer. And there are things we can do to hold off our getting the disease.

Alzheimer's, Dr. Bartzokis explained, affects the brain's ability to repair itself, which naturally declines with age. "If you live long enough," he told me, "eighty percent of one-hundred-year-olds will have Alzheimer's." Although you can't change the genes that determine the rate at which your internal brain fixers decline, you can, he insisted, protect your normal brain-repair processes by taking steps to fight high cholesterol, diabetes, and hypertension. Lifestyle is critical, both for our parents and ourselves. "Exercise," he said, "produces neurotrophines, which send signals for the brain to repair itself." If the children of today's Alzheimer's patients delay the onset of Alzheimer's long enough, Dr. Bartzokis maintained, "It can literally mean prevention."

Not all Alzheimer's experts are this sanguine. Dr. Bartzokis's UCLA colleague, researcher Dr. John Ringman, declared that the research on lifestyle changes slowing onset has not yet been "conclusively demonstrated." Still, he noted, these health and lifestyle measures are good for you anyway. The research outlook for future Alzheimer's medications, he added, was "very promising."

Trading Places: The Best Education—for Siblings

If you are not here with Mom every day, you may clutch at any evidence that she is not so far gone, despite what the doctors or social workers have told you. Professionals have one universal recommendation for dementia caregivers. Get your sister or brother, somehow, someway, to take your place for at least three days. That is the time required for them to see "the good, the bad, and the ugly," as Barlam puts it.

"I have seen out-of-towners literally transformed by seeing how hard the job is," Dr. Barzokis agreed. "When they see their father getting lost on the way to the bathroom and then not being able to find his way back to the living room, then it becomes more real. It's no longer 'my sister's just complaining because she's always been a complainer.' It's like they've seen God."

After such an experience, professionals say, it is not unusual to have a sister or brother who was totally in denial stepping up and offering to care for Mom or Dad for a spell to give their sibling a vacation.

STRATEGIES FOR COPING WITH DEMENTED BEHAVIOR

Education about dementia now includes an arsenal of tools to help patients' families, tools based on decades of research that shows they work. These practical strategies make it less stressful for me to care for Dad, and they can potentially improve how we deal with one another.

Some techniques aim at alleviating the depression and helplessness many of us feel spending time with our parents. They work best when our parents have midlevel Alzheimer's. University of Washington researcher Linda Teri developed a way to make this time more meaningful to us. If Dad, for example, can no longer plan how he'd like to spend a day, we are asked to think back on what he used to enjoy. We make a list of the things that gave him pleasure. Then we spend some afternoons doing these things with him, perhaps going to a movie, reading to him, or taking a walk in the park. Teri's research shows that these memory-infused activities give *us* a lift.

Other researchers have developed problem-solving approaches to help us deal with some of Alzheimer's most disturbing behavioral symptoms, such as aggressiveness or agitation. If, for example, your mother regularly gets distressed at a particular time of day or in a particular situation, you can think back to when it happened, what occurred just before it happened, and make a guess as to what may be triggering it. Steven Zarit recalled a patient who got agitated in the late afternoons. One day at this time, right before he got upset, he said, "I'm hungry." Zarit suggested his dinner be moved up, and his agitation stopped.

Nowadays much of this research has been turned into easily usable practical advice, much of it available online from the Alzheimer's Association and other resources. Strategies like these were first taught—and still are—in family meetings, scheduled by researchers or therapists at times when all the siblings can be in town. Mary Mittelman, who helped break new ground with such meetings, has seen how teaching these problem-solving approaches affects the entire family. "It helps if the siblings understand how stressful the illness is for the one who is the primary caregiver," she explained. "At the least, they become more empathic. They criticize less, and they may even offer to give respite."

FAMILY COUNSELING HELPS FAMILIES WORK

Family meetings emerged from early research on how to alleviate the sense of burden of Alzheimer's caregivers, who were often overwhelmed and depressed. The meetings were designed to enlist support for caregivers: at a minimum, practical help, and if possible, emotional support. Studies demonstrated that the meetings worked; they lessened the caregiver's burden and sense of isolation, especially when combined with counseling and other kinds of support.

Today there are a variety of options for us to get help coping with a demented parent and with one another. Family therapists and social workers who have deep experience with dementia families can offer aid and support. In addition, there are many ongoing studies on Alzheimer's disease, with researchers based within hospitals and universities. There are also outpatient facilities, which may offer family counseling or therapy as part of their study. All local chapters of the Alzheimer's Association provide referrals to trained family therapists, and some, like the New York City chapter, offer more extensive services with trained professionals on staff. "We have a care consultation room," said chapter president and CEO Lou-Ellen Barkan. "It's like a living room, where siblings often go in together with a social worker. We encourage them to come in together, but sometimes we meet independently with each sibling—whatever is needed. They usually come for help when they are desperate, when there's some dissension in the family, or there's an important decision to be made."

There are many kinds of family meetings. They can include our parent or just the adult children. They can bring us all into the same room together or we can be conferenced in by phone. Meetings can be run by a family therapist, social worker, geriatric care manager, or other professional trained to work with families. Some focus strictly on dividing up what needs to be done. Others probe family dynamics to help us gain insight and resolve some of our deeper issues with one another.

The Hoyts, as they learned too late, really needed such help. While not every family has to meet with a trained professional, virtually every family facing the emotional disruption of dementia could benefit. Unfortunately, we usually don't seek help until we're in big trouble. The advent of Alzheimer's drugs may give some of us a false sense of security. "Now the doctor says, 'here's a pill,'" Zarit lamented, "so they think they've taken care of it." Another reason people don't seek help, Mittelman suggested, is that counseling and support are usually defined for "caregivers" and their families. If you are not doing hands-on care, you may not define yourself as a "caregiver." "Many people caring for a relative with a chronic illness define themselves as a wife, husband, daughter, or son, and think of the word 'caregiver' as someone who is paid to help," Mittelman added.

A NEW FRAMEWORK: IN IT TOGETHER

Most family counseling stresses the idea that caring for a parent with Alzheimer's is the responsibility of the entire family, not any one person. Meetings aim at getting the various family members to take on some part of what is a huge job. They focus on what the parent needs and how each of them will do something. Sisters and brothers don't have to like one another to do this; they don't have to resolve their rivalries. "We try to avoid comparisons between siblings," explained therapist Judy Zarit, who helped initiate Alzheimer's caregiving research with her husband, Steven Zarit. "We tell them that one contribution is not more important than another."

If siblings get along relatively well, she observed, one may offer to take parent chores one weekend a month, for example, or on some other regular schedule. If their lives make it impossible to do anything else, they may be asked just to call their sister once a week. "The sense of burden a caregiver has," the therapist explained, "is not a function of the actual burden but how much isolation the caregiver feels."

If siblings really dislike one another, professional meeting leaders can help them schedule their visits with their parents so they don't have to see one another. If it's their parent they don't like, they are urged to do some of the financial or administrative work instead of spending time close up. Whatever approach meetings take, sibling relationships can improve.

In Mittelman's studies, for example, there are two sessions of individual counseling and four sessions of family counseling. Even with so little time together, she has noticed some improvement in family dynamics: "People get more realistic in what they ask of each other," she said, "and what they say they can give in time or money. There's less criticism and more positive family interaction."

Being forced to work together sometimes improves relationships, Judy Zarit has found. She recalled one deeply estranged sister and brother who met with her to make decisions about breast cancer surgery for their demented mother. The brother had researched the effects of general anesthesia on dementia patients and did not want to allow his mother to have it. His sister, who hadn't had much contact with him over the years, saw him as a heartless man who only cared about the cost of treatment. After much back and forth, listening to his reasons and seeing her brother break down in tears, she realized that he really did care about their mother. He was not the monster she'd remembered from childhood. They agreed on a compromise about the anesthesia that would allow the surgery to proceed. Afterward, Zarit saw a transformation in their relationship. "They developed a new respect for each other," she told me. "Now they actually see each other, and their families socialize a little."

Victoria Mitrani uses family therapy with the dementia families she studies at the University of Miami. In her sessions, families meet together with their parent, who must be able to participate at least minimally. Her therapy, like Mittelman's "counseling" and Zarit's "family meetings," takes a pragmatic approach. "We don't need insight," Mitrani explained. "We need behavior, and sometimes the feelings follow. If you have someone who is resentful or feeling incapable or whatever, if you can just get them to behave differently, the lessening of resentment or the feeling more empowered comes after the behavior." What can happen, she has seen, is that when siblings begin to behave like adults, they start to see one another as adults and let go of some of their child's-eye distortions.

However pragmatic these family counseling sessions, they all deal in some way with ambiguous loss. As Pauline Boss has taught, the therapists can coach these sisters and brothers to accept each other's "truth" about their parent's presence or absence. When families have more in-depth therapy geared specifically to ambiguous loss, they learn that this kind of loss has a name and special challenges. "Then they can more willingly think about what part of their loved one is irretrievably lost and needs grieving," Boss explained, "versus what part of that person is still present to be enjoyed and celebrated." They are also taught to learn a new and difficult skill: As Boss explained it, "to hold two opposing ideas in your mind at the same time: He is here, but he is also gone."

Reinventing the Family and Its Rituals

When our old family structure has collapsed, Boss has found, it is crucial for us—the next generation—to find a way to "reinvent" it and preserve the rituals that hold our family together. Among the most important of these are family celebrations, which can easily slip away when our parent has Alzheimer's. "Like a rusty motor, the family just doesn't go anymore," Boss lamented. She recalled one family who planned to cancel Christmas dinner because their demented father, who had always carved the Christmas goose, knocked it off the table the year before. They couldn't conceive of their clan's holiday dinner without him at the head of the table. As long as he was alive, they felt it was wrong for someone else to take his place.

Then his twelve-year-old grandson suggested a solution. Someone else could carve in the kitchen and let Grandpa serve it from the head of the table, with his mom and uncle on either side to help. "This was a pivotal moment for that family," Boss told me, "about how to continue their lovely tradition but adjust it."

If your parent is in a nursing home, you can bring the holiday dinner or gifts to the dining room there. Or gather around your mother's bed, if necessary. Julie Hoyt recalled her last Christmas with her mother in the nursing home as her family was beginning to heal their rupture. "Some of the family was in town," she related. "We brought eggnog, wine, and cookies and turned on Christmas music. My mom loved a glass or two of white wine at celebrations, so my sister Bett gave her a little through a straw—the only way she could drink now. Bett held the straw to her lips, she sucked in, and when the wine hit her taste buds, my mom's eyes went wide and she began to suck harder." In spite of all the losses with Alzheimer's, these simple moments where a ritual, a tradition, and a long-held memory coincide are the things that keep you going through the pain and sadness.

HOW TO COPE WITH THE EMOTIONS OF DEMENTIA—AND WITH EACH OTHER

Wait for your siblings to catch up.
Even after a dementia diagnosis has been made, we will absorb this reality at different times. I have had many people describe to me the moment their loss crystallized after years of "knowing" it. In one family with five siblings, for example, every one of them had such a moment spaced months or even years apart. One sister described her epiphany to me. "I was sitting, talking to Mom about something interesting and abruptly she got that pleasant, blank, uniform response of someone with Alzheimer's, and I felt a shock go through me. The Mom that I could talk to—she had such interesting

views—she's forever checked out. Oh, my God, that Mom I know is never coming back!"

A whole year later, she witnessed her brother's moment: "The two of us were cleaning up the parents' kitchen," she related, "after they'd moved. It was funny and sad, finding every single drawer and all the counters filled with stuff: old sugar packets, matchbooks, socks, broken dishes, crazy stuff. They were doing this wacky old people's thing, bizarre hoarding. 'Oh, no,' my brother wailed. He started just throwing things on the floor, and then he was weeping. He finally got it."

Get resources and referrals from the Alzheimer's Association—right away!

Whether your parent has Alzheimer's or another kind of dementia, don't wait until you are in trouble. When all your siblings are in town, or available by phone, get education and assistance from your local Alzheimer's Association (www.alz.org) chapter. If your siblings won't join you, start on your own. You will get guidance on how to deal with them as well as your parent. All local chapters provide services for any kind of dementia. They also provide care consultations, referrals to Alzheimer's diagnosticians and family therapists, a twenty-four-hour help line (800–272–3900), support groups, educational sessions, and the Safe Return program to help find and return wandering Alzheimer's patients to their families. In addition, some of the larger chapters, like the New York City chapter, provide more in-depth services, more frequent support groups, and more extensive training for care workers, including a grounding in family dynamics.

Accept conflicting realities.

Remind yourself that it is normal for each of you to have different beliefs about whether your parent is still with you or has departed. No one is "crazy," and no one is "right." You are all hurting and trying, each in your own way, to cope with a long, devastating limbo that cries for resolution—in one direction or another. It may be easier for you to think about your mother as gone; it may comfort your brother to think of her as still very much here.

Pay attention to your well parent.

Don't assume your mother is handling everything or that she is even a reliable source of information about your father. She may be—or not. Be alert for signs that she is not coping well, or that she is in denial. Also think about what your father used to do and can no longer do for her. Maybe there are ways that you and your siblings can fill in.

Voice those "unacceptable" feelings.

When our mother or father has Alzheimer's, it's normal to wish they would die, ending their suffering and ours. As one daughter told me, "My mother was so smart and engaged. Now she's adorable and cute and polite, but she has no quality of life. The woman I know her to be: I don't think she'd ever choose this. I wish she would leave this earth." This daughter did not feel guilty for her wish, but many others do. We often keep such feelings to ourselves lest others think we're horrible sons or daughters. But allowing the thoughts out, somewhere, to someone, diminishes their power, and, Boss said, allows us to begin grieving. In her Alzheimer's support groups, reported Sharon Shaw, a group leader for the New York City chapter of the Alzheimer's Association and a social worker in private practice, the caregivers who say such things out loud are supported, accepted, and comforted. "In support groups," Shaw said, "when someone brings up something they feel guilty about, I often ask what they are 'guilty' of. This question encourages discussion among group members about similar thoughts and feelings and how common they are for caregivers who are not only overwhelmed with caregiving tasks, but also sad and helpless about the inevitable decline of their parent. Of course, group support, along with others admitting to sharing these feelings, is therapeutic and helps members to feel less isolated and less 'guilty.'"

Keep your parent in the picture.

Not everyone can do this, but research at the University of Miami has shown that caregivers who continue relating to their demented parent are less depressed. In one study, Mitrani told me, families were videotaped doing three tasks together: planning a menu, talking about what they liked and disliked about relatives, and discussing a recent family argument. When the families involved their parents in the discussion—by talking to them or looking at them—the caregivers were less depressed, regardless of the depth of their parents' dementia. Like Linda Teri's research on doing a parent's favorite activities with them, this study indicates that remaining connected emotionally to who our parent was can help us now.

CHAPTER EIGHT

GATHERING AT THE DEATHBED: DECISIONS, ACCEPTANCE, FORGIVENESS, LOSS

THE FAMILY HAS GATHERED. The prospect that once seemed so distant, even unthinkable, is now weeks, possibly days, or just hours away. Dad is dying. Or Mom is dying. Our last parent is about to leave us. We are on the brink of losing not just that frail old person, but the remnant of our myths about our parents, that they will always be there for us. And with their passing, we also lose our bulwark against time, exposing our own mortality.

Our readiness depends on many things: how long Mom has been ill; whether she's in pain or extremely demented; how much time we have spent with her in her last months. Our spiritual beliefs about life and death will affect how we feel. But, most profoundly, how ready we are to accept our parents' death depends on how emotionally separate we have become, how much we have learned to relate adult-to-adult to others and to see our parents as the human beings they are. But even those of us who are very far along in this will be tested. Losing a mother or father, whatever our relationship has been, is a defining moment of our lives.

For each of us, this time offers a chance to grow, to understand the reality of life and death. It offers a chance to make peace with our dying mother or father and the kind of parent she or he was. It also gives us an opportunity to make peace with our sisters and brothers, to reach out to them for connection and continuity even as the last person who held us together disappears.

But first we have to accept that this death is actually coming. This is not so easy to do in our culture, since we've been led to believe that there is always something we can do to hold off death—one more medical procedure or technological advance that will save a life.

Discussing end-of-life treatment can be intense even when our family relationships are healthy. The real challenge in making decisions about life-extending treatment is how much we can focus on what our dying parent needs rather than on our own anguish. This is the ultimate test of emotional separation. We must try to see our mother as a separate human being with her own pain and suffering, her own beliefs and wishes about life and death, her own fears and needs as she faces her end. If we can, we will be better able to choose what's best for her or to accept the choice she's made.

Although we cannot prevent the death, we can prepare for it in ways that will make us feel a little less helpless. As siblings, we can learn together about the dying process and what our mother or father requires, physically and emotionally. If we haven't yet done so, now is the time to settle our metaphorical accounts with our parent, saying what we need to say, taking any opportunity for forgiveness, ideally mutual forgiveness.

Not everyone will be able to seize this moment. Even in the closest families, the experience of loss will vary for each of us, given our different relationships to our parent and our individual journeys toward maturity. Compassion for one another is the critical element, whether we have been a frustrated caregiver, a supportive or a distant sibling, a favored or rejected child, or the many shades between. Each one of us, no matter our sins of commission or omission, is losing a mother, a father, a last parent.

THE CHOICES TO MAKE, THE STRUGGLE TO ACCEPT

There was a time, not so long ago, when death was more part of the fabric of everyday life. People usually died at home surrounded by family, sometimes in the same room where they had been born. Now most people die in hospitals or nursing homes. Recently, there has been a movement to change this orientation. "In the hospice community, we speak of cherishing the end of life as much as we cherish its beginning," wrote Samira K. Beckwith, the president of Hope Hospice and Palliative Care in Fort Myers, Florida, in "When Families Disagree: Family Conflict and Decisions." "We know how to embrace birth, but our culture seems to have forgotten how to accept death. As a result, the dying process of a loved one is often a very difficult family experience that can test even the closest relationships."

The choices we face in our generation are new. Our parents had their awful vigils waiting for their parents to die. And often that happened very quickly. But now doctors ask us to tell them ahead of time whether to bring our mother or father back from death! No less a decision than this was demanded from the Washington family, and Epatha, a sixty-three-year-old postal worker, was the sister who had to make it.

EPATHA: SO HARD TO ACCEPT, SO DIFFICULT TO CHOOSE

The three surviving Washington siblings—they'd lost a brother a few years before—were at their eighty-eight-year-old dad's bedside together at a Chicago hospital. The first heart attack had brought him here two months before and a second one this week had sent Sheila scrambling up from Alabama to see him for what the doctors were saying would be the last time. While their father wandered in and out of consciousness, Sheila and Dolores pleaded with Epatha to sign the DNR (do-not-resuscitate) order the doctors were advising. "We don't want Daddy to suffer," Dolores begged. "Did you hear what they have to do to bring him back?"

"It will only hurt him," Sheila admonished. "And for what?"

Epatha, distressed and beset, had some "unkind" thoughts. She wondered whether Sheila was just in a hurry to get back to her new husband in Alabama, whether Dolores just couldn't handle the anxiety of waiting.

"Here's the doctor," Sheila said, turning to address the young physician who'd entered the room. "Talk some sense into her."

Epatha, the second oldest, had been their father's caregiver and was the hospital's contact person in the absence of a signed health-care proxy. A short, motherly woman with a gentle manner, she listened sadly to the doctor patiently explaining again that her father's heart was very weak, he would not survive long or with any quality of life, and resuscitation would subject him to a needless ordeal.

"I don't want him to suffer," she replied, "but he's a strong man, and sometimes the heart can heal itself." She turned to her sisters, tears in her eyes. "You remember what Daddy said to me that time? That he'd want to be kept alive as long as possible? Well, he's a fighter and I think we should give him that chance."

"There is no chance," the doctor said.

Epatha drew herself up, looked the tall, young doctor in the eye, and rebuked him. "That's not for you to say. It's for the man upstairs," she said, pointing heavenward.

"You're right," the doctor conceded, and withdrew.

"How could I sign that paper?" she asked her sisters. "That's signing away somebody's life."

"My sisters didn't know the type of person he was like I did," she explained later. "I'd spent so much time with him lately, and I realized that he was a hell of a man, the way he always worked two jobs to make sure we never went without. And we would talk and talk, and he would tell me the same stories. I would never get tired of hearing him tell me about that old red and gold Buick he loved that got stolen." She paused thoughtfully and her eyes misted. "I guess I was having trouble letting my father go."

For two more weeks, she resisted. Then her father got much worse, and her sisters' pleas got more frantic. Finally, Epatha gave in and signed.

Doctors have told me that acceptance usually comes as the endpoint of a process. First there are repeated hospitalizations, then intensive care. Denial gets whittled away as we see that our parents are not going to get better. If we live far away, we may hold on to denial longer, but we will catch up. " I think most people *do* realize, even though when I'm in California and it's a sunny day, and I'm on the phone, I can think they're not doing everything they can," said Dr. Robert Klitzman, a psychiatrist and bioethicist at Columbia University and the author of *When Doctors Become Patients*. "When you show up and see the situation, you understand the doctors are doing the best they can. Doctors are not in the business of pulling plugs."

We usually need time to process the enormity of terminating life support. Very few of us, doctors say, want to watch our parents deteriorate on a respirator over weeks and months. For Epatha, the passage of time and her father's deteriorating condition pointed the way. Her sisters' protests forced her to confront her own denial. She also reflected more on who her father was and the lessons of his life. In the end, she told me, she called to mind that in a similar dire moment, her dad had signed a DNR for her mom, and he had done it as an act of loving kindness.

SLOW MEDICINE: WHEN LESS IS MORE

Until recently, the trend in modern medicine has been to do more: more tests, more procedures, whatever it takes to keep the body going as long as possible, no matter how old the patient, how painful the procedures, or how limited the benefits. But a small countermovement, known as "slow medicine," has taken root (with Dartmouth Medical Center taking the lead) to make the quality of an old person's remaining days the most important consideration. Operating from this approach, seniors are encouraged, if they wish, to refuse invasive tests, hospitalizations, surgery, and even nutrition. They and their children are asked to weigh the downsides of any treatment against its possible gains. If your ninety-four-year-old mother has multiple degenerative illnesses, does it make sense for her to treat a newly discovered cancer? What would her quality of life be with chemotherapy? Could she ever be independent? Would she want to live longer with her infirmities increasing without end? If her answer—or yours for her—is no, then, depending on where she is treated, you may have to fight the establishment to let her live out her life her way. But, more and more, living wills and DNRs are reining in aggressive treatment that prolongs life in tiny increments but at the cost of terrible pain and indignity.

WHEN THERE'S CONFLICT
ABOUT END-OF-LIFE TREATMENT

Many siblings clash over how to manage the death of a parent, causing ethical and legal dilemmas for the medical establishment to untangle. Doctors, nurses, and ethicists are writing journal articles, giving speeches, recommending that those who deal with patients' families learn to become mediators as well as medical professionals.

Although it is important to make living wills, we have to keep in mind that they are not written with all possibilities in mind, whether, for example, the patient should be given nutrition or antibiotics, or have certain kinds of complications treated. Living wills get overridden all the time, research shows, often because family members don't agree. "If the POA is adamant," said Dr. Ann Marie Sheffels, a family practice doctor in Maple Grove, Minnesota, "then we have a leg to stand on in discontinuing treatment. But otherwise, we have to follow in the direction of keeping them going."

When we don't agree about this, what is it exactly that we're fighting about? Whether we're talking about continuing aggressive treatment or stopping it, keeping Mom or Dad alive with a feeding tube or a respirator, these arguments are invariably about much more. They are about my relationship to Mom versus yours; which of us was closer to her, understood her best, knows her wishes. They are about who cares more for her, who needs to protect her at this, her last, most helpless hour. Competitions to care can blow up into literal life-or-death struggles.

If I have been Mom or Dad's caregiver, I may be so identified with my role that I have trouble letting go. If you live out of town, you may be more dispassionate, see the health picture more clearly. Nonetheless, all other things being equal, elder-care professionals say, those of us who live far away may not be as psychologically prepared for our parent's death as our siblings who have had more regular contact. Even if I update you frequently and accurately, you don't have my experience of day-in, day-out attendance on Mom, conferences with doctors, treatments tried and failed, repeated hospitalizations. You will not have witnessed Mom's pain or confusion on an intimate, ongoing basis.

You will also not have had the same time to talk with Mom,

to ask Dad questions, to engage in a mutual summing up and winding down. If one brother sees his father every weekend and his brother only every three months, suggested psychiatrist Rolland, "Living out of town, I might not have psychologically worked it out to the same degree. And I won't have the same exhaustion factor. There might be a big difference in how ready we are to say goodbye to Dad. Also, providing caregiving has its own healing qualities. So when you're taking care of Dad, you can feel that you're giving back in return for all that Dad may have done for you growing up or over the years. Family members who live at a distance may feel guilty for not being more available to share in caregiving. This is why it is important, where possible, for each family member to have some role."

If one of us is Dad's health-care proxy and our siblings disagree with us, this can set the stage for them to beg, accuse, attack, or sue. The potential for complex family interactions are infinite. Dr. Rolland offers some typical examples. "If I had not had a good relationship with my father and you have the POA, I might lean on you to extend his life because I'm hoping he'll still do something to affirm me. Or, I might want to get it over with quicker."

With so much at stake, my brother might go to court and legally wrest the power of attorney away from me. "The kids can end up doing procedures contrary to what the old person wanted," reported LivHome care manager Sharon Rosenfield. "It's horrible, and hard to dampen the anger."

Framing the Questions Around the Parent's Needs

At these heart-gripping moments, it is all too easy to jump to conclusions about our siblings' motivations. But whether you are trying too hard to cling to your mother for your own sake, or your brother is trying to end it all quickly for his, the answer is to focus on what Mom needs: *She* is the one who's dying. "More important than whether the siblings are on the same page," said Rosenfield, "I need them to allow the parent to be where the parent is." In other words, we must come to realize that this is our parent's journey, not our own.

Before we can focus fully on our parent's needs, it may be necessary to become better acquainted with our own. Hard as it can be, sometimes we need to let ourselves feel the whole muck and mire of it: love, fear, sadness, disappointment, guilt, denial.

Hani Shafran, a marriage and family therapist and geriatric-care manager in Los Angeles, is often called in at such times. "It's all about the kids' own feelings of pushing against death or the impending loss of their parent," she said. "I help them acknowledge their feelings but try to see it from the elder's perspective and to accept that this is their parent's process."

One technique she uses is to ask the adult child to role-play and to speak for their parent. This gestalt therapy technique can help people put themselves in the head of their dying parent. Often they find that they do know their mother's or father's feelings and may actually find themselves using words and expressions their parent might use.

"Then the children can start feeling a little more comfortable with the subject of death," Shafran said, "and think about the parent's approach to extreme measures, yea or nay. Would they want to be hooked up to machines, even if it's very costly? Would they want to die at home, or would they rather be in a hospital and feel like they are fighting to the end?"

Many parents are worried that they will not be allowed to die. It is a nightmare from which they expect us to rescue them. "Asked, would you want to be kept alive in a gown lying half naked getting bedsores as a vegetable," Dr. Klitzman posed, "most people would say no." Most children, he said, do not inflict this on their parents for any length of time.

Ask yourself, professionals suggest, "Is your mother suffering now?" If you want to do an invasive procedure or test, ask yourself what you might learn from it and follow the sequence of consequences logically. If you allowed a biopsy, for example, and your demented mother had cancer, would you treat it? If not, why would you allow an invasive, painful procedure?

Elder-care professionals also nudge the patient's children to think about their parent's spiritual or religious beliefs. Did they find comfort in prayer, certain rituals, or beliefs about an afterlife? If so, then we can use these as a guide. Whatever our decision, however unreal it seems, the end will come. The question then is how best to prepare for it—for our parent's sake and our own.

HOSPICE—A GOOD DEATH

Hospice isn't so much a place as a way of thinking about death. The hospice-care approach assumes that death is a natural part of life and strives to give each person an end of life that is dignified, peaceful, and free of pain—usually in their own home surrounded by family members. If home is not a possibility, there are also freestanding hospices and hospice units within hospitals. Wherever your dying parent is, hospice care usually includes a treatment plan developed by a physician, nursing care, and, if at home, help from a home-care aide.

To enter hospice, people must usually have six months or less to live. They receive end-of-life care dedicated to making them comfortable in body and mind. Although they forgo aggressive treatment or invasive procedures, they might receive some treatment aimed at their comfort, for example, medication for pain. At any point, they can choose to leave, either because they've changed their mind or because they've improved. But, most often, our parents enter hospice because they—or we—have accepted that they are dying.

Along with medical care, hospice also offers counseling from a medical social worker, spiritual attendance by a chaplain, and bereavement services for the family. Trained in family dynamics, these counselors often try to broker peace between parent and child, sibling and sibling. Many hospice programs also offer "respite care," which allows regular caregivers a break from their duties; the patient can be brought to a freestanding care facility for a few hours or even days, or a hospice worker can come stay with the patient at home if that person is too ill to travel.

Siblings cannot always agree about hospice, when they are charged with making the choice, but research shows that families who use hospice have a better experience of death than those who do not.

PREPARING FOR DEATH: LEARNING WHAT WE CAN DO

Once we are past making decisions, we are in a new place—the process of dying. Mom is dying, and there is nothing we can do to change it. But that does not mean there is nothing we can do. Learning how we can reduce her pain and make her more comfortable can help her and us. Having more information, hospice professional Beckwith explained, gives us a greater sense of control. What families of the dying need, she said, is to feel they are helping their parent and that he or she is as comfortable as possible.

Death terrifies us, but learning about the dying process together can help us feel less frightened and reduce our potential for conflict. We can learn what to expect and what the changes in Mom mean, whether she is suffering or not. We find out, for example, that she will begin to move less, talk less, show less interest in what is going on around her, and that her breathing and skin color will change. She may lose a sense of reality, fluctuating in and out of consciousness, perhaps having hallucinations or even delusions. All these changes are typical in a dying person; they are not directed at us.

We learn, very significantly, that she will need less food and water and that this will not cause her pain. There are many unnerving misunderstandings about what is happening to this person we love, a belief that she is suffering when she is not. Education can relieve us of this anxiety. "There are so many misconceptions," said Kathrin Boerner, senior research scientist at Jewish Home Lifecare and associate professor at Mount Sinai School of Medicine. "For example, that people will starve. But, at this point, the body is shutting down, and the dying person doesn't want or need food."

Most dying people fear pain more than death, and medicine relieves their pain; if administered correctly, it does not generally shorten life. From hospice we learn that what Dad needs most is to know he will be cared for and not abandoned, that he will be told the truth and be able to speak the truth, if he wishes—about his life and his death. When parents are conscious, they often want to talk to their children about their dying, but find that the kids head them off, whisper in corners of the room. "When asked how they are feeling," Beckwith wrote, "hospice patients may express that they are feeling alone—even though family members are ever-present." Hospice counselors will ask our dad whether he's okay with our talking to him about his dying; they may ask us to include him in our conversations.

We'll also learn that even in a coma, Dad may still be able to hear us. If we are arguing with one another in his room, we can cause him distress. Whether parents are comatose or not, Rosenfield said, "I try to keep strife away from the parent. They are fragile, some with dementia, all with failing bodies and emotionally fragile. They cannot cope with any of the problems in the sibling relationship."

WHAT OUR PARENT NEEDS:
SETTLING FINAL ACCOUNTS, MAKING PEACE

People who know they are dying prepare in different ways. One distant relative of mine, a tough old bird of seventy-eight, had no children of her own but two stepsons with whom she felt connected, although not intimately. When she learned she had lung cancer and would die within the year, she told no one. She announced that she was selling her house in Washington, D.C., where she'd lived for thirty years with her late husband, and moved back to Boise, Idaho, where she had two surviving cousins to whom she felt close. She bought and furnished a new house. She spent time with people from her youth who still mattered to her. And she set her affairs in order. She was leaving her estate to her stepsons and her diamond ring to her only granddaughter. Without making a fuss about it, she let her stepsons know she had been in and out of the hospital. They visited. Conversations were warm but not direct about her death; she would not have it. When she died, her friends found her will, her deeds, and all her papers stacked neatly on the top of her desk along with the phone numbers of the people who needed to be called. To paraphrase the Frank Sinatra anthem, she did it "her way." This was how *she* needed to prepare for death.

If she'd had children of her own, she might have had different priorities. Parents who know they are dying usually feel a need to get their spiritual lives and their families in order. They look back on what they did right, and what they did wrong, as parents; they feel pride or regret. They think about how their children have turned out and their own part in it. They want to die feeling they have left some positive legacy. Invariably, parents want their families around them, and if anyone is estranged from the parent or from their sisters and brothers, they want to mend the relationships. Sometimes they want to apologize and ask forgiveness. I have talked to hospice counselors who have tracked down estranged children, literally shown up on their doorstep and asked them to come to their dying parent's bedside.

"We often see the parent step up to the plate," said Harriet Puckett, a social worker at Rush University Medical Center and a bereavement coordinator at Heartland hospice. "The parent may say, 'I'm sorry I didn't give you the best childhood,'" Puckett said. "The child can usually accept the apology and it brings peace."

This was true for Lana, a former drug addict, who had not seen or spoken to her mother in ten years. She was so angry at her that when she began getting calls that her mother was dying and wanted to see her, she almost did not go.

LANA: THE HEALING POWER OF A MOTHER'S APOLOGY

When Lana and her older brother, Kevin, were teenagers in rural Wyoming, their single mother got married and had another son and daughter in rapid succession. Kevin was eighteen, close to his mom, and about to move out, but Lana, at thirteen, felt abandoned by her mother, who virtually ignored her and threw all her energies into her new children and husband. In their thirties, Kevin was a cop, and Lana, a data inputter, had turned to drugs. Her brother, shamed and disgusted, froze her out, and her mother spat at her that she was damned and going to hell. Her stepsiblings, who were fond of Lana, tried to intercede, but to no avail.

Lana moved to New Mexico, went into rehab, and learned massage therapy. She spoke intermittently to her siblings when they called her, but she had heard that her mother never mentioned her name without a stream of invective. Lana resolved to act as if her mother didn't exist. For years, she kept that promise to herself.

But her mother, Mary, did exist. As the seventy-five-year-old invalid drifted in and out of consciousness in her bed at home, attended by a visiting hospice nurse, she called out again and again for Lana. The hospice social worker sat down with Mary's other children in the living room. She explained that at the end of her days, their mother, like many old people, needed to feel she had left her family intact. She had noticed how the children who were present had been competing to be the one who best understood their mother. Now she urged each of them to try to let go of any bad feeling toward their siblings and especially Kevin's toward Lana. Kevin had been closest to Lana before their break, but for years he had been furious with her for the pain she'd caused their mother, first with the addiction, then by her absence. But he swallowed his anger and called her again. This time, with the social worker's coaching, he did not yell at her. Instead, he said softly, "Mom *needs* to see you before she dies. She's asking for you. She's crying, and I can't bear the way she's suffering. Please come."

When Lana walked into the house, her siblings scarcely recognized the once-anorexic-looking druggie in the robust, ruddy woman who strode in. Lana went up to her mother's room and was left alone with her. As soon as Mary woke and saw her, she began to weep and begged forgiveness for her neglect and harshness. Lana was stricken at her mother's vulnerability. "I'm sorry, too, Mama," she said, crying.

"I didn't think I could ever forgive my mother for the way she treated me," Lana said. "But I just broke apart when she asked me to forgive her. She'd never apologized for anything before, ever. Until then, I don't think I believed she loved me."

When Lana finally walked out of her mother's room, Kevin, who was standing outside, embraced his sister.

Dramatic deathbed reconciliations like this are rare. Most of us work these things out with our parents over time, often less explicitly. Still, Lana's family illustrates the opportunities we have for healing even at the very end. When our mother or father is the one who asks forgiveness, he or she models how we can treat one another. When we forgive, we make a huge leap in our growth as people. We cease seeing our parent as the source of everything we need or the cause of all our troubles, and we take in reality in a new, more adult way.

WHAT WE NEED: SAYING LAST WORDS

"Children don't want to believe in the death of their parents," William "Chaplain Bill" Rudolph of Chicago's Rush Hospice Partners told me. "Even though their mother is in hospice, they say, 'Yes, she's dying, but I still have time to say what I need to say.' But they *don't* have time."

Rudolph and other hospice counselors I spoke with urge people to speak to their parents early and privately, while they are still conscious. They try to free them from hypocrisy and a slavish conventionality that dictates we express only "good" and appropriate feelings in the presence of the dying. "I encourage them to say whatever they need to say," Rudolph told me. "Total freedom, with no one witnessing it."

Often with a little prodding, he has found, the children will go in, one by one, and shut the door. Every conversation is different. Siblings I spoke with took advantage of these moments. Some asked their mother why she had hurt them by treating them a certain way. Others expressed love or apologized for not being a better son or daughter. At her father's deathbed, grief researcher Boerner told me she asked whether he believed in an afterlife and that they would meet again. "It was extremely comforting after he died," she said. "We agreed we would have some connection." She added that some people ask about their own future and seek guidance about things that might happen.

Even if parents are no longer conscious, hospice experts say, they may very well still hear us. We can make a leap of faith and assume they do hear even if they can't respond. This is truly our last chance, and this conversation, even if it is one-sided, is an important part of how we prepare for their death. We may want to express love, ask forgiveness, or voice anger. Finding it in ourselves to forgive them, even if they have not admitted their mistakes, is a profound step for us.

Speaking of forgiveness, Chaplain Bill Rudolph recalled a mother and daughter deathbed reconciliation that he found very moving. When the mother was in her late sixties and dying, she and her daughter had not spoken for twenty-five years over what Rudolph called "many mutual offenses." Then one day the daughter called her mother and flew up from Florida to see her. "She stood at her mother's bedside and cried," Rudolph related. "She said, 'Mommy, I love you. I'm sorry.' The patient said, 'I love you too, honey.' And she died. I still can't tell that story without crying. . . . How to apologize for what you have done while not accepting blame for what the other person thinks you are guilty of? How to untangle the mess? You can't. Love is the ultimate goal in untangling the mess, so why not start with love and forget the rest, which is what they did. They had no time for the rest, and it didn't matter anyway."

REACHING OUT TO SISTERS AND BROTHERS FOR CONNECTION AND CONTINUITY

Some of us will have had close relationhips with our siblings all our lives. But many of us have come together all these years primarily for our parents or our surviving father or mother. This is the person who kept us connected. What will happen to our "family" now? Making peace with our parents can open the way for peace with our sisters and brothers as well. Whether our father's favoritism has set us against one another or our parents' fighting has split us into camps, the tensions between us are virtually always, at base, about our parents. If I can forgive my father for what he failed to give me, it is much likelier that I can forgive you for getting more or having it easier. If you can forgive Mom for being critical and aloof, it is likelier you can forgive me for taking out my pain on you.

If we have been fighting all this time, odds are tensions will only escalate now. I have heard of a few families where the caregiver felt so angry and abandoned by a sister that she did not even want to tell her their mother was dying. "It's hard to step outside the situation," observed Denise M. Brown of

Caregiving.com, "and say, 'This is my mother's son or daughter, and I have to look out for what's best for her.' But in twenty years, I don't want to feel, O'm'gosh, I was the sibling who kept my sister away from my mother when she was dying."

If we're close, we can comfort one another. If we haven't had the chance to get close before, this can be an opportunity. Consider the Herrera family. Ricardo had three half siblings, including his sister Maria, who initially took charge of their dying mother's care. Maria, if you'll recall, learned to stand up to her mother when she threatened, "Oh, you'll miss me when I'm gone." In the last year of their mother's life, Maria's older brother, Carlos, had shared Ma's care. Now Ma was dying. Their sister Luisa, who'd always battled their mother, flitted in and out, seeking consolation from Maria and trying to offer it. Ricardo flew in twice from across the country. The first time he stayed a week and asked what he could do for his siblings. He shopped, did errands, and spent long hours with their mother so the others could rest. Carlos had always thought of his little brother as self-centered and useless. "But he surprised us," Carlos said. "He went over and above."

The second time Ricardo came, their mother was days from death. At night, the brothers took shifts sleeping by her side. During the day the two men spent hours by her bed, watching the ball game and drinking beer. "We were sitting and laughing and talking trash about baseball players," Carlos recalled fondly. "We reverted back to childhood and how I could beat him at basketball. It was a bonding thing, to remember that connection. Since Ma died, we check in a few times a month and always say " 'I love you.' We never said that before. Ricardo is single and he lives far away. But now he's got someone and he's not alone."

PRESENT AT THE PASSING

The siblings I met had very different notions of what it meant to be with a parent at the moment of death. Some told me they didn't believe their mother would know the difference because she was in a coma. Some said that even if she was co-matose, they felt she would know, or she might know, and it would be a terrible thing for her to die alone. Others told me that whatever their parent's condition, it mattered to them to be there and say goodbye; their siblings might feel they'd said their goodbyes a long time ago. One daughter told me that being there when her mother drew her last breath satisfied a deep need for completion, "like closing the cover of the book, like a law of nature."

Experiencing the Death Together—Yet Alone

We have, in a way, been preparing for this final separation since we emerged from our mother's wombs. All our lives we have moved toward it, developing skills and independence that allowed us to function on our own. Most of us have started families of our own, become parents ourselves, even grandparents. Yet, for all our preparation, this moment is no less immense.

Many of the siblings I interviewed felt a need to describe to me the last moments of their parent's life, every feeling, every slow-motion event as it unfolded. Invariably, they wept as they relived it. Many told me how they and their sisters or brothers had comforted one another, embraced and cried. Some as-sumed that their siblings were feeling the way they were feel-ing, even though that was not the case, as they sometimes realized much later. They wanted to feel this sense of unity with one another as the person who held them together slipped away. Generally they shared enough, and the connec-tion was real.

I felt privileged to hear an intimate account of their mother's passing from three sensitive, articulate sisters in Santa Barbara, California. I was struck by how differently each one experi-enced their mother's death, and I was touched by how much they respected one another's different needs and feelings.

THE MONTGOMERY SISTERS:
A TERRIBLE MOMENT, A JOYOUS MOMENT

Stacy, Elspeth, and Meg Montgomery of Santa Barbara had a rehearsal for their mother's deathbed a full five years before she finally died at the age of ninety. The imperious socialite and former well-known beauty, now a reclusive invalid, had decided to stop eating because she was ready to die. She'd put her affairs in order long ago. After each daughter drove an hour to get there, they found their mother suffering from a bad cold and a lack of attention. Mother soon announced she'd reconsidered her decision.

After this event, Stacy, then fifty-eight and a museum docent, made a decision: to visit her mother regularly every other week. She suggested to Elspeth, a fifty-six-year-old golf instructor, and Meg, a fifty-three-year-old children's boutique owner, that they take turns visiting. They demurred. "I could not handle it," Meg told me, "and Elspeth did not want to."

Stacy didn't blame them. Their mother was not and had never been easy. They'd learned that you could only get along with Mother if you admired her, made yourself fit her image of you, and adopted all her opinions. Only Stacy had always rebelled against this and fought her mother. At this juncture, Stacy felt she'd made her "final truce" with Mom. She resolved to be the kind of daughter *she* wanted to be.

Elspeth mostly stayed away, showing up dutifully when called. For her, every visit was an anxious struggle to hold on to her fragile sense of self. The youngest sister, Meg, had worshipped her mother as "an enchanting, brilliant princess" until Mother scorned her marriage at forty to an Indian physician and rejected her husband. Meg's illusions exploded, revealing her mother, she told me, as "a narcissistic, withholding, judgmental, cruel, lonely, and sad person."

This is the place each daughter had reached in her journey

toward separating from her mother when she was really about to die. Ready to support one another, each sister immediately packed a bag and moved in to help with hospice care. There was no chance of a deathbed apology from Mother. The proud old woman had said offhandedly in recent years that she had been a terrible mother, but Elspeth said, "It was not an apology. She never acknowledged how much she hurt us."

When they arrived, they found her in a hospital bed in the living room, barely conscious. They learned how to administer her pain medication and what to watch for. "I knew she was in hospice," Elspeth said, "but I did not think she would die." Meg had a similar feeling. "Mother looked really bad, but I didn't think the word 'dying.'"

They spent days by their mother's bedside, whispering softly to her and to one another. On the evening of the fifth day, they heard her breathing change suddenly. They circled her. Elspeth stroked her mother's arm. Stacy caressed her hair and wept. "I whispered, 'Sweet Mama' over and over," she recalled. "Meg looked at me like I was crazy."

"Don't you want to touch her?" Elspeth urged Meg.

"I already did," Meg said.

"I didn't want to be hugging or kissing her," Meg said later. "That was sad for me that I felt so distant. So, I said, 'Mom, we're all here with you. You're safe.' And then I started singing 'Summertime,' which she used to sing to us as a lullaby." As she heard the old melody, Elspeth wept harder. Then their mother's breathing changed again, and she was dead. "The moment was terrible," Elspeth said, crying at the memory. "It is one of the worst moments of feeling in my life—that something that had always been was . . . no longer there."

Meg's experience was different. "It was the most powerful thing I'd ever experienced," Meg said, "a sensation of huge power all around me, the power of a life ending." For Stacy, her mother's death had yet another dimension. "I felt almost joyous when she slipped away," Stacy said, "that I had done everything to care for her that she would allow me to do for five years, and that I didn't have any regrets. At the end I could finally give her all the care and love she would never accept before."

The Montgomery sisters were able to love and comfort one another even though they were in such different places as they stood together to witness their mother's passing. For five years, Stacy had been preparing by making those regular, trying visits to her mother. She made them out of compassion and a sense that she was doing for her mother what she would want someone to do for her. "When I turned sixty," she said, "I had a feeling I was not that far from my own death, and it was a humbling experience." In accepting human life as it was and doing what she felt was right for her mother, she felt joy as well as sadness when her mother's life ended.

Elspeth, who had adopted a numb stoicism as her defense against hurt, was so connected to her mother's every nuance of thought and feeling that, at some level, she did not believe she could die. The actuality was devastating.

Meg had prepared a little more, coming to see her mother, as she said, "whenever the guilt level got too high." But in her progress toward seeing who her mother was, she had experienced the stage of crushing disillusionment but had not yet reached the more adult place she would come to later, when she understood her mother was "only human." She told me she felt like an "orphan."

Whatever our feelings, none of us is actually an "orphan," a child without parents to care for us. If we have learned to accept our parents' aging and need for care, to see them as the fallible human beings they are, then we will have grown into our maturity with the intimate knowledge that all of us have a limited time on earth. Now we are truly adults. On our own.

HOW TO HELP YOUR PARENT—AND
YOURSELF—THROUGH THE END

Find out your parent's wishes.
If they won't sign a living will, or even talk directly about their
death, engage them casually about other people's end-of-life
situations: your aunt's, your neighbor's. Try to do it at a family
occasion when your siblings can hear what they say. It's important that everybody know their feelings.

Put your parent's wishes ahead of your needs.
This is hard. You may be desperate to "save" your mom. Or
you may find it harrowing to watch her continue to fight and
suffer to the bitter end. But remember that this is *her* life, her
death. She deserves to have her wishes honored. If your mom
wants to talk about dying, let her. Don't shut her out when she
needs you most.

If you disagree about end-of-life care . . .
Your brother may disagree with you, may even be wrong, but
do not assume bad motives. It is highly unlikely that he is trying to "kill" your father or wants to make him suffer—
regardless of their past conflicts. I spoke to one woman who
accused her brother of hating their mom because he wanted
to take her off life support. Later she realized he'd been motivated by love for their mother. "I see now that he was less emotional than I was and could see the situation more clearly," she
told me. "I wasn't ready to let her go." If your sister has put
your mother on life support against her wishes, don't despair.
She may need just a short time, maybe even just a day or two,
to accept that your mother is dying.

If feasible, use hospice services.
With hospice, you can give your parent the best death possible
with the least pain and suffering. Take advantage of all the education hospice offers and all the counseling services avail-

able. Many hospice counselors will help you and your parent to make peace, if possible, and they will also work to reduce sibling conflict.

Just arrived? Try to learn all you can before you react.
If your father's medical situation has been ongoing, you probably don't know as much about it as your sister who's been there every day. Talk to the nurses and doctors and find out what your father really needs and what you can—and can't—do for him.

To take just one example: pain medication. Chaplain Bill Rudolph has often seen a newly arrived son or daughter insist his mother's meds be reduced: "She's sleeping all the time. I can't *talk* to her." What you may not understand is that some pain medication needs to be kept at a constant level to keep your mother above her pain threshold. If it's reduced, she may seem fine when you talk to her yet end up suffering afterward when the staff can't quickly get her back to where she was. Listen to what the professionals tell you. Get another opinion if you need to, but don't decide based on your own needs.

PART 4

REINVENTING THE FAMILY

FOR OUR GENERATION:

SHARING STORIES,

PASSING ON LEGACIES

CHAPTER NINE

MOURNING AND MOVING ON: ALONE AND TOGETHER

THE MILLER SISTERS—Judith, Pennie, and Marcy—planned the funeral observances for their mother as a celebration of her life and the family she loved. Her death had been long expected, so the sisters had time to gather their husbands and partners, their teen and adult children, a few cousins, and other relations. Everyone arrived bearing photos and mementos, which her grandchildren arranged in an artistic display. After the burial, the entire group trooped to a nearby restaurant. "Mom had just enough money left," Judith explained, "to fly the grandkids in and take everyone out to dinner. She loved our far-flung extended family, and she would have loved to have us all come together. This party was on Mom."

Judith, Pennie, and Marcy each told me separately how grateful she was to have her sisters by her side. "The sister support system we developed to care for Mom continued beautifully through her dying and death," Pennie said. And this "sister support" persisted by phone and email when they scattered to their respective cities and lives. Nonetheless, over the months and years ahead, each made her own internal journey through grief, and this was something each sister had to do alone.

It used to be thought, not so long ago by some very smart people, that losing an elderly parent was really no big deal. But the psychological thinking has changed. Now we better understand that losing a parent, even one who is very old, is a life-changing event. Although the experience is different for each of us and different with each parent, it is profound. Losing our last parent may be even more so. Although it is not a tragedy, it puts us in greater touch with the tragic side of life, which can deepen our appreciation of life and help us grow as people.

Loss is at the heart of human experience. Life changes, and every change, even the good ones, means the loss of something. When we love anyone, we understand that, one way or another, we will inevitably be separated. We expect this with our parents, but that does not make losing them easy. Our job in healthy mourning, students of the human psyche say, is to accept that they are gone, make that reality part of us over time—make *them* part of us—and move forward with our lives.

Though we may stand together at the funeral with our sisters and brothers, comforting one another, each of us has to grieve in our own way in our own time. No one should tell us our mourning is too slow or fast, too dramatic or too subdued, too tender or too callous. By the same token, we should not judge the way a sister or brother mourns. There is no wrong way to grieve, though we must learn to differentiate mourning, which moves us forward, from depression, which holds us back.

With memorials and rituals, we can share our loss, be supportive of one another, and begin to see our parents within a fuller, more mature context. And we can stay connected by adapting our roles and the traditions that made us a family to the realities of who and where we are now.

PLANNING THE MEMORIALS:
GIVE EACH SIBLING A ROLE

Every culture has its own rituals for treating the bodies of its dead and mourning the loss of a family member. Invariably, we do this together, with family and friends. We gather at a particular place: a funeral home or house of worship, a grave site, a private residence, or a public venue. Certain words are pronounced, songs are sung, food is shared. We repeat sentiments or phrases our ancestors before us said on such occasions, words we have grown up hearing at such solemn moments. We also improvise and make the ritual fit the person we've lost, our mom or dad.

Done in a meaningful way together, these ceremonies can bring solace. Whenever possible, each sibling should have a role, either in planning or in the ceremony itself. In one family, all the siblings were relieved when the sister who felt left out—not a caregiver, not a POA—asked about what readings they should have at Mom's funeral. They immediately put her in charge of the selections.

In another, larger family, the siblings were each assigned a role based on their talents and how they were feeling. "My musician brother," one sister told me, "handled, naturally, music. My younger brother, totally at loose ends in his grief, was kept busy picking up flowers, getting the program printed, and running errands. I wrote the eulogy, soliciting input from each sibling and allowing them to edit as they wished. It united us and we took comfort from working together."

So think ahead, if possible. Consider each person's emotional state and abilities, and make everyone feel a part of this enormous passage, and a valued person in the family.

MOURNING ALONE: THE INTERNAL PROCESS

Some of us are ambushed by the ferocity of our grief for our parents. Let's say that my mother has been in ill health for years; she's almost ninety or even older. I have expected her death for a long time. My friends and colleagues take her death as a natural occurrence, send a card, and think no more about what my grief might be. But it can be huge. "It surprises middle-aged people," said family therapist Dorothy Becvar, author of *In the Presence of Grief,* "that they're so done in by the death of their parents. They think that because they've expected their parent to die that it isn't going to be that hard. Well, it is."

For many of us nowadays, our parents' longer life spans have given us a chance to develop mature friendships with them. Especially after they've been widowed, our parents may become more intimate companions. Many people told me that when their mother or father died, they had lost a "best friend."

With our last parent's death, we lose any remaining shreds of the mythical parent of childhood who could protect us from all the dark scary things in the closet, all the things that we feared would hurt or destroy us. One middle-aged daughter told me, poignantly, how she felt a spasm of grief for this mythic mother several years after her real mother had died. Fighting cancer, she had a sign that it might have returned. "I couldn't get my results right away," she said, "and it panicked me. I suddenly missed my mother so badly. I wanted *Mommy,* the mommy of my childhood. When I was scared as a child, I'd put my head on her lap for comfort. And I missed that."

"Being a middle-aged 'orphan,'" Becvar noted, "turns out to be a pretty big deal. People feel, 'Who do I turn to now?'" Adult children I interviewed spoke of an existential pain. "My secure place in the world was gone," one bereaved daughter told me. "When my parents were alive, I had a kind of tether that held me to reality, and that reality was that I came from my parents, the roots were there and visible. But now that's gone."

Many people were able to turn this loss into something positive. It brought maturity and growth and, for some, liberation. "The death of a parent," sociologist Debra Umberson wrote, "initiates a rite of passage into a new adult identity. Most adults find a way to view themselves not necessarily as a better person but as a different person—as more responsible, less focused on work, more like or different from their parent, or as a different kind of parent with their own child. The death of the parent transforms the adult child into the adult who is no longer a child—into an adult who glimpses personal mortality and finds a way to become his or her own parent."

The Rhythm of Grief

It used to be thought that we mourn for a given time—one year, two years—and then our grieving is finished. We don't think this anymore, either. "We don't 'get over it,'" Pauline Boss told me. "We live with it." For most of us, the first year is hardest, with every "first" a sharp pang or deep ache—the first birthday, first spring, first Christmas, and, especially, the first anniversary of the death. There are bad days and worse days and others that seem perversely fine. Then when we've been okay for a while, something—such as a song, a scent, or a street corner—evokes a pain so keen it floors us. Or the mere passing of time makes the loss sink in: *Oh. So this is what "forever" feels like.*

Even after our most intense period of mourning, our grief resurfaces, sometimes sharp and fresh. When we reach important milestones in our lives, such as a big birthday, the wedding of a child, the birth or graduation of a grandchild, grief for the parent who should have been there, to whom this moment would have meant so much, weaves through our happiness. The older we get, Stanford psychologist Laura Carstensen once told me, the greater our capacity for feeling both sorrow and joy together, each one partaking of the other. I think that losing people we love, yet holding them inside us, teaches us this duality.

Every new loss, even a small one, touches on and reawakens our earlier losses. The death of my mother's old cat may send me into convulsive sobs two years after my mom died. Who am I crying for? The cat? Yes, and for Mom and the transience of everything. Several bereaved people told me how the death of their second parent unleashed again, or for the first time, their grief for the parent who died first. Some told me they had not really mourned the first time; they had avoided it, had thrown themselves into caring for their other parent. But finally, their grief caught up with them.

MAKING THE LOSS PART OF US—AND EMERGING WHOLE

Recognizing that our mother or father is *gone*, truly taking it in, requires time. In the first weeks, and maybe for years afterward, we think, "Oh, I have to tell Mom . . ." Maybe we even reach for the telephone. Let's say you wear a ring that used to be on your father's finger but is now on yours. I may use a sugar bowl that used to sit on my mother's kitchen table. But her kitchen is a place I will never go again; she is not there. Her sugar bowl, which I see every day, helps me integrate her loss.

Some of us take longer to do this. The human spirit is endlessly inventive in avoiding pain. I may keep my mother's old bathrobe hanging on a hook in the room where she stayed, as if she will walk in and put it on any minute. Some of us, in the aftermath of the death, distract ourselves so that we do not feel the pain of grief. We immerse ourselves in work or become embroiled in some new crisis. We fight with one another, for example, over who gets Mom's dining table or Dad's tool chest, and this ferocious emotion takes up the space where our grief would be, if we let ourselves feel it. (Such conflict is a whole subject in itself, which I will discuss in the next chapter.)

Grieving takes time but not only time. We have to make internal adjustments to not having parents and to being whole without them. If, years after my mother's death, I still get a knot in my stomach cooking the holiday soup because I could never season it right for her, this could be a sign that I have not fully incorporated her loss. I know she is dead, of course, but I still feel as if she were about to walk in the kitchen and taste the soup. If my father left me his business, but I still behave as if he is looking over my shoulder and second-guessing my decisions, then I haven't taken in that he's gone, that this is my business now. I can make whatever decisions I think are right and enjoy my triumphs or deal with the consequences of my mistakes.

If we have truly mourned, we can move forward with our lives—invest ourselves in other people we care about, put more energy into our work or things we'd like to do: get healthy, take up running, learn piano, go traveling. If we don't move forward, it may be because we feel ambivalent, angry, or guilty. But it may also be possible that we're depressed. If, for example, years after my mother's funeral I can't set a wedding date because she won't be there to stand up with me, that is probably depression rather than mourning. The same is true if you can't start building on the lot Dad helped you pick out because he'll never get to see the house. We may feel sadness that they won't be there to share these things with us, but we can think how they would have enjoyed them.

How do we reach this better place? By taking something of the dead person inside us, Freud said. "To resolve grief," Pauline Boss explained, "you have to say to yourself, 'I can let them go.' But you are more likely to let someone go if you also hold on to parts of what they left behind that you might hold dear: a recipe, a piece of jewelry, a phrase—or do just the opposite in reaction to what you disliked."

Many of my interviewees spoke of the parts of their parents they carried inside. One grieving son talked feelingly of being a faithful family man like his father, who went to work early every morning and put aside his own "druthers" for the sake of his family. A mixed legacy, he said, but one with which he felt content. A daughter in mourning told me, "I learned a lot about family responsibility from Dad. And organization. Whenever I have to pack a car, a box, or anything, I think of my dad, and if anyone comments on it, I say I'm my father's daughter." Others spoke of the various likes and dislikes they shared with their parent or of shared physical traits, like the same eyes or hands. Some emphasized the ways they felt they had learned to be different from their parents. "My mother never needed anyone," one daughter told me. "I don't want to be isolated like that. So I make sure I maintain my friendships."

Reaching this place of feeling our parents are gone—but we are still whole—is harder when we have not made peace with who they were, before they died. If I feel guilty and need to make up to my father because I treated him shabbily or never valued him enough, I may be mourning the saint I have made him into rather than the man he really was. If you feel angry at your mother for her neglect or harsh judgments, you may scarcely feel the pain of her loss. It's also harder to mourn when you still yearn for something you will never have. In her research on parent loss, Debra Umberson said, "The pain of unresolved yearning for a certain kind of parent resounded through my interviews with bereaved adults. Yet it seems that those who manage to create a sense of resolution following the loss are often transformed in positive and adaptive ways."

There are tremendous possibilities for growth with the loss of a parent, but before this is possible we need to mourn fully. And to do this we may have to keep working on our relationship with our mother or father. They may be gone but our relationship with them never ends. We can still learn to understand them better, and to make peace with the kind of relationship we had.

Care manager Hani Shafran often helps bereaved adults with this process. Many of their parents never expressed love or gratitude, either because they were demented at the end or because they did not speak in such terms. "This older generation has trouble expressing emotion," she said, "making amends or taking pride. When the parent can only talk about concrete stuff and not feelings, there is an ocean of unsaid stuff." Shafran suggests that mourners role-play and speak as if they were their mother or father. "It helps the child to give a voice to what a parent would say if they could, and the children come up with it."

Such an exercise may not have been enough for Meg Montgomery, whose feelings for her mother were complicated and intense. She'd felt distant at her mother's deathbed, and also sad that she felt so little. It would take time before she could mourn for her mother and integrate her loss. But she kept working at their relationship, and her reward was being able to grieve for her.

MEG: LEARNING TO MOURN HER MOTHER

Although she cried nearly every day in the weeks after her mother's interment, Meg was not feeling "devastated," she said, the way she had after her father's death. She had missed him, missing talking to him in that special way the two of them had. "I did not miss her," she told me. "I missed the fact that I had a mother. I felt an emptiness." In fact, the place where Meg's mother should have been—internally—was empty.

For whom should she mourn? The "enchanting, brilliant princess" Meg had thought Mom was when she was younger? That mother didn't exist anymore. She'd been replaced by the "narcissistic" and "cruel" woman who'd rejected Meg's marriage and husband. How could she grieve for her?

But Meg's relationship with her mother was a work in progress. Over months and years, she began to let go of her anger at her. For Meg, the process involved therapy and support groups, but most of all, just life, relationships, and the passage of time. "It happened as I watched my child grow," she said, "as I saw my husband's parents grow older."

As Meg became less angry, she was able, internally, to put the two caricatures of her mother together to form the whole person she had been: a woman with her own vulnerabilities and limitations, her own strengths and attractions. When Meg saw her this way, she began to mourn in earnest. Her sadness did not feel bad. In fact, it comforted her. Because now she felt that she'd had a mother. "I felt I lost her when she rejected my marriage," Meg explained. "Now I've reclaimed the good parts of her."

With this transition, Meg found herself remembering the aspects of her mother she enjoyed. Three years after her mother's death, she felt her mother's presence in the things they'd done together—the crossword puzzle, gardening, tying scarves in intricate ways. "I've been missing Mother more as time goes by," she told me. "Every time I'm gardening and I see a tulip bulb come up, she comes up too in my mind. I'm glad she taught me those things."

Meg had grown a great deal in her grieving. Sometimes she felt guilty that she had not done more for her mother in her old age, but she made peace with this, too. Increasingly, her sadness turned into quiet satisfaction. "I've just turned sixty," she related. "I was taking a walk outside on Sunday, trying to figure out how old I was when my mother turned sixty. I realized that was a happy time for her in a not-very-happy life. I felt glad she had some happiness." She paused and said earnestly, "It feels *good* to have good feelings about my mother."

HELPING ONE ANOTHER MOURN AND MOVE FORWARD

Although mourning is an internal process for each of us, there are ways we can help one another through it. Many sisters and brothers told me how they had comforted one another immediately after their parent's death, at the funeral or wake. In the months and years that followed, they also reached out, talked through their feelings, and listened to one another. Unfortunately, there were people who felt the same need but were put off by their sisters' or brothers' way of coping. That is a great shame and probably an unnecessary deprivation. "Family members who cannot share their experience of loss," the family therapist Monica McGoldrick wrote in *Living Beyond Loss: Death in the Family,* "are kept from one of the most important healing resources: each other."

Understanding Our Different Ways of Mourning

I may not cry at the graveside, or at all, while you can't stop weeping. I may not even be aware that today is Mom's birthday, but you can hardly get out of bed. I may feel sad but a little relieved while you feel helpless and abandoned. Maybe I want to tear through their house to get rid of their things right away, but you need more time.

Many things influence how we mourn: our personalities, our gender, the speed at which we process emotion, how long our parents were sick, whether they had dementia, whether we were caregivers or not—and, very significantly, the kind of relationship we had with them. Yet in our grief, we often don't take these things into account; we may not even realize that mourning can take many and various forms. Grief scholar Boerner has seen a vast range of responses to the death of a parent. Mourners move at different paces, she said, and in different ways. One may take in the death better by talking, the other by not talking. The important thing, she said, is that "these can all be normal styles of mourning."

Some people I met were able to share their loss with their sisters and brothers. Others judged one another's mourning and distorted its meaning. If I can feel my pain, but I can't see yours, I might think, "You don't care." It's almost impossible that this is true, but in the upheaval of our own emotion, we can make such rash assumptions. "Everybody's wound up in their own grief," explained Becvar, "and it's really hard to look out and see how what we are doing is affecting the others around us."

Although Emma and Mitch, middle-aged professionals in New York City, were very close as siblings, this lack of understanding divided them at their father's funeral. Just when Emma most needed her "best friend" Mitch, she could not bear to be around him because of what she imagined he was feeling.

EMMA AND MITCH: HER DEVASTATION, HIS QUIET SADNESS

Since the funeral three weeks before, Emma, a fifty-year-old art librarian, was feeling cut adrift from her adored brother. The Manhattan church had been filled to overflowing. There was no one in their community—friends, family, colleagues—who did not know how this sister and brother and their families had suffered during their father's decade-long deterioration from Alzheimer's.

In her eulogy, Emma, a delicate, pixieish woman whose voice quavered, spoke tenderly of the father of her childhood who carried her to bed, rubbed her chest during her frequent bouts of bronchitis, called her his "honey." Mitch, a fifty-four-year-old leadership consultant, spoke next. A tall, barrel-chested man with a craggy face, he began, "My father was hard on me when I was a kid, very tough." Mitch told stories about how his dad, the man-from-Montana married to a fashionable and excitable woman from Milan, had struggled, with sometimes comic results, to keep up with his cosmopolitan and verbally gifted family. He also spoke about what good chums they had become.

Emma was stunned by her brother's criticism and tone. Growing up in their affluent Upper East Side neighborhood, the children of a legal printer who worked all hours to support them, neither of them, she felt, had ever given him credit for what a wonderful man he was. "We were spoiled little shits," she told me, weeping. "It was always about us or

Mom. He never got the accolades." At the funeral, she felt, "Daddy, this is *your* day." Then her brother had made jokes about him and said things that were "unkind and ugly and dishonored my father." After the service, she forced herself to hug her brother, but she didn't want to speak to him ever again.

A week later, still distraught, she told Mitch her feelings. When he tried to explain, she yelled through her tears, "You don't give a flying fuck about Daddy!" "Oh, Emma, how can you say that?" Mitch responded. "I grieved for Daddy ten years ago."

In their mourning, this sister and brother differed in just about every way possible. They illustrate the gamut of variations, starting with their personalities. Emma was intense, verbal, and volatile. Mitch was steady and even-tempered. He relied on patience and a dry sense of humor to get him through hard times. "I'm like my father in this," he told me. "I don't enjoy public mourning. But my grieving is no less." At the funeral, he reflected, "I guess I was going for a cheap laugh, to relieve the solemnity."

Emma and Mitch were also on opposite sides of the gender divide, something Emma did not take into account. In our culture, women usually cry and show their feelings more, said therapist McGoldrick, who has studied these gender differences. Women find comfort in observing mourning rituals, being with others, talking about their feelings. They find that retelling the experience of the death and remembering the person gives them relief. In their initial grief, they tend to focus more on their relationships, less on practical things.

Men, on the other hand, she noted, feel powerless at a death. Afraid of losing control of their feelings, they look for ways to feel in control. They focus on solving problems, doing their work, keeping busy. They grieve in private and are often uncomfortable with others' grieving. Sometimes they avoid mourning altogether, drink too much, or act out in other ways.

These are generalizations, of course. I have met sisters who differ along these gender lines and brothers who have been open and expressive mourners. As gender roles evolve with time, these differences may diminish. Still, it's important for us to understand that gender does influence how we mourn; sisters should not judge their brothers as uncaring because they show less emotion.

If our mother or father suffered a long decline or had dementia, we may begin grieving at different times. When Mitch told Emma he had grieved ten years before, he was being literal. He had started to mourn when his father was diagnosed with Alzheimer's. "In a sense," Mitch said sadly, "my father had been leaving for quite a while; bits and parts and aspects of him left over time."

Emma, on the other hand, saw him as present until the very end. "The sicker he got," she told me, "the more I loved him. Even after he lost the ability to speak, there were moments when I would walk into his room and his face would just light up when he saw me with this beatific look."

Just as all siblings, Emma and Mitch had different relationships with their father and were at different places in learning to relate to him as a person. The point Mitch had wanted to make in his eulogy, he explained, is that he had long ago forgiven his father's strictness with him when he was a child. As a young man, his father had treated him differently and they'd bonded.

Emma had spent her adolescence and young adulthood embarrassed by her father's social awkwardness and verbal limitations, and she'd felt ill at ease when talking with him. She was only beginning to recognize his sterling qualities when he became ill. Stricken with remorse and compassion, she needed to make it up to him through devotion and a kind of hero worship.

Like all family dynamics, our differences in mourning are

complex. If I have been the caregiver, for example, I may miss this role and the structure it gave to my life, and even experience depression. If I was not around much, I may not have been ready for Mom to die. Or, like Mitch, I may have prepared for it years in advance, maybe even wished for it as a release from suffering. "Often it's the sibling who was not around who has delayed and complicated grief," social worker Cibuzar said. Taking account of our varied experiences can help us feel more compassion for one another.

Sharing Stories: Putting Our Loss in Perspective

When I last spoke to Emma and Mitch, they were spending time together again, but it was still hard for Emma to talk about her father with him. I hoped that in time she would. I had seen how talking together, comparing notes, filling in blanks in the family history, had helped other grieving siblings. Over time, they helped each other round out their picture of their parents to see their family in greater dimensionality. If their family had been troubled, this was especially helpful. "Sharing memories and stories of the dead," McGoldrick observed, "can help family members develop more benign, less traumatic perspectives on the role of those in their lives. . . . If events cannot be mentioned or if the family 'party line' cannot be expanded upon, it is almost impossible for family members to make sense of their history."

I was moved by the way the Herrera family helped one another transcend their childhood abuse. If you recall, Maria had brought her mother to live with her and had worked hard not to baby her. One brother, Carlos, helped her; another, Ricardo, lived far away. Maria's older sister, Luisa, and her mother were still at odds when the old woman died. Yet despite grieving in different ways, they all comforted one another. They also helped one another gain perspective on their mother. This was especially dramatic for Maria and Luisa, who were at opposite poles in their feelings about their mother.

MARIA AND LUISA: HELPING EACH OTHER MOURN THEIR MOTHER—AND UNDERSTAND HER

Maria had forgiven her mother for staying so long with their abusive stepfather. Yet the memories lingered. "I used to get physically sick before he came home," Maria recalled. "I never knew what he would find to punish us for." Maria just took the beatings, she said, but Luisa was "a fighter. She'd get in his face and scratch him."

Luisa had forgiven nothing. She had grown from rebellious teenager to chain-smoking cosmetics-store tycoon, driving a Mercedes, issuing orders to the extended family, and insulting her mother at family parties. "I hate her," she often told Maria, who believed her sister was speaking out of pain, not hatred. While their mother was dying, neither Ma nor Luisa asked forgiveness of each other. Luisa rushed in and out of the hospital, bringing people food, looking distressed. She never cried, not then or after her mother's death. "I know she's in pain," Maria said, "and I want to hug her, but hugging my sister is like hugging a rock. She believes to cope is to be hard."

For all that, Maria found her sister to be gentle with her after their mother died. As Maria wept, seeing the chair her mother sat in, the coffee mug she drank from every day, Luisa would call and speak carefully to her, not criticizing their mother the way she had done before. This respect for each other's feelings allowed them to talk and help each other make sense of their loss. Maria missed her mother, her "best friend." Luisa was convinced her mother hadn't loved her. She lived with guilt: She thought Ma died thinking Luisa hated her. Irrationally, Luisa even feared retribution from beyond.

When a beloved granddaughter nearly died from a high fever, Luisa told Maria she thought their mother was trying to take the baby away to punish her.

"How can you think Mommy would do that?" Maria asked

her. "Luisa, listen, which of your children do you love the best?"

"I love them all," Luisa replied.

"Think about it," Maria begged her. "How can you say Mommy didn't love you? She loved us all."

After a long silence, Luisa said simply, "Okay." Afterward, she never again said her mother didn't love her.

This tempering of perspective worked two ways. Although Maria had a more balanced view of her mother, a woman who'd made mistakes, not a saint, she still saw her only through her own eyes. As the months went by, Luisa brought up things Maria had forgotten or had never known. Once, Luisa told Maria about her long stay in Mexico with their grandmother. Her little cousins blamed her for breaking a vase, she recounted, and her grandmother was always hostile to her afterward. Luisa was four years old at the time, and that year was a lifetime to her.

"How could Mommy let you go away for a year?" Maria exclaimed.

"That's the mother I knew," Luisa replied bitterly. "You didn't know her."

"I really felt for my sister," Maria told me. "I was so little then, I didn't remember much." Looking back, she realized that her mother had just married her stepfather when she sent Luisa away. Was that why? Maria didn't know. What she did recall clearly was the day Luisa came home—an angry little girl of five—and demanded a lick of three-year-old Maria's ice-cream cone.

"No, it's mine!" Maria refused.

"Give me a lick," Luisa demanded, "or I'll punch you in the nose."

"I said no," Maria recalled with a peal of laughter, "and she punched me right in the nose."

Maria then became thoughtful. "We all thought my sister was lucky to get away."

Maria and Luisa were a perfect example of what I understood family therapist Evan Imber-Black to mean when she told me, "Holding differences is one of the hardest things for siblings. I tell adult siblings who are in therapy with me, 'It's okay that we're in different places. It's okay that we see things differently, and we don't have to batter each other over the head to see it the same way.' How many moments are there where somebody feels exactly the same as we do? Not too many. But to have someone listen to our story and then we listen to theirs: That's a connection."

ADAPTING OUR FAMILY AND TRADITIONS
TO STAY CONNECTED

After our parents die, what holds us together? If we're lucky, affection and a wish to be connected. Even those of us with mixed feelings about one another usually feel a bond. It's made of family history, memories good and bad, and a yearning for continuity in the face of death. During this time of grief, I have seen many people feel a compelling pull toward their siblings. In the absence of their parents, they have found new ways to be together.

During our parents' long decline, many of us will have begun reorganizing ourselves to take on some of their roles. I may keep everyone in touch, plan or host get-togethers, send everyone photos. Someone else, maybe my brother, will offer advice of the kind Dad used to give, about how to start a fire, fix the car, flatten a bent key. Maybe my sister will be the repository of the family recipes or lore.

Our traditions, the way we did things that made us different from other families, can now provide an important source of connection to one another, to our parents and our past. These may be small, everyday traditions, like how we set the table with the napkins folded at angles, how we always put tons of sugar in the tea. Maybe we told the same jokes over and over, chiming in on the punch lines. If we all used to call Mom or Dad on Sunday, we may now call one another.

Our holiday rituals are probably even more important. But in order to continue them, we have to adjust them. Various people told me how they adapted their customs to fit their new generation. The ones who lived near one another may have had an easier time, but they still had to make changes. With so many in-laws and grandkids, we may not find it practical to gather at the same table the way we did when our parents were alive or when they were healthy. Yet we can still connect at holidays. The Herreras, for example, no longer all gather at Luisa's for Christmas dinner. Too many people, too hard. But on Christmas morning, Carlos first drops by Luisa's house, then has the holiday meal with Maria's family. And Luisa's kids call Aunt Maria every year to ask again how Grandma made the tamales.

The Kristal sisters, who still kid the youngest, folksinger Abbie, for running away from their family chaos, get together on most holidays. Instead of their dad giving out the presents, though, his two grandsons perform this ceremony with an attempt to imitate his brio and humor. At Thanksgiving, the oldest sister, Ginny, carves the turkey. "After Dad got sick," she said, "that became my role, and he taught me well. I can carve a mean turkey."

If we live far apart, we may just call one another to say, "Merry Christmas." Maybe on Thanksgiving, I call my brother at halftime to talk about the game. My sister may send us all photos. These small things make siblings feel they are part of one another's lives. Although they may get together infrequently, they think of one another as family, people who will be there for them in time of need.

HOW TO GET THROUGH GRIEF, SEPARATELY AND TOGETHER

There is no easy way to grieve, but there are things we can do to help us move forward. Here are a few:

Create everyday rituals to help you take in the loss.

Grief can sometimes take over your life, penetrating every corner of it. Or you can shunt it aside while immersed in a busy life. Make time for it, time set aside for reflection or crying or whatever form your mourning takes. Sitting in a special place with photos of your parents, writing your feelings in a journal, visiting their graves or a place that resonates with their memories: All these can help you feel your grief without being consumed by it.

Don't ignore special days.

On important days such as birthdays, anniversaries, or Father's Day, do something: light a candle, have a meal with your mom's favorite food, raise a glass to them, plant a bulb in your garden. When possible, reach out to your sisters and brothers on these days. Even if they're not aware of what day it is, it can still feel good to connect.

Make something that belonged to your parents your own.

Using something of theirs can remind you of them even as it helps you take in the reality that they're gone. Many people I spoke with found this comforting, especially on important occasions. One fiftysomething bride told me she made her wedding dress using swatches of her father's favorite shirt and her mother's laciest blouse. "I felt Mom and Dad were there with me," she said.

Accommodate your sister's or brother's coping style.

Expect that you will not feel the same. And don't expect them to react in ways that are counter to their nature. But reach out. If your brother can't handle your sobbing, don't call him when you need to weep. Call him the next day. He may be able to hear you say, "Yesterday was a hard day for me. I was thinking how Daddy would have been ninety." Your brother may respond with silence or a simple but heartfelt "Yeah, I was thinking that, too." If you are together, a hug can speak volumes.

Adapt old traditions or create new ones.

The first holiday may feel very sad without your parents. But don't completely turn away from your celebrations. With your siblings, if possible, or with your own family or friends, mark the occasion. Celebrate the time of year as you usually do, but set aside some small part of it to honor your parents, with a toast, for example, or sharing photos and memories.

Reflect on whether you are moving forward.

There are many normal ways to grieve, but sometimes we confuse depression with grief. Missing our parents and feeling sad is normal. Feeling stuck, hopeless, and unable to enjoy life may signal depression. Have you given up things you love? Have you stopped working to succeed because you can't tell your dad about your achievements? Have you let some important goal go? If so, be aware of this as something that is not a necessary part of mourning. Try to break through your impasse. If you can't, you may want to get some help.

Think actively about your parents' legacies, positive and negative.

There are many ways to do this. Think about the things they shared with you or taught you to love—cooking, literature, sports, giving parties. These things are part of you, but you may want to remind yourself that these things continue to connect you to your parent. Some people were helped by taking up causes they felt would honor their parents. Others, feeling liberated from their mother's or father's disapproval, took off in new directions where they'd never dared to go before.

I met people who dedicated themselves to not making the mistakes their parents made. "I wanted to do something for my mother," one woman told me. "So I thought, 'I will try not to have the traits she had that I knew she didn't want to have, like being defensive and nasty to people. I could be like that, too, dictatorial and outraged at the grocery store. Now I'm seldom like that."

During these meditations and conversations, look for a way

to give up any anger you may still feel toward them. "Maybe they were doing the best they could," Becvar suggested, "and maybe that wasn't so wonderful. But if we can understand where the older generation is coming from, maybe we can forgive them that they couldn't be what we wanted them to be."

CHAPTER TEN

INHERITANCE: WHAT OUR PARENTS HAVE LEFT US, WHAT WE CARRY AWAY

ADRIANNE'S FATHER WAS DEAD, but his power to hurt her remained very much alive. Earlier her mother had told the fifty-eight-year-old teacher that their will split everything equally among the three kids. But after Adrianne's mom died, her father made a new will, leaving her only 10 percent. Adrianne, a passionate gay activist living in San Francisco, was sure she knew his motive: He did not recognize her twenty-five-year relationship with her partner, Lois. Adrianne, a graying, full-figured woman who expressed herself with emphatic gestures, spoke to me with Lois at her side on the sofa. The two women resembled each other in that way that long-married people do, but Lois was more soft-spoken and serene.

"I was hurt, shocked, appalled," Adrianne continued, "hit by a wave of homophobia. But this was not out of character for my father. Money speaks, and the money stood for so much. Ten percent, forty-five, forty-five: What a statement about who we, a same-sex couple, are—and who we are not."

Our parents' will is, in some sense, their last word to us, weighted with powerful symbolic messages of love, approval, and trust. It also conveys very tangible dollars and property, which we probably want or need. We've been expecting to get something, maybe even relying on it, with or without reason. It's possible to see our inheritance as a tangible continuation of our parents' caring. Ideally, each of us feels "fairly" treated. Most of the people I interviewed did not have a problem with what their parents left them or how they divided it. But when an inheritance does leave us feeling cheated or punished, it can destroy sibling relationships, drawing on the same unresolved hurts and rivalries that have beset us in the twilight. We may feel, correctly or not, that our parents have wronged us and our siblings are to blame.

Anything unexpected or unwelcome about our inheritance can reveal new information about who our parents were, how they felt about us, our siblings, and the world. At the least, we need to understand why our parents did what they did. They may have had reasons that can be opaque to us, and completely out of line with the principles that we think should guide inheritance. The professionals (attorneys, accountants, therapists) who have seen every permutation of financial planning, good and bad, witness a range of motivations, often multilayered. Mining their experience and looking at our parents from a new vantage point may help us make sense of why our parents acted as they did. Difficult as this sometimes is, it offers us an opportunity to see the world more through our parents' eyes, to better understand who they were and to reconcile ourselves to what they left us.

If our parents' legacy is patently unfair or problematic, it offers us an opportunity to transcend their behavior as parents and to rework our relationships with our siblings. This is not, of course, an opportunity anybody goes looking for. An unjust inheritance is one of the hardest things to surmount. If we are the ones who feel cheated, we'll probably get angry with our siblings for our parents' actions, just as we did as little kids. But we have choices now. If I am a "winner" in the inheritance sweepstakes, I can, if I choose, share my portion. If I'm a "loser," I can choose my connection with my brother over a bitter fight that leaves me with no family at all. We all have choices.

While fights over family money fuel more lawsuits than tussles over teapots, most of us are likelier to argue over the stuff from our parents' house: a storybook or a chair, a baseball cap or a tablecloth. If we can talk about what these things mean to us and devise a system for dividing them, we can end up recovering memories and, probably, having some of the things we treasure.

INTERPRETING THE "WHY": THE REAL AND SYMBOLIC MESSAGES OF OUR PARENTS' LEGACIES

Shortly before his death, Adrianne's father told her the terms of his will. She didn't like what he said and didn't believe the explanation he gave, but at least he told her himself. Some parents don't tell us anything, so we're left wondering why. If we're disappointed, we may attribute symbolic meanings that our parents never intended, that probably don't reflect their feelings about us.

Why don't they tell us? Many reasons, some good, most not so good. Parents of a certain age, those who lived through the Depression, often feel differently about money than their boomer children; certainly more private. "The World War II generation," St. Louis attorney Scott H. Malin told me, "doesn't want to tell their kids what they have or how they'll leave it. They think it's none of their business, and whatever they get, they should be thankful for."

Some recent surveys found that elders are more willing to discuss their wills than their kids think they are, but most of the financial professionals I queried say their clients find inheritance talk uncomfortable. According to a survey by the Allianz life insurance firm, nearly two thirds of parents have not talked to all their children about how they are leaving their money or why. Talking about this stuff, said financial planner Elizabeth Arnold, author of *Creating the Good Will,* "requires parents to take an honest look at their family dynamics. Money can be a symbol of everything, and these conversations can be very uncomfortable."

But a lack of explanation can be devastating. Lawyers have told me of grieving children calling them up to ask why their parents left them less than their sisters or brothers. Often, lawyers are not permitted to share the reasons, but in many instances the causes are not what the heirs think. "If kids don't get the same as their siblings and don't know why," Malin told me, "they usually imagine the worst. That's something they'll have to live with for the rest of their lives."

I talked to one bereaved son who imagined all kinds of painful things when his mother left him less than his sister. He obsessed about it. Was it because his sister had been her caregiver? Was it because he hadn't brought his kids to visit their grandma often enough or that his wife was cool to her? Was it because she loved him less? "I was surprised at how much this ate at me," he said. "The idea that maybe my mom died mad at me kept me up nights." Finally, his aunt told him that his mother had been worried about his sister and thought he didn't need the money. She said his mom was proud of him and how successful he'd been.

Is "Equal" What's "Fair"?

It's not surprising that this son expected his mom to divide her money in half. It's an automatic assumption in our culture. Generally, when we think "fair," we think "equal," just like when we were kids and we eyed our piece of cake suspiciously to see whether it was a millimeter smaller than our sister's. In fact, research shows that the great majority of parents do leave their children equal portions. So if our parents have split their estate right down the middle, that should be okay with everyone, right? Well, not so fast.

Even if our parents have been scrupulously even in dividing their estates, some of us will not be happy. If I've been keeping score since childhood, I may feel shortchanged once again: "They sent him to Harvard! I went to State U," I may protest. You may object, "She had a twenty-thousand-dollar wedding, but I eloped and saved them a bundle." Most parents, inheritance expert Arnold told me, don't keep score that way. Their attitude, she said, is " 'Sorry, that was done; it's over. You had the same options. You made different choices.' "

Wait! What if my parents lent my brother large amounts of money in adulthood, which he never repaid? Or they helped my sister buy a house? Shouldn't they deduct this money from their inheritance? Some parents do, but most are very reluctant, research shows. Parents feel that when they die they want to wipe the slates clean, to forgive all debts. This may not seem "fair" to us. It may reflect unhealthy family dynamics. But it is what most parents feel they need to do.

When the Will Is Not Equal

Parents do not see their will primarily as a symbolic message. It distributes real property that can make a far greater difference in one child's life than another. Gerontologist Elaine Brody told me that how to divide their estate was a frequent and anguished subject of conversation among the widows at her upscale California condominium. "They worry about how to leave their money," she told me, "to the poor versus the affluent child, the married versus the divorced daughter."

Worried parents want to make sure that all of us will be "okay" after they're gone, and this need often trumps their wish to be evenhanded. One seventy-four-year-old mother in Texas told me how she'd come to her decision. Since a truck-driving accident, her forty-two-year-old son, a commercial trucker, had been on disability and living with her. His doctors said he couldn't live alone. "I want to give my son the means to make choices and have independence and be his own person," she told me, "so I decided to leave him the lion's share, sixty percent. But I'm not going to lie to you. It was a very difficult decision, and I struggled close to a year to make it."

If our parents handle this well, they explain their reasons to us, as this mother did to her other children. We may still feel it's not fair. The truck driver was "disabled," but I may feel my perpetually unemployed sister has been "enabled," and I may be right. "One of the most bitter results of considering need," Minnesota therapist and planner Susan Zimmerman told me, "can be providing larger sums to children who have made poor life choices, effectively rewarding them for their 'screw-ups' while punishing their siblings for hard work by shorting them on inheritance amounts." This happens, and, good or bad, it's our parents' decision.

On the flip side, some parents, especially if they're wealthy, believe in leaving more to the kids who've performed well or behaved in accordance with their expectations or values. "As parents get older," financial planner Michael Leonetti explained, "some look at their kids more as people, not just as their children. They ask, 'How is this person leading his life? Does he share my values? Is he carrying on my legacy?'"

Occasionally, I have found, parents leave more to the child who cared for them. Usually, though, they don't, even though I may feel I deserve more because I've been the caregiver and my sister has done nothing. Should we be rewarded financially for caring for our parents? This is a hotly debated issue. Among parents, the most common way of thinking is that caring for them should be a labor of love. California elder law attorney Zoran Basich, a founder of the nonprofit Grey Law group, put himself squarely in this camp. "Morally, I think it's wrong. If I take care of Mom, that's because I want to, not because of the money."

Sometimes parents leave more to one child than another because they want to keep the money in the "family." But who counts as "family?" When the parents are leaving money to the children of their current marriage as well as their kids by previous spouses, this can become a very thorny question. Step-kids? The bias in our culture is still in favor of blood relatives although affection can sometimes overrule this principle. "Step ties are very complicated," McMaster University sociologist Carolyn Rosenthal told me. "Inheritance depends on the length of the ties and the way the family has knit together."

The expectation that one's inheritance should go to blood relations is powerful. It is embedded in our legal system and our thinking, maybe even in our DNA. If we reflect on our own lives, how many of us without children (who invariably inherit) would leave our estates to our best friends, the people we may love most? Most people I know would probably name their siblings or nieces and nephews, even if they were not very close. Money-to-blood is a powerful assumption and one that often goes unquestioned. We, however, may feel that blood is no longer an adequate definition of family in this day of multiple marriages and nontraditional unions.

Adrianne felt so devastated by her father's will because she saw it as a repudiation of Lois as her family. "This never would have been done to a heterosexual couple with children," she said emphatically. I sympathized with her. Still, I thought she was confusing two issues, whether a partner is "family" and whether any couple, gay or straight, has children. The issue of "issue" is the essence of legacy for many people. What they have worked for in their lives, what they leave behind, is their immortality. Most people want to leave it in a way that goes to their posterity, by blood or adoption, or to people or causes in which they feel invested. I've talked to parents who left one married child less than another because they didn't want the former's husband or wife, whom they disliked for whatever reason, to end up with their money.

Finally, yes, our parents are driven by emotions, some unconscious, when they make their wills. For any number of reasons, perhaps because of a rough patch in their personal or financial circumstances, they may feel that one of us got less from them, emotionally or materially. My mother may want to leave more to my brother. He's the family underachiever and she feels partly responsible so she wants to make amends.

Our parents may not be self-aware enough to understand all the reasons that inform their decisions. They may use any of these rationales—need, performance, blood—to explain a less conscious agenda. They may not admit, even to themselves, that they feel guilty toward you, hurt by my lack of attention, or vengeful toward our brother. They may act out of blatant favoritism, gratitude, desire to punish and belittle, dislike for our partner, racism, sexism, or homophobia. If that is the case, our challenge is to make peace with who our parent was. Maybe my father was a bastard. Maybe your mother was weak. No question each was complicated and imperfect. The question for us now is how to come to terms with our feelings about our inheritance and about our parents.

Coming to Terms with What Our Parents Left Us—and Who They Were

Before we can understand our parents' motives, we need to take a hard look at our own assumptions. We may be operating out of some irrational internal calculus for determining what's "fair" and what we are "owed." The same hook of childhood emotions that has colored our perceptions throughout the twilight may be warping our ability to think rationally about this explosive issue. Maybe I think I should get more because Dad hated me, while you think you should get more because he loved you best. Our sister thinks she's "owed" most because she did the most for Mom. Maybe she's so convinced she's "owed" that she gets Mom, in her dementia, to sign a will leaving everything to her or uses her power of attorney to clear out Mom's bank accounts. Clearly illegal, but probably arising out of the same kind of emotional calculus, just more out of control. If that's what she's done, then litigation may be the right course for you. Maybe.

If I'm one of these aggrieved siblings, however, it makes no sense for me to sue you because Mom and Dad weren't "fair" to me according to me. Community Health Sciences professor Bonnie Lashewicz, of the University of Calgary, studied lawsuits in Canada in which people sued a sibling who inherited their parent's house. It's common in Canada, she explained, for frail, aging parents to enter into a "family agreement," usually verbal, in which they say they will leave their house to a child who agrees to move in and care for them. "It might be the youngest," Lashewicz said, "or the one unmarried and/or childless, or perhaps the one who is unemployed and needs the assets."

The people who sued offered a variety of legal arguments for challenging these wills, but the crux of their arguments, Lashewicz found, was that the inheritance wasn't fair. The ones who sued felt they had done just as much for their mom as their sister, or that the caregiving sister was really dominating Mom and didn't give her great care—beliefs that may have been true and just as possibly were distortions of reality. These feelings, Lashewicz found, had often been festering for years. Courts, however, don't judge what's "fair." They focus on what the will says and whether the parents were of sound mind when they made it. In the great majority of the cases Lashewicz studied, the court affirmed the parents' will. Effectively, they ratified the parents' decision and their right to make it.

In cases like these, we need to consider the possibility that Mom knew very well that the caregiver would not be much help, that this arrangement was a convenient fiction for her because she was worried about her son, who didn't seem to be managing life well, whatever the causes. Leaving him her house may have been her way of trying to ensure that he'd have a home after she died.

Ultimately, we come back to whether we can make peace with our parents. This was Adrianne's challenge, and she rose to it. Her feelings of hurt were not irrational, but they were ferocious. She could have let herself be consumed by anger; she could have dismissed her father as a homophobe and bastard, pure and simple. But she did not go that route. She tried to understand him as a man.

Although he gave her a reason for her disproportionate inheritance, she still struggled to understand why. He told her that her siblings had more family responsibilities and needed the money more. He told her sister that he didn't want the money to go to Adrianne's partner, or after Lois's death, to the gay causes she supported. He told her brother something else.

"Who knows what he believed?" Adrianne said. "Maybe it had something to do with wanting his money going to his offspring. Maybe, on some level, he didn't even know. So I'm left needing to make my own story."

The story she crafted took account of her father as a hardworking, responsible man who cared for and about his children. On the negative side, he was emotionally removed and limited in understanding. An Armenian immigrant, he was, she said, prejudiced in ways large and small. "I know he was proud of my accomplishments," she said, "and in his own messed-up way, he loved me, but he screwed up as a father. What he did was wrong."

In writing her own story, Adrianne also created a good ending for it. After her father died, she and Lois used her small inheritance to fund a foundation to assist needy gay and transgender kids, many of whom had been kicked out of their homes and were living in shelters. The foundation, which Adrianne named after her loving and accepting mother, helps the kids with small contributions toward job training or education.

"I feel it redeems the situation for us," Lois put in, "and to some extent, redeems her father."

Hurtful as this passage was, Adrianne felt she had grown from it. "I could be back there where I was," she reflected, "bitter and disgruntled and pissy. But I choose not to do that. I feel great about helping these kids. It really is redeeming, and it takes the sting away."

All of us have the same kinds of choices. We can choose to be bitter and angry. We can challenge the will in court even if it reflects our parents' wishes. Or we can accept our parents as imperfect, make our peace with who they were, and move forward in our lives.

BEING PRACTICAL, REMAINING COMPASSIONATE

It's easy for disagreements to break out during the execution of a will. One of you, maybe several of you, will be stubborn, for example, about selling the house for what it's "worth" (a common dilemma, real estate brokers tell me). Most of us want to believe our parents' house is worth more than it really is. Don't rely on an emotional valuation. Bring in appraisers who have no vested interest. But also be aware of the potential symbolism of the house or other property to your sister or brother. If, for example, his share represents Mom's appreciation for his having taken care of her, then tell him how much Mom appreciated it (if she did) and how much you appreciated it. People have told me that being sympathetic about their siblings' emotions—while remaining rational about the dollars—has helped oil the wheels.

HOT POTATO, HARD DECISIONS: WHEN SIBLINGS WRESTLE WITH AN UNJUST WILL

It's rare that an unjust or punitive will by parents does not damage sibling relationships. Although Adrianne did not blame her sister and brother for what their father had done, she did hold them responsible for how they reacted. Her brother endorsed the will; her sister offered to share some of the money, but only during Adrianne's lifetime; it could not pass to Lois but would revert to Adrianne's nieces. Those relationships were never the same.

For others, knowing their parents' reasons for dividing their resources a certain way can offer siblings a chance to honor their original intentions. "If the siblings have heard their parents' explanation," said mediator Brigitte Bell, "they can deal with new circumstances, for example, if the youngest was left more because he was least established but now he's well employed and the oldest has lost his job." In a case like this that Bell recalled, three siblings redivided their parents' estate so that each got a third rather than the oldest getting a lesser amount.

If one of us gets a bigger inheritance than the other, and either or both of us feel the will is "unfair," we have a dilemma and an opportunity. What do we do? Maybe nothing. Or maybe we can rework our relationships with one another in a positive way. "When a will has been a bit of a hand grenade thrown into the sibling relationship," therapist Evan Imber-Black told me, "it takes some work among them to look, hopefully, collectively, at what happened and deal with their relationships in the present. Or the will can freeze what's going to happen forever among those siblings."

Ideally, we should talk to one another about the inheritance, why it happened, whether it is just, and whether anything should be done to change it. Being willing to try depends on other questions: How much do we value our relationship? What would we like it to be in the future? Most of all, what kind of people do we want to be?

"Winners": Deciding the "Right" Thing to Do

You may think that if I get a bigger share, I win. Actually, I may be quite uncomfortable having received more than you. Some people beg their parents not to leave them more because they don't want to be in this position. If I do get more, I am likely to have very complicated emotions. I may feel sad, guilty, entitled, deserving, or vengeful; probably several things at once. I may really squirm if you look to me to right this alleged wrong.

Suppose our parents left their estate in a way that we ourselves recognize as unjust, prejudiced, or punitive. Do we have an obligation to rectify it? No, but we can, if we choose, refuse to participate in our parents' game and reach out to the sister or brother they've injured. Will we reap gratitude and an amazing sibling bond? Not necessarily.

"You have to be willing to go down a one-way street," family therapist Monica McGoldrick said, "whether the other person can reach back or not. I think that's what differentiation is all about; coming to realize that the only choices we have in life are how we are going to relate, not how other people are going to relate. To me, a lot of the most existential work of therapy is helping people be the kind of person they want to be, not based on how the other person treats them."

Paul, a sixty-seven-year-old private school headmaster in Virginia, thought this way. He didn't want to be the kind of person who would accept money given to him in order to spite his sister.

PAUL: CORRECTING AN INJUSTICE

When Paul's stepmother died, she left him three quarters of her estate, most of which was money that had been his father's, and the rest to his younger sister, Lucy. To Paul, this felt wrong though he could have justified it. He could have repeated to himself his stepmother's mantra: "Your sister did nothing for your father the last half of his life, and she did less than nothing for me." Paul could have told himself he deserved the money for all his late-life attentions to this woman who had cared for his father. Legally, the money was his.

Paul consulted a lawyer, who could help him figure out how to share it. Tweedy, bald-pated, with a silver goatee, Paul was a man comfortable in his own skin. Lounging in an easy chair in his book-crammed study, he told me that he had long ago forgiven his late parents for the traumas they inflicted on him in childhood. These were horrible alcohol-fueled fights, divorce, and stressful remarriages. His sister got the worst of it. "When my mother remarried," he explained, "I had left for boarding school, leaving her in the lurch. . . . Well, she felt that, while I was thrilled with my new independence."

Lucy had never gotten over the damage. "I tried to tell her," he said, "that when our parents were younger, they were confused like us and that she should stop being angry. But that just made her angrier." When Paul told Lucy he would share the money with her, she accepted his decision as "fair."

In equalizing his inheritance, Paul did what he felt was right for two reasons. He wanted to think of himself as a fair and honorable person. Also, it mattered to him that he and Lucy, and their respective children, continue to be family to one another. He empathized with her lifelong unhappiness even though he believed she could have done more to help herself.

For his magnanimous decision, what did he get back from her? Not a lot. "She did not go all to pieces with gratitude," Paul noted dryly. "But, truthfully, I was not hard-up and could afford to do it. There was an injustice I had the power to correct, and I would have felt guilty if I had not. So, doing it gave me a certain amount of self-gratification, if you will."

Undoubtedly, his decision was less complicated than it might have been if his inheritance had come directly from his father. Still, he had gone down McGoldrick's "one-way street" and felt good about where he had come out.

SHOULD THE EXECUTOR GET SOMETHING EXTRA FOR DOING ALL THAT WORK?

If you've ever cleaned out a house and gotten it ready for sale, you know what a grueling, time-intensive job it is.

Add in the challenge of dealing with a parent's paperwork and possibly disorganized financial records, and you're talking about still more time. Unfortunately, many parents do not think about this when they write their wills, and the sibling who ends up with these chores rarely gets financial compensation. If it's not in writing, it's unlikely the executor will get paid. But if siblings agree that this sister or brother should get something, especially for giving up paid work to do it, one rule of thumb, says Colorado elder-care attorney Mark D. Masters, is to pay whatever you'd pay per hour to a house cleaner, a painter, an accountant, etc. It may not replace the lost income but it's something. And if the executor does a good job, and is sensitive to each person's feelings, his or her siblings may want to express their gratitude.

In one family, for instance, when one sibling handled all such executor duties with no compensation built in to the will, her siblings mutually agreed to do a "giveback" of money after the second parent died and the family house was sold. In this case each sibling contributed what he or she was capable of contributing, and also based their individual amounts on how much they'd been able to help their sister, but in another family siblings may prefer to contribute equally. There is no hard-and-fast rule on this, but it could be a goodwill gesture worth considering.

"Losers": Making Peace with the "Wrong" Decision

If our parents have left us less or left us nothing, we have an even greater opportunity for growth. Let's face it: It's harder not to get the money, especially if the inheritance comes with hurtful messages. If I am disinherited because of my parents' blatant prejudice, this may be terribly unjust, but should I expect my sister to fix it? Probably not. "Most people take the money and run," reported McGoldrick, who's worked with siblings on both sides of the inheritance question.

If I feel unfairly treated by my parents, my challenge is to get past what they've done and to try to have the best relationship I can with my siblings. I can ask my brother whether he thinks the will is fair. I can ask him to share the inheritance with me. But it's not reasonable to expect that he will. Nor is it fair to blame him for what our parents did.

Rachel, a fifty-one-year-old real estate broker in Vancouver, British Columbia, had exactly this challenge. She knew that her parents had disinherited her for marrying out of her faith. She forgave them, but she had a much harder time forgiving her sister for not sharing their estate with her.

RACHEL AND REBECCA:
STRIVING TO OVERCOME A LEGACY OF HURT

"You know, you're cut out of the will," Rachel's seventy-nine-year-old mother casually remarked.

This was one of the first things she'd said to her daughter after almost twenty-five years of silence. Rachel, a petite woman with a crown of brown curls and an animated manner, was so happy to see her mother again that she didn't care about the will. Then.

Growing up in their orthodox Jewish home in Brooklyn, Rachel was close to her parents, especially her mother. "My role was to make Mom happy," she told me. "Mom had a hard life, but she was a firebrand, and I admired her." Rebecca, four years younger, disliked their strict, old-fashioned parents, and looked to her big sister for love and guidance about real life.

When Rachel moved to the Pacific Northwest for graduate school, something completely unlooked-for happened: She fell in love with a non-Jew. They moved in together. When her parents found out, she and her boyfriend got married. From that time on, for more than two decades, her parents treated her as if she were dead, rejected her pleas to see them, returned her letters, refused even to acknowledge her children. Rachel was devastated.

At the time of Rachel's marriage, Rebecca was eighteen and still living at home. She told her sister she felt abandoned. Through all the years, she, and eventually her husband and children, stayed close to Rachel, but she complained repeatedly to her sister: "It's not fair. I have to deal with them."

When their eighty-three-year-old father had a stroke, Rebecca's sense of burden exploded. "Mom," she demanded, "I can't handle this alone. You have to let her come." So Rachel reentered the family fold. She flew in from Vancouver for every crisis. She brought her children to meet her father before he died. Over the next three years, she spent long hours in person and on the phone comforting her grieving mother. Mom appeared grateful and even gave her small, sentimental presents: her father's watch, his gold fountain pen. Never an easy woman, she also gave her plenty of her characteristic criticism. Then she, too, died.

While the sisters were sitting shiva at their parents' home, Rebecca and her husband followed Rachel into a bedroom and asked her to sign a document agreeing not to contest the will. Grieving, upset, outraged, Rachel refused. "I thought it was wrong," she said.

After the funeral, tense emails passed between the sisters. Rachel never intended to challenge the will, but her sister's attitude hurt her. "I waited for her to give me something," she related, "anything—a pin, some keepsake, but no. I never told her this hurt me. I imagined her defending herself by saying, 'This is Mom's wish.'"

Eventually, Rachel decided to put it behind her. "I was conscious growing up," she said, "that I had no grandparents and a really small family. So the idea of allowing something to truncate our family, that made me decide to come to peace with it. You can buy jewelry or a house. But you can't buy family."

Rachel decided to get past her anger and hurt and accept her sister as she was, with whatever limitations she had. She valued their relationship more than the money and more than making a point. It was the right decision: The peace she made in the family sent its vibrations down through the next generation when Rachel's daughter moved to New York and Aunt Rebecca took her under her wing.

But there was another path to growth that Rachel was unable to pursue: to see her mother more realistically. The obstacles to this were overwhelming. She and her sister had grown up in a home where it was more than unsafe to be separate—it was suicidal. If you broke the family rules, you were considered dead.

So instead of holding her mother responsible for her actions, Rachel blamed her sister. Rachel told me that she did not expect her mother to change the will their father had written. "She would never do that," Rachel told me. "Because he made the money." Yet, because of her mother's warmth to her after her return, because Rachel needed to believe her mother was a loving person, Rachel believed that her mother "expected" her sister to give her part of the inheritance.

Rachel had no evidence for this. Her mother could certainly have changed her will had she wished. But Rachel gave her mom a pass. During her midlife years, when most people grow to see their parents more realistically, Rachel was living in exile. Her longing and her guilt were so profound that she was blocked from making this leap. If she had made it, she would have had to confront the painful possibility that her cherished mother was, at the least, rigid, and at worst, vindictive.

Rebecca, at some level, still blamed Rachel for abandoning her instead of blaming the parents who banished her sister. Even though Rebecca did not hold with their strict beliefs, she followed their rules. She never saw herself as a separate person who had a choice about how to live her life or how much to do for her parents.

If the sisters had been able to talk about the will, Rachel

might have asked Rebecca if she thought the inheritance was just. She might have asked whether she'd share it or give her a keepsake. Unfortunately, Rachel could not talk about this because she was afraid Rebecca would tell her exactly what she feared to hear: that this was what Mom wanted. So the sisters made an imperfect peace, which is often the best we can do. We live in imperfect families, and grief over losing our parents magnifies the pain of hurtful legacies. But even a partial peace that leads to connection and continuity is better than none at all.

DIVIDING MEMORIES:
THE LEGACY OF TABLES AND TEAPOTS

Most of the time, our parents' wills prevent more conflicts than they cause; they spell out who gets what. Many families handle this without fighting at all. But if we do disagree, we're likelier to fight about their "stuff"—the furniture, household objects, and mementos that are often not explicitly addressed in the will. In fact, research shows, we're five times more likely to fight about our parents' possessions than about their money or other property.

In a typical family, rarely will parents and siblings decide, together and in advance of the last parent's death, who gets what. If there have been any discussions at all, usually they've been casual and piecemeal. Maybe I ask Mom if I can have the china set when she doesn't need it anymore, and she says yes. I regard this as a solemn promise, but my mom immediately forgets and may sometime later, just as offhandedly, agree to give it to my sister. Or my father may casually tell my sister-in-law she can have it. So when we're actually at the point of dividing the things, when we're grieving and overemotional, we can find ourselves in a free-for-all.

The actual dispersal of the stuff may also be haphazard. If I live near Mom, I probably won't think twice about taking something or wonder whether you might really want it. If we get together to do this, we can find ourselves back in the house of childhood, with one of us bossing the others around and old competitions flaring up.

Even when we try to divide things fairly, we can run into problems. What's equitable, for example, when you weigh two baseball cards against a Queen Anne table? What if the family sat around that table every holiday of their lives? What if the baseball cards are worth thousands of dollars? In "Who Gets Grandma's Yellow Pie Plate?," her study of how siblings divide the stuff, University of Minnesota family social science professor Marlene Stum found that when people were grieving or selling the family home, they were especially sensitive about the things they grew up with. Making these decisions immediately after a death, Stum's study participants told her, was "'too much loss to cope with at one time.'"

I recall a pair of middle-aged sisters in Wisconsin who described what it was like to go through their mother's things and find the Uncle Wiggly book she'd read to them as children. In that moment, both felt magically transported back into their childhood selves, feeling how prized—and how fragile—these brief idylls with their aloof mother were. These women, both over sixty, told me they fought over who should have the crumbling storybook, with both ending up in tears. Finally, the older sister managed to climb back into her adult self. She saw that her sister needed the book more than she did. So she let it go, sadly.

Other people told me they fought because their sister or brother didn't understand that something of Mom's or Dad's was important. I recall one sister and brother whose relationship was rocked by a rocking chair, which he had unthinkingly given away to a neighbor. "She went nuts when I got rid of it with the rest of my folks' old junk," he told me. "I had to go to my neighbor and beg for it back."

When we're in an emotional state, we don't think clearly. If we did, we'd realize that all of us couldn't possibly have the same memories attached to a plate, a hammer, or a painting.

The only way to know what something means to someone is to ask. Many of the folks Stum interviewed said that afterward they'd felt sorry they hadn't asked their siblings what various things meant to them or whether they wanted something.

From the outside, it's easy to see how easily the rocking chair incident could have been prevented. She should not have expected him to read her mind, and he should have asked her what she wanted before disposing of it. But when we're on the inside, this is not so easy to see. Grief scholar Dorothy Becvar has seen this kind of conflict often among grieving family members. "Be caring," she advises. "Be sensitive. Recognize that everybody has something they might like to have."

When we manage to divide the old things without hurt feelings, we may also get to share our memories about them—and have good feelings when we see them again. One brother from a large family told me, "Whenever I go to one of my sister or brother's houses, I'm always surprised when I see something from the old house. And it brings things up: 'Oh, you got that old lamp. Remember when Jerry knocked it over and Dad caught it like a football before it hit the floor?'"

The things are scattered, but we can stay connected. And the chairs and teapots can remind us of our shared history.

DEALING WITH THE DYNAMICS OF INHERITANCE

IF YOU HAVE RECEIVED LESS THAN YOU THINK IS FAIR . . .

Think like a parent.
Imagine that one of your adult children is struggling financially or emotionally. Think about what you might want to do to safeguard one, to make amends to another. Then think like your parents, people of a different generation. What does their legacy mean? Do not assume it has anything to do with how much they loved you.

Put the responsibility where it belongs.
Your parents have made the decision, not your siblings. If you are hurt or angry, try to examine who your parents were and make peace with that. If you feel a terrible injustice has been done, calm down and try to talk it through with your siblings. You may all learn something. There is even the possibility of redressing the injustice, partially or in full.

Think about the kind of relationship you want with your siblings.
Inheritance splits apart more families than almost anything else. Do you want to be part of an angry, fragmented family? Is justice more important? Is money more important? Maybe it is, but just think about it. Most of all, think about the kind of person you want to be.

Try family therapy before you hire a lawyer.
If you believe you have literally been robbed, that your sister or brother has tricked your demented mother into signing an unfair will, allow for the possibility that you might be mistaken. See whether your sibling will consent to family counseling or mediation. If not, you will have to decide whether you want to hire a lawyer or simply walk away. You may not care, but you should know that if you do sue, your relationship with that sibling will almost certainly end. On the other hand, if you believe that fraud or other illegalities have occurred, litigation may be the right answer.

IF YOU HAVE RECEIVED MORE THAN A SIBLING . . .

Think about whether your parents have acted fairly.
Have they always pitted you against your sister or brother? Is this will one more example? Is this a legacy you want to perpetuate? Be willing to talk the will through with your siblings, and try not to be defensive. If you feel the inheritance is unjust, you can decide whether you want to do anything about it.

HOW TO DIVIDE THE STUFF WITHOUT DIVIDING THE FAMILY:

If possible, try to postpone the division.
Wait until the first shock of grief has passed. If this is not possible, keep in mind that everyone is grieving, whether they are showing it in a way you recognize or not. Hurt feelings about who gets Mom's or Dad's things can last a long time and poison relationships. So tread delicately.

Expect that you will have different ideas about what is fair.
This is normal, says Stum. If you go in expecting the division to be equal, you will find distribution nearly impossible. You can find yourself in the position of King Solomon, faced with having to divide the baby in half.

If you are the one who must deal with the possessions, give everyone notice.
When you're ready to deal with the stuff, to distribute it, sell it, or throw it out, send all your siblings an email at the same time. Ask whether there is anything they specially treasure. Indicate that expressing their preference does not guarantee getting the item, but at least the question can be discussed and settled in a fair way.

If you are far away from the stuff:
Speak up. Don't be embarrassed to ask for a memento just because you feel guilty you were less involved in caregiving. You might send all your siblings an email suggesting that you all might want something and that a system could be created for dividing things fairly. But be aware that getting rid of the stuff is often a huge job and what you suggest may not be practical.

Pick a system and include everyone in devising it.
As Stum points out, when people have input on how decisions will be made, they are likelier to consider the outcome fair. As for the system itself, there are many rational ways to go. You

can let people choose one item at a time in an order selected by chance. You can divide the valuable stuff from the sentimental stuff and allow people to choose in order from each list. Talk about what these old things mean to you. Listen to one another's stories—and learn.

CHAPTER ELEVEN

THE SIBLING GENERATION: SUSTAINING THE FAMILY CONNECTION INTO THE FUTURE

NOW WE ARE THE OLDEST GENERATION. Our connection to our original family is with our sisters and brothers. If we have grown as people through these challenging years, those of us who always had strong ties will probably be even closer. Perhaps we have rediscovered one another and unexpectedly become friends. If we came from troubled families, it's possible we've overcome some of the dynamics that divided us. Unfortunately, we can't all get past the family hand we're dealt, and this crisis may have driven some of us further apart.

The people I met fell into all these camps. The closest siblings often gathered for holidays or celebrations or just because they wanted to see one another. They talked, they sent photos. Their kids knew their cousins, and together they moved forward with a strong sense of connection. The stories of other families were still evolving.

Russell, the St. Louis CEO, for example, had always been fond of his sister, but his years of caregiving had frayed their relationship. When I interviewed him shortly after his father's death, he'd described himself as "resigned" to having some limited relationship with her after their mother died. Three years later, their bond felt qualitatively different. They spoke often and got together regularly. "I've dealt with my anger at my sister now that we're . . ."—Russell smiled ruefully—"'orphans.' Maybe I'm mellowing, or she's maturing, I don't know, but I'm getting to like my sister more."

Of all the families I met, the Herrera half siblings, who'd suffered an abusive childhood together, seemed most grateful to have rediscovered one another as adults. Carlos got close to Maria as he helped her care for their mother, an experience that enriched and surprised him. As their mom was dying, he saw how his brother, Ricardo, came through for them as a caring adult rather than the selfish young man he'd remembered; and Carlos finally learned to look beyond his older sister Luisa's abrasive style and empathize with her pain. He was almost rhapsodic when he talked about his sisters and brother. "To me, it's remarkable," he said. "We're not little kids in that abusive household clinging to each other, but adults choosing to be warm and loving to each other. I'm amazed at what my siblings and I have not only survived but moved past."

In a much less happy place were the Hoyts, who were ambushed by the dynamics of dementia. If you recall, their family unity was shattered when the younger siblings "stole" their parents from their hometown. When I last checked in on them, their father had recently died, one year after their mother. The six siblings and their families were preparing to assemble for a joint memorial service in their hometown, as requested by their parents. Julie, the youngest, who'd moved her parents to her house, was hopeful about the reunion. She had taken some baby steps toward mending some of the ruptured relationships. Bett, the middle sibling, did not expect much. After the service, she wondered who would bring them all together again. "I can't play the role my mother did," Bett said, "because she was truly kind and knew how to forgive. I am some distance from that place, but I strive for healing, my own and my family's." She described their family as "broken." Maybe they never would heal their rift. Some families don't. On the other hand, the Hoyt siblings were still raw with mourning. It was possible that in time they might learn to forgive one another as other siblings I met did.

TOO LATE TO MAKE UP?

With the initial pain of mourning behind them, many of the people whose lives I followed seemed more philosophical and more tolerant of their siblings' foibles. Sociologist Debra Umberson found, as I did, a greater willingness in people to forgive their siblings after their parents were gone.

I detected in people more willingness to reflect on what went wrong in their sibling relationships and found them more open to what part they themselves might have played. A full year after her mother's death, Katrina, a fifty-nine-year-old social worker in Philadelphia—a professional fixer-up of other people's relationships, as she pointed out ruefully—began to consider her own role in her estrangement from her sisters.

KATRINA: MAKING THE FIRST MOVE TO MAKE UP

Katrina, an imposing woman with a brisk manner, had not spoken to her sisters, Sharon and Evie, in the year since their mother's funeral. She'd been close to them all her life, but they had disappointed her during the years she cared for her mother. "My sisters were remarkably not there for me," she said.

Katrina had been happy to have her ailing mother move in. She'd always felt close to her and rarely incurred her criticism or wrath as her sisters had. She'd lived her life the way her mother expected, was always obedient, married the "right" sort of man. "I didn't separate emotionally from my mother until I was forty-five," Katrina said wryly, "when she told my daughter that girls were less important than boys. That's the first time I challenged her."

After her mother's stroke, Katrina found caring for her much harder. Her sisters lived far away, and as the sick woman faded, Katrina longed for her sisters' company. She hinted as much. Sometimes she remonstrated that their mother needed more attention from them even though Mom was past knowing the difference. After her mother died, Katrina mourned her mother and nursed her resentment.

During our first conversation, Katrina began thinking about why she'd received so little help from her sisters. When she'd asked them to spell her so she could attend a conference or a wedding, they obliged. But she rarely asked. In their family, one didn't ask for oneself. Faith, obedience, and sacrifice were the family virtues.

"My sister Sharon," Katrina fumed, "sat in that chair and said, 'If you need anything, just ask me. You know I don't like to volunteer.' But she knew I would never ask."

Or did she? Obviously their family dynamics were deeply entrenched. Katrina missed her sisters and decided to make the first move. "If I'm the one who's angry and hurt," she told herself, "why should I sit in my stew and do nothing?"

Katrina contacted Sharon, sixty-one, also a social worker, and Evie, forty-nine, a full-time mother of three. She told them she felt sad they were out of touch and asked them to fly in to meet with her. "I had not heard their voices since my mother's funeral," Katrina said, brimming up. "Sharon said she'd tried to write but couldn't find the words."

After months of complicated logistics, they gathered from different cities in a hotel room on a lake, furnished with a conference table, a couch, and a coffeemaker. "Here, I bought this blouse," said Sharon, tall and trim. "It's too big for me. Would you like it?" Katrina felt like walking out before the meeting even started. "All our lives," she explained, "I was a size twelve, and Sharon was a size twenty. Then after we turned fifty, our bodies just reversed. And now she was rubbing my nose in it."

Fortunately, Katrina understood that her impulse was childish; she forced herself to squelch it. Despite the rocky start, their meeting turned out well. As the sisters sipped coffee and nibbled pastries, Katrina explained how sad and angry she'd felt during those years of watching her mother fade. "I was so lonely," she told them.

Sharon and Evie both made heartfelt apologies. Sharon, whose relationship with their mother was contentious, maintained that she'd done what was appropriate for their mother. "But I regret," she told Katrina contritely, "that I didn't do more for you."

"I tried reaching out," Evie said, defending herself timidly. She was smaller and rosier than her sisters. "I sent cards, but you never acknowledged them. So I stopped trying."

Katrina tried to explain, tactfully, that Evie's cheery inspirational cards, with religious messages meant to be uplifting and hopeful, had struck a false note with her. "At the time," Katrina told Evie, "I didn't know how to explain that the tone wasn't helpful. So I didn't answer."

Each sister began to voice her thoughts about what she could have done differently. Some things they discussed easily, like how Sharon's hard relationship with her mother got in the way of her being able to help Katrina more. Other topics, such as their mother's sexism and favoritism toward her grandsons, were awkward, and they agreed to set them aside. But Katrina and Sharon were quick to agree with Evie's earnest observation: "It's a shame we haven't gotten together before this."

After two hours, they'd agreed on one definite goal: to meet and talk like this at least once a year.

Then they went shopping.

"What's so hard is that first step," Katrina told me. "People don't know what to say, so no one reaches across the table. And these discussions are so difficult that even people like us, who do it for a living and come at it with good intentions, can falter pretty badly and find it hard to take their own advice."

Katrina made the effort to repair her relationships with her sisters because they had relationships worth mending: They'd once been close. They had resources of mutual affection on which to draw. Also, Katrina had begun to see that she herself had been part of the problem; what happened—and didn't happen—was not all her sisters' fault.

Should we all do whatever it takes to repair our sibling relationships? Not necessarily. We may have nothing worth mending, or it may not be possible. Even if I'm willing to acknowledge my fault, you may never forgive me for things that happened when we were kids, revived and magnified in the twilight. Maybe in our house of childhood, the rules are immutable: We don't forgive. Maybe the only way I can feel good about myself is to see you as the bad guy. Family dynamics run deep. We can't always overcome them. If I reach out to you, but you won't reciprocate, I may have to accept that we can't have a relationship. Not all conflicts can be resolved. Learning to accept our losses and move on is also a sign of growth.

LESSONS OF THE TWILIGHT: PASS THEM ON

Whether our children have been closely involved or far away and hearing about our experience in snatches, they can benefit from our sharing with them the way we've been touched and what we've learned.

Remember the Keller family? I began chapter one with an account of moving day, when these siblings transferred their reluctant ailing mother to an assisted living center. After that day, Arlene, the sister who took charge, went through profound upheavals and uplifts: bickering with her siblings, gaining insights into each person's need to feel needed, watching their mother accept her new situation with dignity and grace. All these things Arlene made a point of sharing with her son and daughter, young parents themselves. She also shared her heartbreak about having to sell the family homestead—along with their amazing find in the attic as she and her sisters cleaned it out. They unearthed the ration books their mother kept for each of them during World War II when their father was away at the front. "How did Mom keep track of all this and raise five kids?" she wondered as she talked this over with her own kids. This story led to intimate talks about parenthood, getting older, and the flow of life. "I share these things about Mom," Arlene says. "I let them *see* this transition."

Let your kids in on your experiences with your parents and siblings. They will learn from the things you did right and the things you did wrong. But, most of all, think ahead to your own aging and how you can ease *their* passage through the twilight transition.

THE SIBLING GENERATION MOVING FORWARD

What will our generation of siblings be like as we get older? If we are anything like those before us, we will only become more important to one another as we age. A graph of siblings' lifelong connection takes on an "hourglass" shape, as researcher Victoria Hilkevitch Bedford described it, lots of closeness in childhood, less as siblings make separate lives in young adulthood, and then a renewal of closeness in middle age and after.

Only a small fraction of us are likely to cut one another off completely. In the group of older siblings studied by sociologist Deborah T. Gold, only 10 percent were hostile and 10 percent apathetic. The great majority maintained some kind of positive relationship with their sisters and brothers, ranging from phone calls on the holidays to being best friends. Their odds of being close were better if they had at least one sister among them, and sisters had the closest relationships of all.

Our generation's sibling relationships will probably be even more essential to us, Bedford asserted. For one thing, we have more siblings than other generations, at least, during recent times; we also have fewer children, and more of us are unpartnered. Living longer, women are especially likely to live many years alone after they are widowed. Furthermore, boomer men have become more involved fathers and caregivers; they may turn out to be more involved brothers as well.

As we get older, the history we share becomes even more valuable. "These are the last people I can talk the language of my childhood with," Katrina said of the sisters with whom she reconciled. She was referring specifically to the Flemish that she learned from her Belgian immigrant parents. But even those of us who grew up learning only English speak a language no one outside our family knows.

My sister is the only one to whom I can say "Uncle Morris" and who will sigh and roll her eyes at the memory of our eccentric, reclusive uncle who sparked a family tempest when he stuffed dinner rolls in his jacket pocket at our cousin's wedding. For sure, she's the only one who will laugh, recalling my father's yelling and frantic searching when I prompt, "Remember when we hid Daddy's winter coat so he wouldn't drive in the storm?"

Even apart from shared references like these, the older we get, the likelier it is that our siblings will be the only people who have known us our entire lives, and who also knew our parents. Our connection can grow more valuable as a source of continuity and perspective—because at every stage of life, we refine our insight into ourselves and our past, and this process of understanding ourselves and our relationships continues as long as we live.

For Russell, sharing memories with his sister has been an important resource as he continues to hone his insight. Until quite recently, for example, he considered himself the better child and superior person. But he's begun to rethink this position. "Sometimes," he reflected, "I think my sister was right to confront my parents and speak up. I'd adopt the posture that they were the parents, and I'd be submissive, or, at least, nonconfrontational. She'd be combative. She'd stand up to them when they gave her bad advice about raising her kids. Now, I think that would have been a better course for me as well."

The twilight transition of our family has been a tumultuous time. It has tested us and changed us. If we're fortunate, it has also taught us a great deal. If we have come through it with stronger sibling bonds, that is a good thing. But even if we have not, we may have learned things that will help us later. As we move forward in understanding the nature of reality, of life and death and the place we came from—our first family—we are likelier to make the twilight an easier time for the next generation.

ACKNOWLEDGMENTS

First, I want to express my gratitude to the many sisters and brothers who shared their intimate family stories with me over several years. They were generous with their time and their emotions and willing to open their deepest feelings to view. They helped me understand the richness and complexity of family dynamics during this tumultuous twilight transition, when our parents' aging and death so challenges us. And they taught me to have compassion for all of us.

I want to acknowledge my late mother and father, whose struggles I understand much better now than while they were living and aging. And I especially want to acknowledge my sister Joyce, who, I am happy to say, remains "family" despite some very difficult years during which I wish I had understood more and behaved differently.

Professionally, I owe a great deal to my editor at Bantam, Philip Rappaport, who saw the potential of this book and whose skilled and sensitive editing helped mold it. My agents, Joanne Wyckoff and Todd Shuster of Zachary Shuster Harmsworth, guided me through the long haul from idea to book proposal to book. I am especially grateful to Joanne for being such a good reader and editor throughout the process. I also want to thank Becky Cabaza for her editorial help and organizational prowess.

I owe a great deal to the many researchers and practitioners in the diverse disciplines that study and address the needs of the aging family. They are too many to name here, but I do credit them in the text or the notes. Elaine Brody's seminal work has been invaluable. I also owe a special thanks to Pauline Boss for her wisdom, friendship, and generous gift of time as well as for her very helpful reading of the manuscript.

Not least are my friends and family. Many friends have contributed suggestions, referrals, and practical advice or just talked me down from the ledge during the really hard moments. I cannot name them all here, but I do want to single out a few whose contributions have been especially constant or substantive (in alphabetical order by first name, which is how I think of them): Adrianne Navon, Alice Feiring, Amy Gillenson, Donna Torrance, Harriet Levin Balkind, Michael Clive, Patricia Kitchen, Shirley Ariker, and Susan Barocas. As for my kids—Sara, Joanna, Justin, Lindsey, and Brennan—I thank them for listening to me talk about "the book" endlessly over many years and letting me know they're with me. I am certainly "with" them.

NOTES

CHAPTER ONE: THE LAST TRANSITION OF OUR FIRST FAMILY

7–8 "In fact, many states had": Elaine M. Brody, "The Philadelphia Geriatric Center: How Did It Happen?," *Contemporary Gerontology* 8:7 (2001): 14–20.

8 Over the following decades, the Philadelphia Geriatric Center: Ibid.

8 In the 1970s, Penn State gerontologist Steven Zarit: Steven Zarit, "Caregiving Revisited: Old and New Perspectives on Families Assisting Elders," M. Powell Lawton Award Lecture, Gerontological Society of America, 2005.

8 Many old people themselves: Dr. Gunhild Hagestad, United Nations Programme on Aging, http://www.un.org/ageing/society_newage .html.

8 Between 1950 and 2000: http://www.nia.nih.gov/NewsAndEvents/ PressReleases/PR2006030965PlusReport.htm.

9 We are the ones who will care: http://74.125.95.104/search?q=cache: ThBDlKMDwx4J:www.familycaregiving101.org/news/keyfindings.doc.

9 We grew up in tremendous prosperity: Karen L. Fingerman and Megan Dolbin-MacNab, "The Baby Boomers and Their Parents: Cohort Influences and Intergenerational Ties," in *The Baby Boomers Grow Up: Contemporary Perspectives on Midlife,* eds. Susan Drauss Whitbourne and Sherry L. Willis (Mahwah, N.J.: Erlbaum, 2006), 237–60.

9 At least half of us live fifty miles: G. Lin and P. A. Rogerson, "Elderly parents and the geographic availability of their adult children," *Research in Aging* 17 (1995): 303–31.

9   This makes us the first native-born: Karen Fingerman and Dolbin-MacNab, "The Baby Boomers and Their Parents," 249.

10 Although studies show that we remain: Ibid.

10 Moreover, many of us became: J. J. Suitor, "Mother-Daughter Relations When Married Daughters Return to School: Effects of Status Similarity," *Journal of Marriage and the Family* 49 (1987): 435–44.

10 Ambivalence in our relationships: K. Lüscher and K. Pillemer, "Intergenerational Ambivalence: A New Approach to the Study of Parent-Child Relations in Later Life," *Journal of Marriage and the Family* 67:2 (1998): 413–25, and I. A. Conndis and J. A. McMullin, "Sociological Ambivalence and Family Ties: A Critical Perspective," *Journal of Marriage and Family* 64:3 (2002): 558–67.

10 Those who have studied us: M. E. Lachman, "Development in Midlife," *Annual Review of Psychology* 55 (2004): 305–31.

10 But most of us also enter midlife: http://www.aarp.org/opinions/othervoices/articles/excerpt_from_death.html, and H. H. Winsborough, L. L. Bumpass, and W. S. Aquilino, "The Death of Parents and the Transition to Old Age," National Survey of Families and Households, NSFH Working Paper 39 (1991), pp. 8–9.

11 A family is a living organism: Michael E. Kerr and Murray Bowen, *Family Evaluation: An Approach Based on Bowen Theory* (New York: Norton, 1988).

14 It was psychoanalyst Erik Erikson: Erik H. Erikson, *Childhood and Society*, 2nd ed. (New York: Norton, 1968), 41.

16–17 Then, in 2004, University of Rochester: D. A. King and L. C. Wynne, "The Emergence of 'Family Integrity' in Later Life," *Family Process* 43 (2004): 7–21.

17 For any family to succeed: Ibid.

CHAPTER TWO: ACKNOWLEDGING OUR PARENTS' AGING

20 I use "mother" more frequently: Elaine M. Brody, *Women in the Middle: Their Parent Care Years*, 2nd ed. (New York: Springer, 2004), 9.

20 Also, when women are widowed: Ibid.

20 In addition, with a majority: http://www.aarp.org/research/housing-mobility/caregiving.

22 Studies show that we think of ourselves: Lachman, "Development in Midlife," 305–31.

22 Scholars of midlife: Ibid.

23 "Scholars who have studied people our age: M. M. Skaff, "The View from the Driver's Seat: Sense of Control in the Baby Boomers at Midlife," in *The Baby Boomers Grow Up*, 185–204.

23 It is a time to be confident: Ibid.

23 This is a time, Purdue family studies researcher: Karen L. Fingerman and Marion Perlmutter, "Future Time Perspective and Life Events Across Adulthood," *Journal of General Psychology* 122 (1995): 95–111.

23 In fact, *we* fixate more on death: Karen L Fingerman, *Aging Mothers and Their Adult Daughters: A Study in Mixed Emotions* (New York: Springer, 2001), 116–17.

23 When WellPoint, a health company: Roper/WellPoint Survey on Life, Health and Aging, 2006, http://www.mywire.com/a/PRNewswire/WellPoint-Launches-Nationwide-Initiative-to/1922551?extID=10051.

23 When University of Texas sociologist Debra Umberson: Deborah Umberson, *Death of a Parent: Transition to a New Adult Identity* (New York: Cambridge University Press, 2003), 165.

24 As Ernest Becker points out: Ernest Becker, *The Denial of Death* (New York: Free Press, 1973).

24 Avoiding the constant awareness: Mario Tonti, "Relationships Among Adult Siblings Who Care for Aged Parents," in *Siblings in Therapy: Life Span and Clinical Issues,* eds. Michael D. Kahn and Karen Gail Lewis (New York: Norton, 1988), 418.

24 "Most children": Ibid.

26 Somewhere along the way: Donald Williamson, *The Intimacy Paradox: Personal Authority in the Family System* (New York: Guilford, 2002).

28 Emotional separateness: Kerr and Bowen, *Family Evaluation.*

30 When our parents are too little involved: Michael P. Nichols with Richard C. Schwartz, *Family Therapy: Concepts and Methods,* 7th ed. (Boston: Pearson, 2006).

30 Therapists describe us as "fused": Ibid.

35 In interviews with healthy mothers over seventy: Fingerman, *Aging Mothers and Their Adult Daughters,* 117.

35 The mothers complained: Ibid.

35 For all of us to work together: King and Wynne, "The Emergence of 'Family Integrity.'"

37 Some scholarship concludes that we leave home: Fingerman, *Aging Mothers and Their Adult Daughters,* xiii–xv.

37 Other researchers argue that we're likelier: Ibid.

37 Some say that some distance: Ibid.

37 Although cultural and ethnic: Ibid.

37 Either way, one cause and/or effect: J. Aldous, E. Klaus, and D. Klein, "The Understanding Heart: Aging Parents and Their Favorite Children," *Child Development* 56 (1985): 303–16.

37 Family therapists say the more important: Nichols and Schwartz, *Family Therapy,* 136.

38 If family members are too fused: Ibid., 121.

38 "We take it as a sign of growth": Ibid.

38 Telltale signs: Ibid., 136.

38 When we are middle-aged adults: Fingerman, *Aging Mothers and Their Adult Daughters,* xiv.

39 Alas, as research shows: A. S. Rossi and P. H. Rossi, "Normative Obligations and Parent-Child Help Exchange Across the Life Course," in *Parent-Child Relationships Throughout Life,* eds. Karl Pillemer and Kathleen McCartney (Hillside, N.J.: Erlbaum, 1991), 201–23.

40 "Whatever the trauma": Tonti, "Relationships Among Adult Siblings," 419.

CHAPTER THREE: WHO'S TAKING CARE OF MOM?

49 Research conducted by Home Instead: http://www.homeinstead .com/resources/4070/default.aspx.

49 Another poll found that 60 percent: Roper/WellPoint Survey on Life, Health and Aging, 2006, http://www.mywire.com/a/PRNewswire/ WellPoint-Launches-Nationwide-Initiative-to/1922551?extID=10051.

52 Some scholars have found, for example: Peggye Dilworth-Anderson, Ishan Canty Williams, and Brent E. Gibson, "Issues of Race, Ethnicity, and Culture in Caregiving Research: A 20-Year Review: (1980–2000)," *Gerontologist* 42 (2002): 237–72.

52 Latinos expect more help: Ibid.

53 After poring over a dozen: V. H. Bedford and P. S. Avioli, "Contradictory Paradigms in Family Care Research: Sibling Systems of Filial Care vs. the Principal Caregiver Model," paper presented at the Gerontological Society of America, San Diego, November 24, 2003.

53 As people grow old and dependent: Tonti, "Relationships Among Adult Siblings," 421–22.

53 "In order to maintain": Ibid., 421.

54 The "typical" caregiver: http://74.125.95.104/search?q=cache:ThBDlKMD wx4J:www.familycaregiving101.org/news/keyfindings.doc.

54 Almost a quarter of primary caregivers: "Miles Away: The MetLife Study of Long-Distance Caregiving," MetLife and National Alliance for Caregiving, http://www.caregiving.org/data/milesaway.pdf.

54 Cleveland State University sociologist: Sarah H. Matthews, *Sisters and Brothers/Daughters and Sons: Meeting the Needs of Old Parents* (Bloomington, Ind.: Unlimited, 2002).

55 More of us are men: "Miles Away."

55 When Towson University gerontologist: Interview and http://www .caregiver.org/caregiver/jsp/content/pdfs/op_2003_workplace_pro grams.pdf.

55 They helped their parents: Ibid.

56 In her psychologically probing: Brody, *Women in the Middle.*

60 This, more than anything else: Interviews, and Brody, *Women in the Middle,* 112.

62 Researchers tell us that the vast majority: Interviews, and Brody, *Women in the Middle.*

63 Penn State gerontologist Steven Zarit: Interview and S. H. Zarit, K. E. Reever, and J. Bach-Peterson, "Relatives of Impaired Elderly: Correlates of Feelings of Burden," *Gerontologist* 20 (1980): 649–55.

63 As Zarit and others studied: Carol S. Aneshensel et al., *Profiles in Caregiving: The Unexpected Career* (New York: Academic Press, 1995).

63 If their cultural or religious beliefs: Ibid., and Dilworth-Anderson et al., "Issues of Race, Ethnicity, and Culture," *The Gerontologist* 42 (2002): 237–72.

64 Workplace studies show that: http://www.caregiver.org/caregiver/ jsp/content/pdfs/op_2003_workplace_programs.pdf.

64 All of this is good advice: B. Ingersoll-Dayton, M. B. Neal, and L. B. Hammer, "Aging Parents Helping Adult Children: The Experience of the Sandwiched Generation," *Family Relations* 50:3 (2001): 262–71.

66 This is not only because there are more: Brody, *Women in the Middle,* 121.

66 Women not only do more: J. L. Yee and R. Schulz, "Gender Differences in Psychiatric Morbidity Among Family Caregivers: A Review and Analysis," *Gerontologist* 40 (2000): 147–64.

66 When sociologists Jill Suitor and Karl Pillemer: Karl Pillemer and J. Jill Suitor, "Making Choices: A Within-Family Study of Caregiver Selection," *Gerontologist* 46 (2006): 439–48.

67 "they do not differentiate": Brody, *Women in the Middle,* 122 (emphasis in original).

68 Theirs is an impossible mission: Ibid.

69 As recent feminist scholarship: Fingerman, *Aging Mothers and Their Adult Daughters,* 4–5, and Diane Shrier, Margaret Tompsett, and Lydia A. Shrier, "Adult Mother-Daughter Relationships: A Review of the Theoretical and Research Literature," *Journal of the American Academy of Psychoanalysis and Dynamic Psychology* 32:1 (2004): 91–115.

71 In her studies of caregiving daughters: Brody, *Women in the Middle,* 93–110.

71 One of her more crowded: Ibid.

71 "These women may present themselves": Ibid.

71 "Although the behavior": Ibid.

CHAPTER FOUR: DAD STILL LOVES YOU MORE

84 "Ours is a 'neolocal' society": Stephen P. Bank and Michael D. Kahn, *The Sibling Bond* (New York: Perseus, 1997), 224.

84 We can use this geographic distance: Ibid.

95 We learn how to compete, cooperate: Ibid., 199.

95 "Achieving a feeling": Ibid., 201.

96 It's likely that Mom and Dad saw: Daniel Eckstein, "Empirical Studies

Indicating Significant Birth-Order-Related Personality Differences," *Journal of Individual Psychology* 56 (2000): 481–94, and Matthew F. Bumpus, Ann C. Crouter, and Susan M. McHale, "Parental Autonomy Granting During Adolescence: Exploring Gender Differences in Context," *Developmental Psychology* 37 (2001): 163–73.

96 On the other hand, I am probably: Bank and Kahn, *The Sibling Bond*, 205–6.

96 If you are the youngest: Delroy L. Paulhus, Paul D. Trapnell, and D. Chen, "Birth Order Effects on Personality and Achievement Within Families," *Psychological Science* 10 (1999): 482–88.

96 As the last one left at home: Judy Dunn and Robert Plomin, "Why Are Siblings So Different? The Significance of Differences in Sibling Experiences Within the Family," *Family Process* 30 (1991): 271–83.

97 What's important to realize: Bank and Kahn, *The Sibling Bond*.

97 When sociologists Jill Suitor: J. J. Suitor and K. Pillemer, "Mothers' Favoritism in Later Life: The Role of Children's Birth Order," *Research on Aging* 29:1 (2007): 32–55.

98 When Suitor and Pillemer asked: J. J. Suitor and K. Pillemer, "Did Mom Really Love You Best? Developmental Histories, Status Transitions, and Parental Favoritism in Later Life Families," *Motivation and Emotion* 24:2 (2000), and J. J. Suitor, J. Sechrist, M. Steinhour, and K. Pillemer, "'I'm Sure She Chose Me!' Accuracy of Children's Reports of Mother's Favoritism in Later Life," *Family Relations* 55:5 (2006): 526–38.

98 Elaine Brody's research found: Brody, *Women in the Middle*, 108.

98 Overwhelmingly, research shows: J. J. Suitor and K. Pillemer, "Choosing Daughters: Exploring Why Mothers Favor Adult Daughters over Sons," *Sociological Perspectives* 49:2 (2006): 139–61.

CHAPTER FIVE: "WE WEREN'T YOUR NORMAN ROCKWELL FAMILY"

109 We expect things from our siblings: B. Ingersoll-Dayton, J. J. Suitor, and K. Pillemer, "Sources of Support and Interpersonal Stress in the Networks of Married Caregiving Daughters: Findings From a 2-Year Longitudinal Study," *Journal of Gerontology* 51 (1996): S297–306.

111 Writing about this shift: Fingerman, *The Baby Boomers Grow Up*, 250–52.

111 The test included such questions: Ibid.

121 What *is* essential: Interviews, and Matthews, *Sisters and Brothers*.

121 If you felt like your mother's least-favored: V. H. Bedford, "Memories of Parental Favoritism and the Quality of Parent-Child Ties in Adulthood," *Journal of Gerontology* 47 (1992): S149–55.

124 "The single greatest impediment": Nichols and Schwartz, *Family Therapy*, 138–39.

126 As Brody found with caregivers: Brody, *Women in the Middle*, 112.

126 Many of the women Brody studied: Ibid.

126–127 Their sisters reported: Ibid., 108–9.

127 When they lived far away: Ibid.

127 When researcher Berit Ingersoll-Dayton: B. Ingersoll-Dayton, M. B. Neal, J. Ha, and L. B. Hammer, "Redressing Inequity in Parent Care Among Siblings," *Journal of Marriage and Family* 65:1 (2003): 201–12.

CHAPTER SIX: WHO PUT YOU IN CHARGE?

135 One AARP study found: http://www.aarp.org/research/reference/publicopinions/aresearch-import-424.html.

140 Research by Rutgers University sociologist: Interviews, and D. Carr and D. Khodyakov, "End-of-Life Health Care Planning Among Young-Old Adults: An Assessment of Psychosocial Influences," *Journals of Gerontology Series B* 62 (2007): S135–141, and D. Khodyakov and D. Carr, "The Impact of Late-Life Parental Death on Sibling Relationships: Do Advance Directives Help or Hurt?" *Research on Aging* 31 (2009): 495–519.

CHAPTER SEVEN: HERE YET NOT HERE

156 With 5.3 million Americans: 2009 Alzheimer's Disease Facts and Figures, http://alz.org/media_media_resources.asp.

156 On the most basic level: Ibid.

156 It takes a heavier toll: Ibid.

156 Like other caregivers: Ibid.

157 The ambiguity of Mom's condition: Pauline Boss, *Ambiguous Loss: Learning to Live with Unresolved Grief* (Cambridge, Mass.: Harvard University Press, 1999).

157 According to the Alzheimer's Association: http://www.alz.org/alzheimers_disease_related_diseases.asp.

158 The term describes a specific: Boss, *Ambiguous Loss.*

168 As psychiatrist John Rolland: John S. Rolland, "Living with Anticipatory Loss in the New Era of Genetics: A Life Cycle Perspective," in *Individuals, Families, and the New Era of Genetics: Biopsychosocial Perspectives,* ed., Suzanne Miller et al. (New York: Norton, 2006), 157–58.

171 But if your sister was depressed: Brody, *Women in the Middle,* 309, and Richard Schulz et al., "Long-term Care Placement of Dementia Patients and Caregiver Health and Well-being," *JAMA* 292 (2004): 961–67.

173 Having a parent with the disease: http://www.alz.org/alzheimers_disease_causes_risk_factors.asp.

173 Nearly a third of Americans: http://www.metlife.com/WPSAssets/88281571601147208287V1FAlzheimersReportFINAL.pdf.

175 University of Washington researcher: L. Teri and R. G. Logsdon, "Identifying Pleasant Activities for Alzheimer's Disease Patients: The Pleasant Events Schedule," *Gerontologist* 31:1 (1991): 124–27.

175 Teri's research shows: Ibid.

175 Other researchers have developed: Interviews, and C. J. Whitlatch, S. H. Zarit, and A. von Eye, "Efficacy of Interventions with Caregivers: A Reanalysis," *Gerontologist* 31:1 (1991): 9–14.

176 Studies demonstrated that the meetings: Interviews, S. H. Zarit, K. E. Reever, and J. Bach-Peterson, "Relatives of Impaired Elderly: Correlates of Feelings of Burden," *Gerontologist* 33:20 (1980): 649–55, and M. S. Mittelman, S. H. Ferris, G. Steinberg, E. Shulman, J. A. Mackell, A. Ambinder, and J. Cohen, "An Intervention That Delays Institutionalization of Alzheimer's Disease Patients: Treatment of Spouse-Caregivers," *Gerontologist* 33:6 (1993): 730–40.

CHAPTER EIGHT: GATHERING AT THE DEATHBED

186 "In the hospice community": Samira K. Beckwith, "When Families Disagree: Family Conflict and Decisions," in *Living with Grief: Ethical Dilemmas and End-of-Life Care,* at http://www.hospicefoundation.org/teleconference/books/lwg2005/beckwith.pdf.

189 a small countermovement, known as "slow medicine": Abigail Zuger, M.D., "For the Very Old, a Dose of 'Slow Medicine,'" *New York Times,* February 28, 2008.

189 Many siblings clash: B. J. Kramer, A. Z. Boelk, and C. Auer, "Family Conflict at the End of Life: Lessons Learned in a Model Program for Vulnerable Older Adults," *Journal of Palliative Medicine* 9:3 (2006): 791–801.

190 Doctors, nurses, and ethicists: Debra Gerardi and Jacqueline N. Font-Guzman, "Conflict at End-of-Life: A Growing Need for Dispute Resolution Practices," at http://culaw2.creighton.edu/pdf/publications/2006FallLawyer34.pdf.

190 Living wills get overridden: Interviews, Joan M. Teno, S. Licks, J. Lynn, N. Wegner, A. F. Connors Jr., R. S. Phillips, M. A. O'Connor, D. P. Murphy, W. J. Fulkerson, N. Desbiens, and W. A. Knaus, "Do Advance Directives Provide Instructions That Direct Care? SUPPORT Investigators. Study to Understand Prognoses and Preferences for Outcomes and Risks of Treatment," *Journal of the American Geriatric Society* 45:4 (1997): 519–20, and Joanne Lynn, J. M. Teno, R. S. Phillips, A. W. Wu, N. Desbiens, J. Harrold, M. T. Claessens, N. Wenger, B. Kreling, and A. F. Connors Jr., "Perceptions by Family Members of the Dying Experience of Older and Seriously Ill Patients," *Annals of Internal Medicine* 126:2 (1997): 97–106.

194 Siblings cannot always agree: Joan M. Teno et al., "Family Perspectives on End-of-Life Care at the Last Place of Care," *JAMA* 291 (2004): 88–93.

194 Having more information: Beckwith, "When Families Disagree."

194 We find out, for example: Hospice Foundation of America, *The Dying Process: A Guide for Caregivers.*

194 She may lose a sense: Ibid.

195 We learn, very significantly: Ibid.

195 Most dying people fear: Ibid.

195 From hospice we learn that what he needs: Ibid.

195 "When asked how they are feeling": Beckwith, "When Families Disagree."

CHAPTER NINE: MOURNING AND MOVING ON

215 "The death of a parent": Umberson, *Death of a Parent*, 203.

218 In her research on parent loss: Ibid., 44.

221 "Family members who cannot share": Monica McGoldrick, "Echoes from the Past: Helping Families Deal with Their Ghosts," in *Living Beyond Loss: Death in the Family*, eds. Froma Walsh and Monica McGoldrick, 2nd ed. (New York: Norton, 2004), 326.

223 In our culture, women usually: Monica McGoldrick, "Gender and Mourning," in *Living Beyond Loss,* eds. Walsh and McGoldrick, 108.

223 Women find comfort: Ibid.

223 Men, on the other hand: Ibid.

225 If I have been the caregiver: K. Boerner, R. Schulz, and A. Horowitz, "Positive Aspects of Caregiving and Adaptation to Bereavement," *Psychology and Aging* 19:4 (2004): 668–75.

225 "Sharing memories and stories": McGoldrick, "Echoes from the Past," 315.

230 Sitting in a special place: Ibid., 322, and Dorothy S. Becvar, *In the Presence of Grief* (New York: Guilford, 2003), 220–21.

CHAPTER TEN: INHERITANCE

235 Some recent surveys: Allianz American Legacies Study, 2005, https://www.allianzlife.com/mediacenter/americanlegacies.aspx.

236 In fact, research shows: M. S. Stum, "Families and Inheritance Decisions: Examining Non-Titled Property Transfers," *Journal of Family and Economic Issues* 21:2 (2000): 177–202.

237 Some parents do, but most are: Ibid.

238 The bias in our culture is still: I. A. Connidis, "Sibling Ties Across Time: The Middle and Later Years," in *The Cambridge Handbook of Age and Ageing,* ed. Malcolm L. Johnson (New York: Cambridge University Press, 2005), 234.

240 Community Health Sciences professor Bonnie: Interviews, and B. Lashewicz, G. Manning, M. Hall, and N. Keating, "Equity Matters: Doing Fairness in the Context of Family Caregiving," *Canadian Journal on Aging* 26 (2007): 91–102.

251 In fact, research shows: Allianz American Legacies Study, 2005, https://www.allianzlife.com/mediacenter/americanlegacies.asp, in M. S. Stum, "Who Gets Grandma's Yellow Pie Plate?," http://www.yellowpieplate.umn.edu/fa.html.

252 Making these decisions immediately: Ibid.

253 Many of the folks Stum interviewed: Ibid.

255 As Stum points out: Ibid.

CHAPTER ELEVEN: THE SIBLING GENERATION

259 Sociologist Debra Umberson found: Umberson, *Death of a Parent*, 172.

263 A graph of siblings' lifelong connection: Victor G. Cicirelli, *Sibling Relationships Across the Life Span* (New York: Springer, 1995), 60.

264 In the group of older siblings: D. T. Gold, "Sibling Relationships in Old Age: A Typology," paper presented at the Annual Scientific Meeting of the Gerontological Society, Chicago, November 19–23, 1986, and "Siblings in Old Age: Their Roles and Relationships," Center for Applied Gerontology, 1988.

264 Their odds of being close: Monica McGoldrick, Marlene Watson, and Waymon Benton, "Siblings Through the Life Cycle," in *The Expanded Family Life Cycle: Individual, Family and Social Perspectives*, eds. Betty Carter and Monica McGoldrick, 3rd ed. (New York: Pearson, 2005), 155.

264 Our generation's sibling relationships: Victoria Hilkevitch Bedford and Paula Smith Avioli, "Variations on Sibling Intimacy in Old Age," *Generations* 25:2 (2001): 34–40.

INDEX

ABOUT THE AUTHOR

FRANCINE RUSSO is a widely recognized journalist known for her alertness to developing trends, especially in her own boomer generation. For nearly a decade she covered the boomer beat for *Time* magazine and in 2004 established a popular niche, becoming *Time*'s boomer expert in her regularly featured "Ask Francine" column. Russo has also developed an enthusiastic following with her frequent articles in such media as *Redbook, Family Circle, Ladies' Home Journal, Self, Glamour,* and *The Village Voice,* where she was a theater critic for more than a decade. Her 2005 *Time* article "Who Cares More for Mom?" attracted wide attention and was the genesis for her book. In 2009 she became a New York Times Fellow at the International Longevity Center. She brings a rich personal history to her writing as a daughter, sister, wife, widow, mother of two, and stepmother of three. She has a Ph.D. in English and lives in Manhattan.